Financing
State and Local
Governments

Studies of Government Finance

FIRST SERIES

Federal Fiscal Policy in the Postwar Recessions, by Wilfred Lewis, Jr.

Federal Tax Treatment of State and Local Securities, by David J. Ott and Allan H. Meltzer.

Federal Tax Treatment of Income from Oil and Gas, by Stephen L. McDonald.

Federal Tax Treatment of the Family, by Harold M. Groves.

The Role of Direct and Indirect Taxes in the Federal Revenue System, John F. Due, Editor. A Report of the National Bureau of Economic Research and the Brookings Institution (Princeton University Press).

The Individual Income Tax, by Richard Goode.

Federal Tax Treatment of Foreign Income, by Lawrence B. Krause and Kenneth W. Dam.

Measuring Benefits of Government Investments, Robert Dorfman, Editor.

Federal Budget Policy, by David J. Ott and Attiat F. Ott. (Revised 1969.)

Financing State and Local Governments, by James A. Maxwell. (Revised 1969.)

Essays in Fiscal Federalism, Richard A. Musgrave, Editor.

Economics of the Property Tax, by Dick Netzer.

A Capital Budget Statement for the U.S. Government, by Maynard S. Comiez.

Foreign Tax Policies and Economic Growth, E. Gordon Keith, Editor. A Report of the National Bureau of Economic Research and the Brookings Institution (Columbia University Press).

Defense Purchases and Regional Growth, by Roger E. Bolton.

Federal Budget Projections, by Gerhard Colm and Peter Wagner. A Report of the National Planning Association and the Brookings Institution.

Corporate Dividend Policy, by John A. Brittain.

Federal Estate and Gift Taxes, by Carl S. Shoup.

Federal Tax Policy, by Joseph A. Pechman. (Revised 1971.)

Economic Behavior of the Affluent, by Robin Barlow, Harvey E. Brazer, and James N. Morgan.

Intergovernmental Fiscal Relations in the United States, by George F. Break.

Studies in the Economics of Income Maintenance, Otto Eckstein, Editor.

Trusts and Estate Taxation, by Gerald R. Jantscher.

Negative Taxes and the Poverty Problem, by Christopher Green.

Economic Evaluation of Urban Renewal, by Jerome Rothenberg.

Problems in Public Expenditure Analysis, Samuel B. Chase, Jr., Editor.

Budget Concepts for Economic Analysis, Wilfred Lewis, Jr., Editor.

Studies in Economic Stabilization, edited by Albert Ando, E. Cary Brown, and Ann F. Friedlaender.

Consumer Response to Income Increases, by George Katona and Eva Mueller.

Alternative Approaches to Capital Gains Taxation, by Martin David.

The Taxation of Income from Capital, Arnold C. Harberger and Martin J. Bailey, Editors.

Tax Incentives and Capital Spending, Gary Fromm, Editor.

The Payroll Tax for Social Security, by John A. Brittain.

Who Bears the Tax Burden? by Joseph A. Pechman and Benjamin A. Okner.

The Economics of Public Finance, Essays by Alan S. Blinder and Robert M. Solow, George F. Break, Peter O. Steiner, and Dick Netzer.

SECOND SERIES

Who Pays the Property Tax? A New View, by Henry J. Aaron.

Federal Tax Reform: The Impossible Dream? by George F. Break and Joseph A. Pechman.

The Individual Income Tax, by Richard Goode. (Revised 1975.)

Inflation and the Income Tax, Henry J. Aaron, Editor.

Federal Tax Policy, by Joseph A. Pechman. (Third Edition.)

Financing State and Local Governments, by James A. Maxwell and J. Richard Aronson. (Third Edition.)

Financing
State and Local
Governments

JAMES A. MAXWELL

and J. RICHARD ARONSON

THIRD EDITION

Studies of Government Finance

THE BROOKINGS INSTITUTION

WASHINGTON, D.C.

Copyright © 1977 by
THE BROOKINGS INSTITUTION
1775 Massachusetts Avenue, N.W., Washington, D.C. 20036

Library of Congress Cataloging in Publication Data:

Maxwell, James Ackley, 1897–1975.
  Financing state and local governments.

  (Studies in government finance: Second series)
  Bibliography: p.
  Includes index.
  1. Finance, Public—United States—States.
2. Local finance—United States. 3. Intergovernmental
fiscal relations—United States. I. Aronson, Jay
Richard, joint author. II. Title. III. Series.
HJ275.M39   1977   336.73   76-54871
ISBN 0-8157-5512-0
ISBN 0-8157-5511-2 pbk.

9 8 7 6 5 4 3 2 1

THE BROOKINGS INSTITUTION is an independent organization devoted to nonpartisan research, education, and publication in economics, government, foreign policy, and the social sciences generally. Its principal purposes are to aid in the development of sound public policies and to promote public understanding of issues of national importance.

The Institution was founded on December 8, 1927, to merge the activities of the Institute for Government Research, founded in 1916, the Institute of Economics, founded in 1922, and the Robert Brookings Graduate School of Economics and Government, founded in 1924.

The Board of Trustees is responsible for the general administration of the Institution, while the immediate direction of the policies, program, and staff is vested in the President, assisted by an advisory committee of the officers and staff. The bylaws of the Institution state: "It is the function of the Trustees to make possible the conduct of scientific research, and publication, under the most favorable conditions, and to safeguard the independence of the research staff in the pursuit of their studies and in the publication of the results of such studies. It is not a part of their function to determine, control, or influence the conduct of particular investigations or the conclusions reached."

The President bears final responsibility for the decision to publish a manuscript as a Brookings book. In reaching his judgment on the competence, accuracy, and objectivity of each study, the President is advised by the director of the appropriate research program and weighs the views of a panel of expert outside readers who report to him in confidence on the quality of the work. Publication of a work signifies that it is deemed a competent treatment worthy of public consideration but does not imply endorsement of conclusions or recommendations.

The Institution maintains its position of neutrality on issues of public policy in order to safeguard the intellectual freedom of the staff. Hence interpretations or conclusions in Brookings publications should be understood to be solely those of the authors and should not be attributed to the Institution, to its trustees, officers, or other staff members, or to the organizations that support its research.

Foreword

STATE AND LOCAL fiscal activity has expanded remarkably since the end of World War II. The expenditures of state and local governments have increased at a higher average annual rate than either the gross national product or the expenditures of the federal government. The corresponding and necessary increases in state and local revenues have been made possible by higher property and sales taxes, greater reliance on income taxes and various user charges, and sharply increased debt.

Perhaps the most dramatic changes have occurred in the fiscal relations among the three levels of government. Federal grants-in-aid to state and local governments, which amounted to less than $2 billion in fiscal year 1949, approached $60 billion in 1976. Not only did the amount of such grants increase very substantially but their structure has been changed in important ways. A general revenue sharing program was enacted in 1972, and conditional grants to finance community development, manpower training, and urban mass transportation have been consolidated under special revenue sharing programs.

This third edition reflects these trends and recent developments and, like its predecessors, summarizes current theories of the incidence of the major state and local taxes, assesses the capacity of state and local governments to carry their debt burdens, and discusses new devices such as property tax "circuit-breakers" and state and local retirement systems. It devotes two chapters, rather than the one in previous editions, to intergovernmental transfers. The statistical and other factual data have been updated throughout.

In preparing this edition, J. Richard Aronson of Lehigh University joined James A. Maxwell as coauthor. Although both worked on every chapter, James Maxwell was primarily responsible for the first six chapters, and Richard Aronson for the last five.

The revision was edited by Alice M. Carroll and indexed by Brian Svikhart. Evelyn P. Fisher checked it for statistical accuracy. Thang Long Ton That and Kathleen Kane provided research assistance. The project was carried out as part of the Brookings Economic Studies program, which is directed by Joseph A. Pechman.

Professor Maxwell died in December 1975. The loss is especially painful for those who were privileged to work closely with him. This book is the last of his many scholarly contributions, all distinguished by a penetrating understanding of state and local finance and inter-governmental fiscal relations.

This is the sixth publication in the Brookings Studies of Government Finance second series, which is devoted to examining issues in taxation and public expenditure policy. The authors' views are their own and should not be ascribed to the trustees, officers, or other staff members of the Brookings Institution or to Lehigh University.

GILBERT Y. STEINER
Acting President

October 1976
Washington, D.C.

Contents

ix

Text Tables

Appendix Tables

Figures

Introduction

Everything has already been told, but as no one listens, we must always be beginning again.

André Gide, *The Return of the Prodigal*

STATE AND LOCAL governments together spend three times as much as the federal government to provide civilian services for citizens. Education, roads, welfare, public health, hospitals, police, sanitation—these are state and local responsibilities, and their cost falls mainly on state and local sources of revenue, although in the last decade federal financial assistance has burgeoned. A surge of state and local activity that began after World War II has not yet lost its force. Rates of state and local taxes have been raised, new taxes have been added, and the bases of old taxes have been enlarged.

Most of the expansion of state and local spending has been for old and well-established governmental functions, rather than for new functions. The most powerful expansion has been for education, a function in the public sector for over a century and a half. The reasons for the sharp growth in this expenditure are plain. The number of children has increased, children now stay in school a longer period of time, and what is taught has become more complex. All this has required more plant, equipment, and trained personnel.

Public welfare and health are other traditional functions for which state and local spending has grown, especially services for the aged. The aged are a growing proportion of the population; a change in mores has pushed more of them out of the family; a revolution in

1

medicine has lengthened their lives and enlarged the range of their ailments that can be treated.

Roads are still another old function for which public spending has soared. In our affluent society, there are more passenger cars than families; the efficiency of transportation by truck has shifted more and more of the carriage of goods to the public highways; deficiencies in construction of urban roads and interstate highways—the expensive kind—have had to be made up.

Traditional functions have not merely grown in size; a vast change has taken place in their content. A state's public health expenditure is now very different from that of thirty years ago; the curriculum of a new regional high school is quite unlike that of the small high schools it replaced; a city throughway bears only a functional resemblance to an ordinary city street. Changes of this sort may be evidence of increased productivity of government in performing its functions. But any such increase has been more than absorbed by changes in quality; it does not bring decreases in government costs. And when the content of the old functions is stable—the services of city clerks, police, tax administrators, custodians, for example—little increase in productivity is discernible. Even more than in the private sector, provision of services eludes technological progress.

What governmental duties, and what means of finance, belong at the state and local, rather than the federal, level? Broad lines of division are constitutionally provided, but history has blurred the lines. Moreover, the boundaries of a locality and of a state are porous, and the effects of state and local financial decisions are not tightly circumscribed within a geographic area. When are these spillovers of national concern? Do these states have too many functions? Have they the sources of revenue appropriate to their functions? Perhaps no neat division of functions is possible or desirable, because some government functions should be handled by joint action, through federal-state cooperation. Such intergovernmental cooperation, discussed in chapter 1, provides structural flexibility in a federal system.

Interstate Comparisons

Chapter 2 provides quantitative background for interstate fiscal comparisons. The essential feature that emerges is diversity, both in overall expenditures and expenditures on particular functions.

Comparisons of state government expenditures are treacherous. One state government may perform functions that in another state are left to localities. Accordingly, a better basis for interstate comparison is the per capita amount spent (and raised) by both state and local governments. Such state expenditure figures diverge greatly: the highest per capita expenditures are more than three times as large as the lowest (excluding atypical Alaska).

What are the reasons? Most obviously, a rich state (in which residents, on the average, have large incomes) will spend more than a poor state, although some states spend considerably more and some considerably less per capita than might be expected. Density of population, urbanization, and so on have less discernible effects on expenditure. Much of the divergence in per capita expenditure, state by state, can be explained by historical and political differences. When relative expenditure on particular functions is examined, once again diversity rather than uniformity is the rule.

A reasonable basis for comparing financial effort, state by state, is the sum of state and local revenues obtained from their own sources, expressed per $1,000 of personal income. Rich states, on the average, do not have to make as great an effort as poor states to raise the revenue to finance an average level of per capita expenditure. The variety of patterns of taxes levied by state governments is as notable as the lack of variety in those levied by local governments. Even when a similar tax is imposed in many states, it is not necessarily utilized in the same way.

Grants-in-Aid

For decades neither state nor local governments have depended wholly on their own sources of revenue. Chapters 3 and 4 examine the grants (intergovernmental transfers) made by the federal government to state and local governments, and those made by state governments to local governments.

Federal grants to local governments, still modest in amount, are growing. The special issue they raise is whether or not the state governments should be bypassed. Federal grants to state governments are, in dollars, much more important, and they have made it possible for states to add many new programs since World War II.

Most federal grants (85 percent) are specific, for particular and limited purposes; their main aim is to raise the level of provision of programs in which a strong federal interest exists. The multiplication of grants in the 1960s was so pronounced, and so confusing to the recipient state and local governments, that a reaction developed that led to experiments with block grants, designed to cover broadly defined functions, within which each state allocates its expenditure among programs. Moreover, in 1972 Congress instituted revenue sharing, allotting general purpose grants to state and local governments for a five-year period.

Federal grants redistribute income among the states. Money is raised through a progressive tax system that brings in more from rich than from poor states. In turn, many grants are allocated by formulas that provide more for poor than for rich states. For what grants is such distribution appropriate? What is the desirable amount of redistribution?

State grants and shared taxes provide nearly 35 percent of local general revenue. In 1973, education received the bulk (57 percent) of such aid, with public welfare second (18 percent) and highways third (7 percent). General support aid amounted to 10.5 percent. Beyond doubt most states have permitted, and even facilitated, the proliferation of local units (over 78,000 existed in 1972); through grants they have perpetuated the existence of inefficient units. The grants themselves have been fragmented in amounts, purposes, and formulas. In many states consolidation would be a clear gain. Moreover, grants should be used as an instrument to speed reorganization of local units.

State Taxes

Chapters 5 and 6 examine the taxes used by state governments. The states pioneered in the use of income taxation in the United States, but two world wars and the depression of the 1930s have led the federal government to become the prime user of this source of revenue. At present the high rates, steep progression, and low personal exemption of the federal tax leave only modest scope for state income taxes. Moreover, with some honorable exceptions, state achievement in taxation of individual income has not been impressive. Diverse definitions of income have bred inequities and magnified the costs of collection and compliance.

Congressional rejection of the general sales tax as a federal revenue source during the 1930s and World War II encouraged state entry, just as strong federal use of income taxation slackened its adoption by the states. Twenty-one states adopted a retail sales tax during the years 1933–38, and eight more during 1947–51. State legislatures were irresistibly attracted by the revenue productivity, and the gradual, somewhat concealed method of payment. The defect of regressivity was sometimes alleviated through exemption from the tax base of purchases of food, clothing, and medicine, and through a sales tax credit against income tax liability. Forty-five states employ the tax, in comparison with forty that tax individual income. The number of states that employ both taxes is growing. In the thirty-six states with both, the sales tax is usually dominant, with income taxation viewed as a supplementary source of revenue.

State taxation of business income has been even less satisfactory than taxation of individual income. In their attempts to enlarge the tax base, states have reached outside their boundaries. As a result, indefensible jurisdictional jostling takes place, made tolerable chiefly by weak administration. State formulas for determining the taxable share of the net earnings of a multistate business create obstacles to interstate trade. State use taxes, levied on commodities purchased outside a state for use within the state, similarly impede interstate trade. Except for conspicuous commodities (automobiles that have to be registered in the taxing state), application of the tax to users is difficult. More and more the states have ordered out-of-state sellers to collect the use tax for them. Should this obligation be limited, through congressional intervention, to sellers who have some definable business connection with the taxing state?

Is there a future in state taxation of income, both individual and corporate? If federal taxes are reduced, might the states move in? Are there devices, such as federal tax credits, by which such a move might be facilitated? Can state taxation of income be satisfactory in the long run without uniformity in definition of income, steps to limit tax conflict, and alleviation of complexities in compliance? The uncompensated drag on the efficient operation of the economic system through multiple definitions of taxable income is likely to become less and less tolerable. Economic integration of the nation proceeds apace; it enjoins a parallel improvement in assessment and administration of taxes.

Death taxes—mostly inheritance taxes—were levied by states long before the federal government, in 1916, enacted an estate tax (on the entire net estate left by a decedent). In the 1920s, mostly for the purpose of checkmating the efforts at repeal of inheritance taxes by Florida and Nevada, Congress provided an 80 percent credit against the federal tax liability for death taxes paid to the states. Since then increases in the federal tax, with no enlargement of the credit, have reduced the importance of the credit. The Advisory Commission on Intergovernmental Relations (ACIR) has recommended enlarging the federal credit both to increase state revenues and, through the imposition of federal conditions, to spur the states toward simplification and coordination of their taxes. So far Congress has not responded.

Local Taxes

The general property tax, once a major source of state revenue, has become primarily a local tax. In 1973 it produced 83 percent of local tax revenue. Its postwar yield has shown a surprising expansibility and, as a result, the tenor of discussion has turned from a search for substitutes to the possibility of reform.

As indicated in chapter 7, the most serious fault of the property tax is inaccurate assessment. The inequity of unequal valuations to taxpayers residing in the same area is obvious. But unequal aggregate assessed valuations from locality to locality also have serious faults: state governments have used these valuations to set ceilings on local debt and property tax rates, and to determine local shares of state grants and county taxes.

A reform movement has been launched that assumes that state governments will be the prime movers in rehabilitating the property tax through the reorganization of assessment districts, professionalization of assessment officers, strong supervision of local assessment practices, and halting state erosion of the local base.

Since the ACIR organized and published its twenty-nine recommendations for property tax reform in 1963 there has been progress. Perhaps the most dramatic change has been the development of the circuit-breaker device, a technique that provides property tax relief without eroding a local government's tax base. The lack of improvement in coefficients of intra-area dispersion in property tax assessment ratios since 1966, however, indicates that property tax reform is not yet complete.

In the 1930s, driven by desperate financial needs, a few large cities enacted nonproperty taxes—New York a retail sales tax, Philadelphia an earnings tax. These examples, which have been imitated by other cities in a limited number of states, are examined in chapter 8. While such taxes have many faults, the persuasive argument in their favor is that no alternatives of greater merit are visible.

Nontax Revenue

State and local governments raise nontax revenue from public service enterprises (such as water, electric power, gas, and public transit companies), and from user charges for noncommercial services. The former, except for public transit, are usually self-supporting, although much debate goes on concerning what sums in lieu of taxes a public enterprise should include as costs. Public transit systems incur substantial deficits; users are subsidized in kind by taxpayers. During the period 1953–73 all categories of public service enterprises showed an increase in the ratio of operating expenditures to revenues. A continuing upward trend in this ratio may provide a warning of future financial difficulties for state and local governments.

The services that hospitals, housing, education, sanitation, and so on, provide are regarded as partly collective or welfare in content, although measurable benefits accrue to individual consumers. Pursuit of welfare objectives through low user charges, however, may be excessive; state and local governments might secure needed revenue from higher charges.

Borrowing

In the postwar years, as chapter 9 demonstrates, most state and local governments have borrowed heavily to finance capital expenditures for highways, buildings, sewerage, and so on. An important and distinctive characteristic of state and local debt is that its interest is exempt from federal income tax.

In most states either statutory or constitutional limitations are placed on the state's power, and the power of its local governments, to borrow. It is not possible to determine whether these restrictions have held down the aggregate amount of borrowing. It is clear, however, that they have stimulated a mushroom-like development of ingenious devices to escape the limitations. The most important device has been the nonguaranteed bond (as distinct from a bond secured for its interest and principal by the full faith and credit of a state or local government). Nonguaranteed bonds, which generally carry higher yields than full faith and credit bonds, now make up about half of state and one-third of local long-term debt.

Have state and local governments issued too much debt? Although debt per capita rose by 65 percent between 1966 and 1973, debt service payments in relation to general revenues have remained constant. The overall picture appears to be satisfactory. However, the financial difficulties encountered in New York City and other metropolitan areas are cause for concern and indicate the quality of debt is not uniform among state and local units.

Budgeting

As explained in chapter 10, the job of budgeting at the state and local levels is one of efficient allocation of limited resources to meet public needs. In most states and a growing number of cities, preparation of the budget falls on the executive, although this desirable practice is often frustrated by the exemption of important agencies from executive control. The next step, examination and appraisal of the budget, falls on the legislative branch. Implementation of the budget follows, with the executive responsible for seeing that funds flow to the designated purposes, in the correct amounts, and at the proper time.

The comprehensiveness of state and local budgets is often impaired by earmarking of revenue from particular sources to particular programs by statutory or constitutional provision. Removing programs from the budgetary process may be justifiable for government enterprises, and also when the benefits secured by particular users of services are linked with the payments collected from them. But in most state budgets, earmarking goes beyond these guidelines. The extent of its use illustrates the widespread mistrust with which voters appraise the wisdom and integrity of their legislatures.

Some kinds of state and local expenditures raise special difficulties in budgeting, notably those that are large and irregular and that yield services stretching into the future. Simply as a matter of procedure, these should be bundled together into a capital budget (which will be a section of the total budget). Should the items in a capital budget be financed by borrowing? Should the rule be pay as you use or pay as you go? A practicable and effective compromise would be for state and local governments to appraise with severity the capital items for which borrowing is approved, and to vary the volume of capital items provided by borrowing, raising it in years of recession and lowering it in boom years. Such a policy would serve to assure some degree of intergeneration equity and would also help in countering cyclical fluctuations in government income.

Trends

Trends in state and local finance are examined in chapter 11. The expectation of some forecasters is that the financial pressures of recent years will diminish during the last half of the 1970s. The projections rely heavily on demographic changes, on anticipated changes in capital outlays, and on growth in various types of federal grants.

Such an optimistic outlook, however, may underestimate several factors. For example, even though a reduced birth rate may make it unnecessary to increase the quantity of certain public goods, the desire to improve the quality of these goods will cause pressure on expenditures to continue. At the same time, the rate of real growth in national income is likely to be modest, so that state and local governments will not be able to count on their tax revenues growing automatically in real terms.

A new area of potential fiscal difficulty for state and local governments is pension fund financing. State and local governments across the nation have been extremely generous in the retirement provisions recently established for their employees. Unfortunately, most of these plans appear to be significantly underfunded. This funding practice would not be a matter of serious concern if strong economic growth were expected. However, since the general economic outlook over the next few years is not bright, and since, in any case, particular communities will not share in the growth that is achieved, it appears that unless an attempt is made to reduce the retirement benefits of people now entering government employ, an increasing share of state and local tax revenues will have to be devoted to financing retirement programs.

CHAPTER ONE

Development of the Federal System

Many considerations . . . seem to place it beyond doubt that the first and most natural attachment of the people will be to the governments of their respective States.

James Madison, *The Federalist*

What's past is prologue.

The Tempest

THE UNITED STATES is a federal union, governed by a Constitution that splits the functions of government between a sovereign central government and sovereign states. The powers of the national government are enumerated in Article 1, Section 8 of the Constitution; the Tenth Amendment reserves to the states all powers neither delegated to the national government nor prohibited to the states. Nowhere mentioned in the Constitution are many of the vital citizen needs that today dominate the domestic scene: education, relief, public health, highways, and so forth. These functions are neither granted to the national government nor specifically prohibited to the states. The assumption is that these are residual state powers.

In addition to the national government and the state governments, a great number (78,269 in 1972) and variety of local governments

10

abound in the United States. Unlike the federal-state relationship, the state-local relationship is not one between sovereign governments. The states are by law the complete masters of these local governments; that is, the relationship is unitary. This concept is known as Dillon's rule, after Justice John F. Dillon of the Supreme Court of Iowa who declared:

Municipal corporations owe their origin to, and derive their powers and rights wholly from, the [state] legislature. It breathes into them the breath of life, without which they cannot exist. As it creates, so it may destroy. If it may destroy, it may abridge and control.[1]

The relations that now prevail, federal-state and state-local, may not seem to conform to these neat legal divisions. Every citizen knows that the practical power of states to alter and control local government is limited, and that the federal government spends money on functions that might seem to belong to the states. In view of the great overlap in the performance of most governmental functions, it is not absurd to ask: What has become of the Tenth Amendment?

The Historical Balance of Federal, State, and Local Power

In the two centuries since the nation was formed, nation-state and state-local relations have not remained static. The power of the states vis à vis the federal government has waxed and waned as the federal structure adjusted to changes in social philosophy and environment. In this century, and particularly in the 1930s, major shifts in both absolute and relative terms have occurred in the functions, expenditures, and revenues of all levels of government. In the 1930s, many observers predicted the obsolescence of federalism; since World War II, however, a new intergovernmental equilibrium has emerged in which state and local vitality is manifest.

These developments are reviewed in the following section, which focuses on the relative contributions during this century of federal and state-local governments to overall expenditures for civil purposes, and relates these to periods of significant change in the evolution of American federalism.

1. *City of Clinton* v. *Cedar Rapids and Missouri River RR. Co,* 24 Iowa 475 (1868).

The First Century of Federalism

In the years of the Confederation, 1781–88, the states were so strong that they threatened the survival of a national government. Congress had no real power to administer, and especially to finance, its limited functions. Expenses of the national government were allocated to the states; each state was supposed to raise its allotment through its own officers. The results were nearly disastrous, and yet attempts to strengthen the financial powers of Congress by amending the Articles of Confederation failed because of the requirement of state unanimity. The feeling grew that the Articles provided the wrong kind of government. A strong nation would emerge only with a government that could levy taxes for its own use through its own officers.

Federal powers were greatly increased in the new Constitution—written in 1787, ratified by the necessary number of states in 1788, and effective March 4, 1789. Congress received the power "to lay and collect taxes, duties, imposts and excises, to pay the debts and provide for the common defense and general welfare of the United States."[2] This meant that, in addition to exclusive control over customs, it was to have concurrent jurisdiction with the states in practically all fields of taxation. In the first decade of its existence, the national government exercised—and even extended—its financial powers. The debts both of the Confederation and of the states were successfully refunded, custom duties were assessed by national officers, a system of federal excises was established, and a Bank of the United States was created.

Despite these vigorous steps, the divisive forces latent in the new federalism revived. During the next sixty years the state governments gained such strength that, once again, they threatened the existence of the national government. Geographic expansion brought into the Union new states with diverse sectional interests, and, in addition, the old cleavage between North and South was deepened by the spread of cotton and slavery. Most statesmen, obsessed with the perplexities of federalism, came to believe that national functions should be held to a minimum in order to preserve the Union.[3]

2. Subject to the qualification that "all duties, imposts and excises shall be uniform throughout the United States."

3. These developments are examined in James A. Maxwell, *The Fiscal Impact of Federalism in the United States* (Harvard University Press, 1946), chap. 1.

The deference paid to the states did not succeed. Instead, the sectional rift deepened until the nation drifted into the Civil War, which settled the issue of national supremacy by force. The Union was not a compact among the states; the national government was entitled to enforce its constitutional decisions in the face of state objections.

The effect of the Civil War and of events subsequent to it—such as carpetbag government in the South—was to diminish the prestige of the states. When, in the last two decades of the nineteenth century, many southern states remade their constitutions, extensive and crippling restrictions on legislatures and executives were imposed. Scholars, observing these trends, had forebodings about the future of the states. They foresaw a continuing gravitation of power toward the national government.[4]

What was federal performance at this time? James Bryce, although aware of many defects, was favorably impressed, and certainly this judgment is correct if comparison is made with performance before the Civil War. But the scope and range of federal activity were very modest, as the next section indicates.

Revival of the States

Around the turn of the new century, the state governments began to stir. A look at overall governmental expenditures in 1902 provides a base from which change may be judged. In table 1-1 only expendi-

4. John W. Burgess, professor of political science at Columbia University, observed in 1886 that legislative and judicial powers were "gravitating towards the national government," and that police powers were "passing over to the municipalities." This was not, in his opinion, a "pendulum-swing"; rather did he forecast that "in the twentieth century, the commonwealth will occupy a much lower place in our political system, the Nation a much higher, and the municipalities a much more distinct and independent sphere." ("The American Commonwealth: Changes in its Relation to the Nation," *Political Science Quarterly*, vol. 1 [June 1886], pp. 32–34.) In 1890 Simon N. Patten, professor of political economy at the University of Pennsylvania, found an economic explanation for the decline of the states. This was the absoluteness of the boundary lines—"the unchangeableness of the territorial extent of our states." The remedy would be to create "natural boundaries for each state" and thereby restore vitality. ("The Decay of State and Local Governments," *Annals of the American Academy of Political and Social Science*, vol. 1 [July 1890– June 1891], pp. 39–40.) In the opinion of other contemporary observers, the inert performance of the state governments was not compensated for by vigor at the local level. James Bryce, in 1888, critical as he was of the states, declared that "the government of cities is the one conspicuous failure of the United States." (*The American Commonwealth*, vol. 2 [London: Macmillan, 1899], p. 281.)

Table 1-1. General Expenditure for Civil Functions by Federal, State, and Local Governments, 1902 and 1973[a]

Level of government	Amount, in millions of dollars		Percentage of civil expenditure	
	1902	*1973*	*1902*	*1973*
Federal	230	57,838	18.5	24.2
State	134	67,264	10.8	28.2
Local	879	113,822	70.7	47.6
All	1,243	238,924	100.0	100.0

Sources: U.S. Census Bureau, *Historical Statistics of the United States: Colonial Times to 1957* (Government Printing Office, 1960), pp. 722–30; and Census Bureau, *Governmental Finances in 1972–73*, pp. 17 and 21. In all tables and figures, years are fiscal unless otherwise noted.

a. General expenditure excludes amounts expended in utilities, liquor stores, and insurance trusts, which are approximately offset by receipts; it includes intergovernmental transactions net of duplicative transactions between levels of government. Federal expenditure for civil purposes has been calculated by deducting from total federal general expenditure ($565 million in 1902 and $163,147 million in 1973) the amounts spent on national defense, international relations, veterans (not elsewhere classified), and interest on the federal debt ($335 million in 1902 and $105,309 million in 1973). All state and local expenditures are regarded as civil. These assumptions are faulty. Some portion of interest on federal debt was incurred for civil purposes and some portion of state-local expenditure for war-related purposes. Because reckoning them would be conjectural, these and other refinements have not been attempted.

ture for civil functions is considered; defense expenditure is excluded, since in this book the intergovernmental balance of power is a major issue. A decision to spend more or less for defense is, beyond dispute, a federal function; no question is raised of encroachment on, or withdrawal from, the state-local sphere. Attention should therefore be focused on spending for civil purposes. In 1902 this totaled $1,243 million; federal spending amounted to $230 million (nearly one-fifth of the total); state and local spending was $1,013 million, and local governments spent appreciably more than both federal and state governments together. The relative importance of local governments is, perhaps, the striking feature of governmental expenditure at this time. By 1973 great changes had occurred. Federal spending was almost one-fourth of the total; state spending as a percentage of the total had increased more than two and one-half times since 1902; local spending had experienced a great relative decline.

Table 1-1 hides a decision concerning the classification of intergovernmental payments, that is, payments by the federal government in the form of grants and shared taxes to state and local governments (and similar payments by the states to local governments). Against which level of government should these sums be charged? A choice must be made in order to avoid double counting. When the federal government raises $1 million that it gives to state governments to spend for, say, highways (instead of spending the $1 million directly

Table 1-2. General Expenditure for Civil Functions by Final Disbursing Level and Originating Level of Government, 1902 and 1973

Year and level of government	Amount, in millions of dollars		Percent of civil expenditure	
	Final level	Originating level	Final level	Originating level
1902				
Federal	230	237	18.5	19.1
State-local	1,013	1,006	81.5	80.9
All	1,243	1,243	100.0	100.0
1973				
Federal	57,838	99,504	24.2	41.6
State-local	181,086	139,420	75.8	58.4
All	238,924	238,924	100.0	100.0

Source: Same as table 1-1.

for its own purposes), the $1 million can be charged either to the state government, the government that makes the final disbursement, or to the federal government, the originating level of government. If the state government is chosen for the charge, the total expenditure of the final disbursing level of government (the level that receives the grant) is larger, while that of the originating level of government (the level that pays the grants) is smaller, than when the opposite alternative is chosen. Table 1-2 shows the two sets of figures for 1902 and 1973. Since federal intergovernmental payments were not important in 1902, the percentage distribution of federal spending for civil purposes under the alternative choices is almost identical. But by 1973 the spread was great because of the growth of federal intergovernmental expenditure to $41,666 million. When the reckoning of civil expenditures is made by assigning intergovernmental expenditures to the final disbursing level, relative federal expenditures have risen only modestly from 18.5 percent of the total in 1902 to 24.2 percent in 1973. But when the comparison is made by assigning intergovernmental expenditures to the originating level, relative federal expenditures have risen sharply from 19.1 percent to 41.6 percent. The key is federal intergovernmental payments.

The Quarter Century 1902–27

What happened in the years between 1902 and 1973? In the period 1902–27 the absolute amount of spending for civil purposes rose

**Figure 1-1. Percentage of General Expenditure for Civil Functions
by Federal and State-Local Governments, Selected Years, 1902-73**

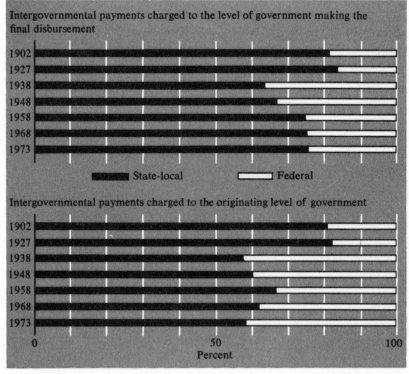

Source: Table A-1.

rapidly, but again the relative shares of the levels of government—
federal versus state-local—changed little (see figure 1-1 and table
A-1). In the 1920s the federal share declined slightly because concern over the large hangover of expenditures from World War I
stimulated the feeling that citizen demands for new and better public
services should be directed to state and local governments. Federal
intergovernmental payments were unimportant and whether they are
charged to the disbursing or originating level of government, the
federal share of civil expenditure for 1927 in figure 1-1 is around 17
percent.

In the years from 1902 to 1927 there was little change in the proportion of total taxes collected by each level of government. The state
share did increase somewhat (see table A-2). Major alterations did
take place, however, in the structure and composition of taxes (see

Figure 1-2. Relative Use of Various Taxes by Federal, State, and Local Governments, 1902, 1927, 1938, 1948, and 1973

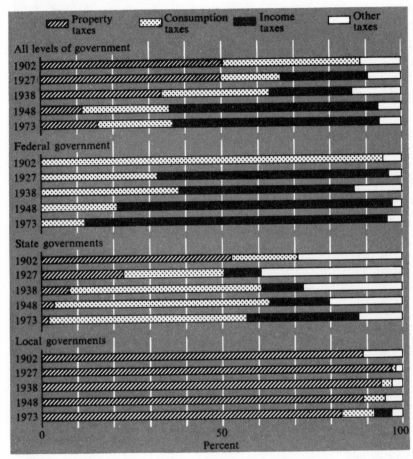

Source: Table A-2.

figure 1-2). In 1902, income taxation was so small that it was not recorded separately; by 1927 it accounted for 64 percent of federal and 10 percent of state tax revenues. In 1902 taxes on consumption were dominant at the federal level (95 percent of the total) and significant at the state level (18 percent); in 1927 their importance at the federal level was declining, and at the state level was increasing. Only at the local level was there little change in tax composition. Both in 1902 and in 1927 the property tax provided almost all of local tax revenues.

One main feature emerges from this summary of government finances before the Great Depression of the 1930s: with respect to expenditure for civil functions, the federal government, vis à vis state and local governments, played a small role, and one that seemed unlikely soon to grow. With respect to taxation, however, the federal government had been pushed by World War I to move strongly into taxes on income, both individual and corporate. In the 1920s the rates of these taxes were sharply reduced, but there was no repeal; the framework was retained. Nonetheless, state governments had reason to be content with their prospects. They were assuming new functions and extending their control over old ones. New and productive revenues in the form of taxation of motor fuel had been discovered and developed; joint occupancy of income and death taxation with the federal government seemed practicable since federal rates were low.

The Depression of the 1930s

The decade of the 1930s brought more drastic change to the intergovernmental financial structure in the United States than had the preceding 140 years. The force behind the change was a depression without precedent in its intensity and duration. A powerful shift in social philosophy developed when it became clear that state and local governments could not cope with obvious relief and welfare needs. Local governments simply ran out of money as property tax collections declined and tax delinquencies rose, and as they found themselves unable to borrow. State governments came to the rescue, but their efforts were both laggard and inadequate. After 1933, federal intervention took place on a large scale, at first mostly by emergency programs of public works, work relief, and direct relief. Then in 1935 the Social Security Act provided a federal program of old-age insurance, a federal-state system of unemployment insurance, and an extensive system of grants for public assistance which pushed state and local governments into these programs and reimbursed them for about half of their costs. Other governmental programs proliferated. Sometimes the new expenditure was wholly federal; quite often joint federal-state financing was provided.

Thus the 1930s brought a major intergovernmental redistribution of expenditure for civil purposes (see figure 1-1 and table A-1) The most remarkable change was the increase in the federal contribution in the form of intergovernmental grants, the bulk of which was in the form of emergency grants for the Federal Civil Works Administration, the Public Works Administration, and the Federal Emergency Relief Administration, although after passage of the Social Security Act in 1935 expenditure on regular grants grew steadily. Direct federal spending also grew.

Overall tax collections of the federal government and the state governments rose, between 1927 and 1938, by 59 percent and 95 percent, respectively (see table A-2), whereas local tax collections declined slightly in absolute terms.

In the 1930s, judicial doctrine showed a centralizing bias. For half a century after 1880 the Supreme Court had marked out a fairly clear boundary between federal and state activities; it stood as referee to solve jurisdictional disputes. Whether in response to shifts in social philosophy or as a reaction to contradictory precedents, a new judicial interpretation emerged in the 1930s that "accepted a reading of the general welfare clause that places no discernible judicial limits on the amounts or purposes of Federal spending."[5] The Supreme Court became unwilling also to place restraints on government regulation of economic affairs.

In the 1930s a critical chorus arose, repeating much more vehemently than in the 1880s that the states were obsolete and should be scrapped. Simeon E. Leland, a well-known professor of public finance, believed that the states should become "administrative areas" of the national government. It was, he avowed, anomalous to have forty-eight states fumble ineffectively with similar problems. An eminent political scientist, Luther Gulick, was equally specific. The states were no longer vital organizational units; "dual federalism" was an artificial concept since state governments could not deal "even inefficiently with the imperative, the life and death tasks of the new national economy." What had they done, what could they do, about regulation of utilities, about protecting bank deposits, about social insurance? These programs were "mostly national in scope. It is extremely wasteful, and in most cases impossible, to solve them state by state."[6] No one spelled out the timing of the dissolution of the states; fulfillment could presumably await the millennium.

5. U.S. Commission on Intergovernmental Relations, *A Report to the President* (The Commission, 1955), p. 29. This report, known as the *Kestnbaum Report*, was prepared under the chairmanship of Meyer Kestnbaum.

6. These and similar references are given in W. Brooke Graves, *American State Government* (Heath, 1936), pp. 746–53.

Three decades later, the entire analysis and indictment seem un-realistic. The economic disaster that struck the United States in the 1930s required a reallocation and also an enlargement of govern-mental functions. Realization of this necessity did not come easily. A period of fumbling, of debate over governmental responsibilities, and of improvisation was inevitable. Only gradually could a new alignment of functions, and especially of governmental finance, evolve. When this came the federal structure was found to be intact, and the states as units of government had gained in strength.

Postwar Resurgence of State and Local Spending

Before this revitalization occurred, World War II intervened. Even more than in World War I, state and local finances were put on a standby basis. As federal spending in the years from 1940 to 1944 expanded tenfold (from $10.1 billion to $100.5 billion), state and local spending declined (from $11.2 billion to $10.5 billion).

But when the war ended the federal government rapidly disman-tled its military establishment and prepared to reestablish its prewar pattern of activities.[7] State and local governments prepared to catch up on deficiencies in public construction resulting from depression and war. On the surface their finances seemed strong: revenues were abundant, and never had interest rates on state and local securities been so low. The cold war, followed by actual war in Korea and Vietnam, soon impaired the optimistic outlook because it brought to a halt, and then reversed, the drop in federal tax rates. State and local governments, instead of occupying sources of revenue vacated by the federal government, had to compete with the federal government for the taxpayer's dollar.

Postwar state-local expenditures show a sizable relative and abso-lute increase. They represented 6.9 percent of the gross national prod-uct in 1948, and 14.0 percent in 1973 (see table A-3). Higher stan-dards of public demand for education, welfare, public health, highways, housing, and so forth, required state and local action. Even when intergovernmental payments are attributed to the originat-ing level, the distribution of spending for civil purposes in 1948 and 1973 shows that state and local governments held their position (see figure 1-1 and table A-1).

7. Through the Employment Act of 1946, the federal government assumed the new function of promoting economic stabilization. This did not, however, require provision of new federal programs.

Between the years 1948 and 1973, the federal share of tax collections decreased from 74.0 percent to 57.7 percent, while the state and local shares grew. A surprising feature was the recovery of the property tax. During the 1930s it lost ground precipitously. After the war it revived and showed considerable strength (see figure 1-2 and table A-2). The state governments discovered that income taxation could be a useful source of revenue; it contributed 16 percent of their revenue in 1948 and 31 percent in 1973.

Functional Distribution of Expenditures

This brief historical review of governmental finances indicates that while the nation has been buffeted by strong economic forces, federalism in the United States has been flexible. The division of aggregate governmental expenditure for civil purposes—federal versus state and local—changed in the 1930s with growth in the federal share and decline in the state-local share. The shift is more emphatic when federal grants are reckoned as federal rather than state-local expenditure.

What rationale can be offered concerning the division of functions between the federal government on the one hand, and state-local governments on the other? The framers of the Constitution had a rationale; they drew lines that set limits to the powers of the national government. The lines were not clearcut in 1788, and they are much more blurred today. The scope of government has grown, and the economy of the nation is much more integrated. As a result, the concept of the separation of governmental functions, federal versus state-local, has been replaced by another concept of federal-state relations, "cooperative federalism." In 1955, the situation was summed up this way:

Under current judicial doctrine, there are still limits on the coercive powers at both levels [National or State], but the National powers are broad and the possibilities by means of spending are still broader. The crucial questions now are questions of policy: which level ought to move? Or should both? Or neither? What are the prudent and proper divisions of labor and responsibility between them? These are questions mainly for legislative judgment, and the criteria are chiefly political, economic, and administrative, rather than legal. The emphasis is on mutual and complementary undertakings in furtherance of common aims.[8]

8. *Kestnbaum Report,* p. 33.

The case for decentralized decision and administration remains strong, but federal participation in finance, coupled with modest federal coordination and guidance, is currently thought to be consistent with performance of governmental tasks at the state-local level.

A modern rationale for "cooperative federalism" can be developed through analysis of the benefits derived by people from governmental services. Some of these services are collective and national in nature. The clearest instance is national defense where government considers the need of citizens in the aggregate, not individually. As a logical consequence, government raises the revenue for this expenditure by general taxes which are assessed on individuals according to standards of equity. The collective nature of the benefits dictates that this substantial expenditure must be allocated among taxpayers according to whatever standards the legislature deems appropriate. At the other end of the spectrum, government renders services that are semicommercial in nature: certain individuals are the direct beneficiaries, the government charges them for the service, and individuals may choose to consume whatever amount they wish. A modest collective interest is present (else provision would be left in private hands), but it is veiled. Examples are the postal service, toll highways, and water supply.

Between these extremes all other governmental services may be ranged according to the relative importance of their collective, compared with their individual interest. Thus, educational services are rendered to individuals who thereby receive direct benefits; but these services are also beneficial to the whole society. This spillover of benefits creates a strong collective interest of such importance that the cost of primary and secondary education is defrayed by general taxes, not by charges to the recipients. Many important features of public health services also have a spillover of benefit to the whole society. Welfare services form another distinguishable group of the large in-between category. Here also the benefits accrue directly to recipients, but society is collectively benefited because provision of these services satisfies deeply ingrained humanitarian feelings. Moreover, linking individual benefit with individual payment would be absurd since the recipients are, by definition, without means. In short, finance by general taxation is inevitable and appropriate; government provides the services as a collective duty.

How can these generalizations be applied in deciding between federal or state-local provision of a particular government service? One that is rendered to the nation as a whole (collectively)—defense, for example—is clearly federal; so also is one that, although noncollective, should be provided uniformly to individuals in all states—postal services, for example. The outlook of each state and local government is, on the other hand, circumscribed; the services each provides are for individuals in a limited geographic area. Some variation of type and level of provision is acceptable, and even desirable. Sometimes, however, the benefits from a state or local service spill over and have an impact outside its boundaries. Primary and secondary education is one obvious example. Although the spillover undoubtedly reaches beyond the boundaries of a locality or a state, this national interest has not until recently been recognized by Congress through federal grants-in-aid. Provision is left mainly to local governments because direct benefits accrue to individuals in a locality and because local (and state) governments are strongly responsive and sensitive to the demands of citizens concerning details. The cost is provided through taxes levied at the local and to a smaller extent at the state level.

Public welfare services are another bundle of functions performed mainly at the state-local level of government. The benefits accrue directly to individuals; responsiveness of government to the variety of individual needs is vital; detailed administration is inevitable. The services are rendered mainly to needy persons. During the depression of the 1930s, the opinion emerged strongly that some minimum level of provision should be achieved over the nation. Since this would not result if the states were left to their own devices, federal assistance by grants was enacted. Thereby, state and local governments were stimulated to offer welfare services, not indeed at a uniform level, but so that a minimum level for recipients was feasible even in poor states.

In the years since World War II the most important civil functions provided by government, measured by relative expenditure, have been education, public welfare, highways, and health and hospitals. Together, as table 1-3 shows, they have accounted for more than half the total. Education has always been far in the lead. Expenditure for public welfare rose sharply in the 1930s and is now in second place.

What shifts have occurred in the relative expenditures of the different levels of government? When the figures used are those of direct general expenditures—when intergovernmental transfers are re-

Table 1-3. Percentage Distribution of General Expenditure for Civil Functions by All Levels of Government, 1948, 1958, 1968, and 1973

Function	1948	1958	1968	1973
Education	29.2	28.1	32.0	31.7
Highways	11.6	14.5	10.8	8.0
Public welfare	8.1	6.3	8.3	11.3
Health and hospitals	7.3	7.8	7.8	7.8
Other	43.7	43.4	41.2	41.2
All	100.0	100.0	100.0	100.0

Source: Table A-4. Figures are rounded.

Table 1-4. Percentage of Direct General Expenditure for Civil Functions by the Federal Government, 1958, 1968, and 1973

Function	Intergovernmental payments excluded			Intergovernmental payments included		
	1958	1968	1973	1958	1968	1973
Education	5.4	5.6	8.1	9.3	16.5	19.5
Public welfare	1.3	12.3	12.6	48.9	60.4	57.4
Highways	1.6	1.2	2.9	18.5	30.5	30.4
Health and hospitals	23.7	28.7	25.8	26.0	35.4	35.3

Source: Tables A-4 and A-5.

Table 1-5. Federal Intergovernmental Payments for Selected State-Local Civil Functions, 1958, 1968, and 1973

Millions of dollars

Function	1958	1968	1973
Education	653	4,727	8,666
Public welfare	1,799	5,407	12,097
Highways	1,478	4,291	5,276
Health and hospitals	110	718	1,766
Other	795	2,910	13,861
Total	4,835	18,053	41,666

Source: *Governmental Finances in 1958*, p. 16; *in 1967–68*, p. 22; *in 1972–73*, p. 22.

garded as spent by the level making the final disbursement—the shifts in federal versus state-local levels appear, with the exception of the public welfare category, to be slight (see the first three columns of table 1-4). But the federal government, in addition to its direct general expenditure, made growing intergovernmental expenditures (see table 1-5), and if these are credited to it (included in federal spending), the federal share rises significantly. The two sets of graphs in figure 1-3 show that the federal share of the expenditure for educa-

Figure 1-3. Percentage of General Expenditure for Selected Civil Functions Contributed by Federal and State-Local Governments, 1958, 1968, and 1973

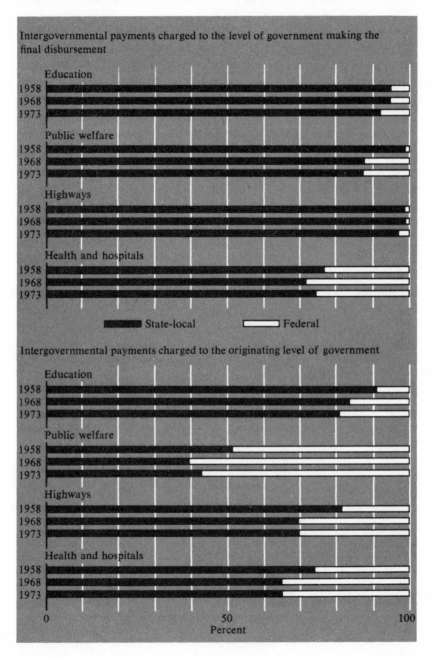

Source: Table 1-4.

tion in 1973 can be figured at 8.1 percent or 19.5 percent; for public welfare at 12.6 percent or 57.4 percent; for highways at 2.9 percent or 30.4 percent.[9]

In short, the overlapping of governmental activities, federal and state-local, increased significantly in the fifteen-year span. Although certain services are still performed at the state-local level, the federal government has greatly enlarged its provision of grants. By specifying conditions for receipt of the grants, it indicates the existence of some national interest in performance of the services.

Apologia for Federalism

The direct expansion of federal power, so forceful a trend in the 1930s, has not continued, but the indirect expansion, through grants, has persisted and even deepened. The states are, so it seems, geographic units that can handle many functions more flexibly, and therefore more in accord with heterogeneous citizen demands, than the national government. State boundaries must be accepted as immutable, and so therefore must their diversity in population, resources, and area. But this diversity is no greater than that of many sovereign nations—and not merely those newborn in the past decade.[10] Through their very existence the states, over the decades, have acquired loyalties and affection that lubricate the machinery of government.

More philosophical reasons may be advanced for a belief that, if the states did not exist, there would be need to invent them. One reason, put cogently, is that the states are laboratories in which limited, and therefore safe, experiments in government or administrative techniques can be made. Such experiments, even when they fail, may have more than mere negative value. They may indicate why and

9. The year 1958 is selected instead of 1948 because in 1948 federal spending for education and hospitals was enlarged abnormally by military payments.

10. The populations of the largest American states in 1972 were approximately equal to those of these well-established nations: California 20.5 million, Colombia 22.5 million; New York 18.4 million, East Germany 17.0 million; Pennsylvania 11.9 million, Netherlands 13.3 million; Texas 11.6 million, Australia 13.0 million; Illinois 11.3 million, Hungary 10.4 million; Ohio 10.8 million, Belgium 9.7 million. (U.S. Census Bureau, *Current Population Reports,* series P-25, No. 500, "Estimates of the Population of States, by Age: July 1, 1971 and 1972," p. 2; and United Nations, *Demographic Yearbook, 1972,* pp. 141–44.)

what kind of federal action is needed. Oklahoma's experiment in guaranteeing bank deposits failed, but it and similar attempts by other states disclosed defects that could be, and were, remedied by a national scheme in 1933 that created a federal corporation to insure bank deposits. In the early years of the twentieth century, state and local governments experimented with techniques of government budgeting and accounting. To these experiments the federal Budget and Accounting Act of 1921 owed a great deal. The Wisconsin income tax of 1911 preceded the federal income tax of 1913. The federal Social Security Act of 1935 grew out of much state investigation and some experimentation with old-age insurance, unemployment insurance, and public assistance. Marked progress here had to wait on federal intervention; yet with respect to unemployment insurance and public assistance, Congress chose to act through the techniques of cooperative federalism. The state governments were pioneers in the use of measures of fiscal capacity in grant programs, and the Highway Safety Act of 1966 was built wholly on state experience over many years. An awareness and appreciation of federalism might not only enable Congress to decide what cooperative programs are appropriate, but conversely to reject programs that are inappropriate.

Nearly a century ago, Woodrow Wilson noted the value of the states as training grounds in the practice of government: "The governorship of a State is very like a smaller Presidency; or, rather, the Presidency is very like a big governorship. Training in the duties of the one fits for the duties of the other."[11] The case for federalism, in the minds of many men, rests on a still more exalted and abstract merit: that state and local governments are bulwarks of democracy. Only where the people of a nation have adequate powers of decision can they develop a public spirit, and the specific knowledge and techniques that give life to free institutions.[12]

Despite a solid performance in postwar years, however, state governments have many structural flaws which need remedy. In 1959 the Commission on Intergovernmental Relations was set up to reappraise

11. *Congressional Government* (Houghton Mifflin, 1885), p. 253.
12. George C. S. Benson, "Values of Dencentralized Government—1961," in George C. S. Benson and others, *Essays in Federalism* (Claremont Men's College, Institute for Studies in Federalism, 1961), pp. 5–16, makes an eloquent case for federalism. See also Terry Sanford, *Storm Over the States* (McGraw-Hill, 1967), especially chap. 12, which includes examples of state leadership.

federalism, and to "study the means of achieving a sounder relationship between Federal, state, and local governments."[13] Its distinguished membership included fifteen persons appointed by the President, five by the president of the Senate, and five by the Speaker of the House of Representatives. Its report—the *Kestnbaum Report*—contained important criticisms of state government. The six members who were, or who had been, state governors did not dissent. Many state constitutions, the report declared, "restrict the scope, effectiveness, and adaptability of State and local action"; there was a "real and pressing need for the States to improve their constitutions."[14] State legislatures should provide a more equitable system of representation.[15] The power of governors was unreasonably limited by the establishment of independent agencies and boards, by the election of numerous state administrative officers, and by the lack of control over budgeting. State legislatures fettered their own power, and that of the localities, to tax and borrow; they earmarked too much revenue; they created, and should mitigate, tax conflicts.[16]

These organizational defects impaired performance of government functions. They diverted to Washington demands from citizens that should be met at the state level; they cast doubt on the logic of federalism—that the states possess political and economic capacity appropriate to their political powers.

Another recent development, raising new doubts about the logic of federalism, has been the growth of metropolitan areas. Urban concentration of population and resources is an old phenomenon. But in postwar years disturbing trends have emerged which, if not new, strike the social conscience of the nation more forcibly and aggravate the disparities between the service and tax areas inside the metropolis, especially in the Northeast and Midwest.

In the metropolis a core area, embracing the central shopping and business districts, shows signs of obsolescence. A suburban area

13. *Public Papers of the Presidents of the United States: Dwight D. Eisenhower, 1953*, p. 140.

14. *Kestnbaum Report*, pp. 37–38. See also Committee for Economic Development, *Modernizing State Government* (CED, 1967); and CED, *Modernizing Local Government to Secure a Balanced Federalism* (CED, 1966).

15. In 1964, the Supreme Court held that the "equal protection" clause of the Fourteenth Amendment requires each state to have a legislature so chosen that, in both houses, each member represents substantially the same number of people. *Reynolds* v. *Sims*, 377 U.S. 533 (1964).

16. *Kestnbaum Report*, especially pp. 38–47 and 93–99.

sprawls outside, attracting business and residential units from the center.[17] In or close to the core area, fresh slums emerge which accelerate the decay and underline problems of health, welfare, and education. How should the governmental duties of the metropolis be handled? Measured in terms of per capita income, or property, or wealth, the metropolis appears to have a large fiscal potential. The difficulty lies in determining how the potential can be exercised: the metropolis is not a single governmental unit governed by one legislative body; instead it embraces a large number of independent jurisdictions. The supply of services—such as water, sewage disposal, and law enforcement—should be organized and administered with an eye to the needs of the whole area; in fact, decisions are often obstructed or postponed while fragmented jurisdictions debate their respective fiscal responsibilities. The resources of the area cannot be mobilized for an efficient assault on its problems. Sometimes the metropolitan area spreads across state borders, necessitating negotiation and agreement by sovereign units.

The Advisory Commission on Intergovernmental Relations (ACIR), in a study of the country's thirty-seven largest metropolitan areas, found a concentration of high-cost citizens in many of the central cities. For example, while 27 percent of Maryland's population lived in Baltimore, 71 percent of the state's expenditure on aid for dependent children was in Baltimore; and Boston, with 14 percent of the population of Massachusetts, accounted for 38 percent of the state's expenditure for such aid. Large central cities in the United States have to spend more than the suburbs for police and fire protection and sanitation services, and must educate "an increasing number of 'high-cost' underprivileged children."[18]

Is federal intervention indicated? If so, should it be through direct federal programs or through conditional grants? If the latter, should the grants be funneled through state governments, or should they go directly to local units?[19] What should the state governments do? In

17. For an analysis of the effects of fiscal variables in intraurban population shifts, see J. Richard Aronson and Eli Schwartz, "Financing Public Goods and the Distribution of Population in a System of Local Governments," *National Tax Journal*, vol. 26 (June 1973), pp. 137–60.

18. *Fiscal Balance in the American Federal System* (GPO, 1968), vol. 2, pp. 4–6.

19. In 1974 $32.2 billion of the $46 billion of federal aid to state and local governments was budgeted to be spent in standard metropolitan statistical areas. See "Special Analysis O," *Special Analyses, Budget of the United States Government, Fiscal Year 1976*, pp. 237 and 244.

1969 the Advisory Commission on Intergovernmental Relations suggested that the states assume substantially all of the costs of elementary and secondary education in order to equalize educational opportunity. And in 1973 the commission concluded that the remedy of intrastate disparities is the job of the states, not of the federal government.[20]

Has American federalism the flexibility to meet and adjust to these new stresses? Rational solution of urban problems often requires reform of state and local political and administrative structures. If reform is postponed, or fails, centralization will be encouraged because, in present circumstances, the separate interests of the states will not be allowed to transcend a strong national interest. The federal government will not be content to act merely "as the bracket to a series of algebraic symbols."[21] The centripetal forces of modern society demand a flexible federalism. Efficient governmental administration will not, in the long pull, be sacrificed for the sake of tradition.

20. Advisory Commission on Intergovernmental Relations, *State Aid to Local Government* (Government Printing Office, 1969), pp. 14–16; and ACIR, *Financing Schools and Property Tax Relief—A State Responsibility* (Washington: ACIR, 1973).

21. Harold J. Laski, *Studies in the Problem of Sovereignty* (Yale University Press, 1917), p. 280.

CHAPTER TWO

Fiscal Performance
and Capacity

There is a great deal of difference between Peter and Peter.

Don Quixote

THE DIVISION of governmental functions between a state government and the local governments that are its creatures varies widely among the fifty states. The quantitative evidence in the form of expenditures is, however, hard to interpret, most obviously because of state inter-governmental transfers. Some state governments take over and perform functions that others leave in local hands and assist by grants-in-aid. In the former case, performance of functions may, with some qualifications, be regarded as centralized, that is, the state governments make a relatively large part of direct general expenditure; in the latter case, performance is decentralized. Table 2-1 shows the ten state governments that in 1973 spent the highest and the ten that spent the lowest proportions of total state-local direct expenditures. Two states with the highest percentages, Alaska and Hawaii, are new states where local units of government have had little chance to become entrenched, and this fact explains their centralization. But no such simple explanation will serve for the other high states, or for the states with low percentages where relative decentralization seems to prevail.

Table 2-1. Percentage of State-Local Direct General Expenditure by Selected State Governments, 1973[a]

Highest states	Percentage	Lowest states	Percentage
Hawaii	80.5	Iowa	37.2
Vermont	64.6	Missouri	36.8
Alaska	63.6	Maryland	36.2
West Virginia	61.5	Indiana	35.0
Kentucky	58.6	Ohio	34.8
Delaware	54.7	Wisconsin	33.6
Maine	54.1	New Jersey	31.3
Rhode Island	53.9	Minnesota	28.8
Oklahoma	52.8	California	28.3
South Carolina	52.4	New York	22.5

Source: U.S. Census Bureau, *Governmental Finances in 1972–73*, p. 51. In all tables and figures, years are fiscal unless otherwise noted.

a. General expenditure is that for all purposes other than specifically defined utility, liquor store, and insurance trust operations. Direct general expenditure excludes intergovernmental expenditure.

The fact is that interstate comparisons of state government finances (or of local government finances) are treacherous, and may be quite misleading about the relative levels of services provided by the states. More revealing comparisons can be made, state by state, of aggregates or subaggregates of state plus local expenditure and revenue. Such figures, when expressed per capita or per $1,000 of personal income, provide a more useful measure of state-by-state differences in governmental provision of services and collection of revenues.[1]

A per capita measure of expenditure has limitations chiefly because population (the denominator) is by itself an inadequate proxy for expenditure needs. Some groups in the population—for example, dependent children and the aged—require extra public expenditure. States differ in meeting their responsibilities here, and refined measurement should allow for such interstate variations. A per capita expenditure basis is rough also because it makes no allowance for price or quality differences, state by state, of public goods. Educational services may be cheaper in Mississippi than in Massachusetts, or it may be that, if account is taken of quality, the reverse is true. A similar uncertainty exists with respect to the pricing of other governmental services. Moreover, state variation in expenditure is not explicable

1. Robert L. Harlow, "Factors Affecting American State Expenditures," *Yale Economic Essays*, vol. 7 (Fall 1967), pp. 263–308, tests the hypothesis that differences in the structure of government are a partial explanation of variations in state current expenditure.

wholly by objective needs and financial capacity; noneconomic and intangible factors, which stem from different historical backgrounds, are important.

This brief enumeration of some of the factors that might affect the levels of state and local expenditure has two purposes. First, it warns that the measure of differences used below—per capita general expenditure—is imperfect; second, it indicates that a more refined measure would be difficult to construct.

For reasons mentioned later, figures of state and local revenue, when expressed per $1,000 of personal income, are not unambiguous measures of revenue effort.

Patterns of Aggregate Expenditure

For the fiscal year 1973, state and local general expenditures for the nation averaged $863 per capita. All general expenditures made by state and local governments are included in this figure, whether the funds were provided from their own sources or by federal grants.

Some idea of the spread among states in per capita state and local expenditures in 1973 is given in the following list:[2]

Per capita expenditure, in dollars	Number of states
Under 600	1
600–49	4
650–99	7
700–49	9
750–99	4
800–49	6
850–99	4
900–49	3
950–99	4
1,000–49	1
1,050–99	3
1,100–49	1
Over 1,150	3

These figures include funds from the federal government; in order to secure figures of per capita expenditure by states from their own

2. Derived from U.S. Census Bureau, *Governmental Finances in 1972–73*, p. 45. The states that spent over $1,150 are Alaska, $2,376; New York, $1,319; and Hawaii, $1,311; Arkansas had the lowest expenditure, $549.

Table 2-2. States with the Highest and the Lowest Per Capita General Expenditure, Excluding Federal Grants, 1973

Highest states	Per capita expenditure, in dollars	Expenditure relative[a]	Lowest states	Per capita expenditure, in dollars	Expenditure relative[a]
Alaska	1,759	267	North Carolina	439	67
Hawaii	1,061	161	Kentucky	437	66
New York	1,058	161	South Carolina	425	65
Delaware	906	138	Alabama	413	63
Nevada	871	132	Mississippi	368	56
Washington	816	124	Arkansas	313	48

Source: Table A-7.

a. The expenditure relative is computed by dividing a state's per capita state-local expenditure by the national average, $658. To compute the New York relative, for example, $1,058 ÷ $658 × 100 = 161.

sources, federal grants must be deducted. For 1973 per capita state and local expenditure, less federal grants, was $658.[3] The six states with the highest and the six with the lowest per capita expenditure on this basis are shown in table 2-2. New York, one of the highest states, spent $1,058 per capita in 1973. Arkansas, the lowest state, spent $313. The figures of per capita state-local expenditures can be made more readily comparable by assigning the value of 100 to the national average ($658), and computing relative numbers that express how much each state spends in relation to this national average. Table 2-2 shows that New York has an expenditure relative of 161 and thus spent from its own sources 61 percent more than the national average; Arkansas, with an expenditure relative of 48, spent 52 percent less than the average. Thirty-two states spent less than the average, eighteen states more.

Efforts have been made to discover and measure the significant variables (other than population) that explain the diversity among the states. The most important other variable or "cause" is income. In general, more will be spent by state and local governments in a "rich" state—one with a high per capita income—than in a "poor" state. The state-by-state relationship between per capita income and per capita state-local government expenditure, excluding federal grants, is presented in figure 2-1. The general pattern shows that income and government expenditure tend to rise together, with expen-

3. See table A-7 for per capita figures for all states, before and after deductions for federal grants.

Figure 2-1. States Ranked by Per Capita Income, 1972, and Per Capita General Expenditure, Excluding Federal Grants, 1973

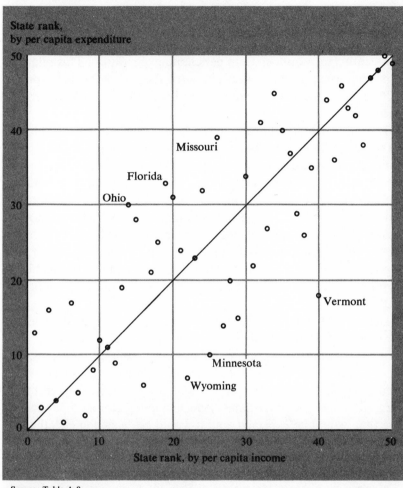

Source: Table A-8.

diture rising somewhat less sharply than income. For every 10 percent increase in a state's per capita income, state-local expenditure increases, on the average, by approximately 6 percent.

This average relationship has many exceptions. More often than not, states that rank low in per capita income have a higher rank in per capita expenditure; conversely, states that rank high in income quite often have a lower rank in per capita expenditure. And some states spend much more, and some much less, than one would expect in terms of their per capita income. For example, Connecticut and New Jersey, which in calendar year 1972 ranked first and third in terms of per capita income, ranked thirteenth and sixteenth in terms of per capita expenditure in fiscal year 1973. Vermont and Utah, which ranked fortieth and thirty-eighth in per capita income, ranked eighteenth and twenty-sixth in per capita expenditure. This relationship is not true for all functions; in particular, it is not true for public welfare. Here, per capita expenditure is usually larger in poor than in rich states.

The influence of other quantifiable variables has been explored, notably population density (population per square mile) and urbanization (percentage of population living in urban places). As population density increases, per capita state-local expenditure tends to decrease, but not uniformly and not for all functions. Per capita expenditure for police and fire protection tends to rise with population density. Increase in urbanization has a modest tendency to increase per capita expenditure, but not that for highways. Moreover, the population density and urbanization variables are themselves highly correlated and not independent; their effects, therefore, cannot be added.

Except for the distinct relationship between per capita income and per capita expenditure, statistical analysis of factors that affect state expenditures indicates considerable diversity among the states. Explanation of the diversities is to be found in historical background or political philosophy, rather than in quantitative facts. For instance, Virginia spends much less, and Louisiana much more, on public welfare than would be expected, and it would be "a safe guess" that the explanation lies in "differences in the political philosophy of the Byrds and the Longs."[4]

4. Glenn W. Fisher, "Determinants of State and Local Government Expenditures: A Preliminary Analysis," *National Tax Journal,* vol. 14 (December 1961), p. 353. In a subsequent article ("Interstate Variation in State and Local Government Expenditure," *National Tax Journal,* vol. 17 [March 1964], pp. 57–74), Fisher related per capita expenditure in 1960 to seven variables and secured a higher correlation than for the three variables (per capita income, population density, and urbanization) he considered earlier. In the later study he found a high negative relation between the levels of expenditure and the percentage of low-income families in a state. Seymour Sacks and Robert Harris ("The Determinants of State and Local Government Expenditures and Intergovernmental Flows of Funds," ibid., pp. 75–85) used the same three variables and included federal aid and state aid per capita as additional independent variables. They found that the significant

Table 2-3. Per Capita Expenditure and Percentage Distribution of General Expenditure, Excluding Federal Grants, of State-Local Governments, by Function, 1973

Function	Per capita expenditure, in dollars	Percentage of total spending
Education	311	47.3
Highways	66	10.0
Health and hospitals	58	8.8
Public welfare	56	8.5
Interest	32	4.9
General control	18	2.7
Fire protection	13	2.0
Other	104	15.8
Total	658	100.0

Sources: *Governmental Finances in 1972–73*, pp. 24, 45–48, and 52; and *Social Security Bulletin*, vol. 37 (October 1974), pp. 27 and 32.

Functional Distribution of Expenditure

In 1973, as table 2-3 shows, education was by far the most important type of spending of state and local governments. It absorbed $311 per capita, or 47.3 percent of total general state-local expenditure after deduction of federal grants. The per capita expenditure for other functions, and the percentage spent for each, are also given in table 2-3.

What state-by-state variation in per capita functional expenditures is found? This is examined by first calculating the expenditure in each state for each major function as a percentage of total state and local expenditure. If, for example, Maine—a poor state—spent approximately the same percentage of its total expenditure (less federal grants) on education in 1973 as Connecticut—a rich state—this would indicate that the function was appraised similarly in the two states even though their actual expenditures (expressed either per capita or per $1,000 of income) were quite different. These relative proportions of total state-local expenditure spent by the states in 1973 on selected functions are given in table 2-4.

increase in federal aid in the forties and fifties, notably for welfare, had been an important determinant of state and local expenditures. Allen D. Manvel, examining the number of state and local government employees per 10,000 inhabitants in an attempt to discover state patterns, concluded that, while economic capacity provided some explanation, "traditions and geographic and demographic characteristics" were at least as influential ("Regional Differences in the Scale of State and Local Government," *National Tax Journal*, vol. 7 [June 1954], p. 120).

Table 2-4. Variation in Expenditure of States by Percentage of State-Local Expenditure, Excluding Federal Grants, by Function, 1973

Function	Mean	Standard deviation	Coefficient of variation[a]
Education	50.72	6.47	12.76
General control	2.80	0.50	17.86
Financial administration	2.29	0.53	23.14
Highways	12.68	5.15	40.62
Interest on general debt	4.64	1.66	35.78
Fire protection	1.81	0.66	36.46
Public welfare	6.98	2.81	40.26

Sources: *Governmental Finances in 1972–73*, pp. 45–48; and *Social Security Bulletin*, vol. 37 (October 1974), p. 32.

a. The coefficient of variation is computed by dividing the standard deviation by the mean, and then multiplying this by 100. For example, for the series showing expenditures on education as a percent of total state-local expenditures, the standard deviation is 6.47 percent and the mean is 50.72 percent. The coefficient of variation is therefore 12.76 percent.

The extent of state variation in proportionate expenditure on different government functions can be measured first by calculating the standard deviation by states for each major function, and second by calculating the coefficient of variation—a percentage that expresses mathematically the degree to which the states vary in their proportionate spending on a particular function. The lower this percentage, the more similar the proportionate amounts spent by the states; the higher the percentage, the greater the variance.

The coefficients of variation for state-local spending, shown in table 2-4, indicate that variation in expenditure for education is modest. This expenditure falls into two parts, that for local schools and that for higher education. The low variation is explicable by the relative similarity of expenditure on local schools. Variation in expenditures for the other functions is much greater than that for education. Apparently, expenditure preferences of state and local governments for most functions are quite diverse from state to state.

Measures of Revenue Effort

Comparisons of state expenditures gain in cogency if they are related to a measure of revenue effort in which the revenues collected by state and local governments from their own sources are related to a relevant, uniform base. Here state personal income seems to be suit-

Table 2-5. States Collecting the Highest and the Lowest General Revenue from Own Sources per $1,000 of Personal Income, 1973

Highest states	Revenue per $1,000 of income, in dollars	Effort relative[a]	Lowest states	Revenue per $1,000 of income, in dollars	Effort relative[a]
Vermont	207	128	North Carolina	140	87
New York	204	126	Illinois	139	86
Alaska	200	124	Indiana	138	86
Minnesota	194	120	New Hampshire	136	84
Wisconsin	193	120	Missouri	134	83
Nevada	188	117	Ohio	134	83

Source: Table A-9.

a. Effort relatives are computed by dividing a state's revenue per $1,000 income by the national average, $161. Thus, for Vermont, $207 ÷ $161 × 100 = 128.

able.[5] Table 2-5 shows the revenues raised by state and local governments from their own sources per $1,000 of personal income for the six highest and the six lowest states in 1973. Vermont, the state exerting the greatest effort according to this scale, collected $207 per $1,000 of personal income; Ohio, the lowest state, collected $134. Nationally, the average revenue per $1,000 of personal income was

5. The income base is not unambiguous. Should it mean income produced, or personal income received by residents of a state? Both have been examined in a staff report of the Advisory Commission on Intergovernmental Relations, *Measures of State and Local Fiscal Capacity and Tax Effort* (ACIR, 1962). The report develops as another measure the representative tax system, which can be used to estimate the amount of revenue that state and local governments could produce, state by state, if they levied a cross-section of taxes currently in use by all state and local governments. This cross-section—established by identifying, weighting, and assigning rates to the present tax structure—provides an estimate of a state's tax capacity; when related to actual tax collections, indexes of a state's tax effort are obtained. These indexes vary significantly from the income indexes for some geographic areas (see ACIR, *Measuring the Fiscal Capacity and Effort of State and Local Areas* [Government Printing Office, 1971], pp. 10–20). For 1966–67 in twenty-nine states per capita personal income gives lower figures for relative fiscal capacity than does the representative tax system. In states where mining or tourism is an important element in the economy, the revenue potential of severance taxes and certain kinds of sales taxes lifts revenue capacity. So also in states where agriculture is an important element because "farming is not completely monetized and has some lingering elements of barter economy that are not fully reflected in income statistics" (ibid., p. 11). The representative tax measure may prove to be a useful measure of capacity. But the figures have been computed only for 1960 and 1967, whereas yearly figures of personal income in relation to state and local revenues are available, and, for this practical reason, are used in this book.

Table 2-6. Revenue Effort Compared with Expenditure Relative of Six States with Lowest Per Capita Expenditure, 1973

State	Expenditure relative	Effort relative
North Carolina	67	87
Kentucky	66	91
South Carolina	65	94
Alabama	63	91
Mississippi	56	103
Arkansas	48	87

Source: Tables A-7 and A-9.

$161. By assigning the figure of 100 to this national average, relatives can be computed for each state that express its effort compared to the national average. The effort relative for Vermont is 128, indicating that its receipts per $1,000 of personal income were 28 percent above the national average; the effort relative for Ohio is 83, or 17 percent below the national average.

Examination of the effort relatives shows, as might be expected, that the revenue collections of some rich states (for example, Illinois) are low in relation to personal income. This does not mean that they have low expenditure relatives.[6] Rich states can make above-average per capita expenditures while making a below-average effort. For example, the expenditure relative for Illinois in 1973 was 104; its effort relative was 86. Conversely, as table 2-6 shows, the expenditure relatives for the six states with the lowest per capita expenditure are all appreciably below the relatives indicating their revenue effort. The conclusion obtrudes that poor states would find it difficult to raise the level of their per capita expenditure to the average. In 1973, for example, South Carolina could have lifted its per capita expenditures to the national average only by lifting its revenue effort well above the national average.

Patterns of Tax Preference and Utilization

In examining the use of taxes by state and local governments, a major difference should be borne in mind. Local governments throughout the nation show little variety in the type of tax they utilize. In 1973, 83 percent of their tax revenue was from the property tax,

6. See table A-7.

and in sixteen states this figure topped 95 percent, as the following distribution shows:[7]

Percent of revenue	Number of states
40–45	1
45–50	0
50–55	1
55–60	0
60–65	0
65–70	5
70–75	2
75–80	6
80–85	7
85–90	5
90–95	7
95–100	16

The plight of many local governments is well known. Despite strong incentives and vigorous efforts, they have been unable to diversify, and they need help from the state level.

State governments, however, show great variety in the use and the weight of their taxes. Fifty years ago states relied heavily on the property tax which provided more than one-third of their tax revenue. Licenses for motor vehicles and operators were a poor second in importance, death and gift taxes third, and corporation income tax fourth (see table 2-7). By 1973 the first three had lost ground, while two old sources—motor fuel tax and individual income tax—had gained. Three new tax revenues—on general sales (usually levied at the retail level), alcoholic beverages, and tobacco products—had emerged, and the first of these won top rank over the whole field by a wide margin. The main target of state taxes now, therefore, is consumption. The pattern of major state tax revenue sources in 1973 is shown in figure 2-2.

This pattern took shape in the 1930s. In 1927, for example, taxes on sales of specific items brought in 28 percent of state tax collections (of which 58 percent was from taxes on motor fuel); none of the revenue, however, was from general sales taxes. Property tax was losing favor as a source of state revenue, and the expectation was widespread that diminished federal reliance on income tax would bring increasing use by the states. As indicated in chapter 1, this ex-

7. *Governmental Finances in 1972–73*, pp. 31–33.

Financing State and Local Governments

Table 2-7. Percentage Distribution and Rank of Major Sources of State Tax Collections, 1922, 1938, 1948, 1968, and 1973

Type of tax	1922	1938	1948	1968	1973
	Percentage of total state tax revenue				
Sales and gross receipts	14.1	53.4	59.9	57.6	54.5
General	...	14.3	21.9	28.7	29.1
Selective	14.1	39.2	38.0	28.9	25.5
Motor fuel	1.4	24.8	18.7	14.2	11.8
Alcoholic beverage	...	5.6	6.3	3.1	2.7
Tobacco product	...	1.8	5.0	5.2	4.6
Other	12.8	7.0	8.0	6.4	6.4
Income	10.7	12.2	16.1	24.0	30.9
Individual	4.5	7.0	7.4	17.1	22.9
Corporate	6.1	5.3	8.7	6.9	8.0
License	31.5	16.0	14.5	10.6	8.5
Motor vehicle and operators'	16.1	11.5	8.8	6.8	5.3
Miscellaneous	15.4	4.5	5.7	3.8	3.1
Other	43.7	18.4	9.6	7.7	6.1
Property	36.7	7.8	4.1	2.5	1.9
Death and gift	7.0	4.5	2.7	2.4	2.1
Miscellaneous	...	6.1	2.8	2.8	2.1
	Rank in importance as source of state tax revenue				
Property	1	4	8	8	9
Motor vehicle and operators' license	2	3	3	5	5
Death and gift	3	8	9	9	8
Corporate income	4	7	4	4	4
Individual income	5	5	5	2	2
Motor fuel	6	1	2	3	3
General sales	...	2	1	1	1
Alcoholic beverage	...	6	6	7	7
Tobacco product	...	9	7	6	6

Sources: Census Bureau, *Historical Statistics of the United States: Colonial Times to 1957* (GPO, 1960), pp. 727–28; and Census Bureau, *State Government Finances in 1968*, pp. 20–22, and *in 1973*, pp. 19–21. Figures are rounded.

pectation was not fulfilled. With the Great Depression, states did turn to taxation of individual income—six states enacted such a tax in 1933. But in those dreary years the falling yield of income tax was distressing to state governments. The unfamiliar and unpopular retail sales tax, however, did bring in the revenue, and a trend started that has not yet lost its force.

While the number of state governments utilizing particular types of taxes does not indicate the weight of the taxes, it does reveal a rough pattern of state preferences. Table 2-8 shows that, in 1973,

Figure 2-2. Major Sources of State Tax Collections, 1973

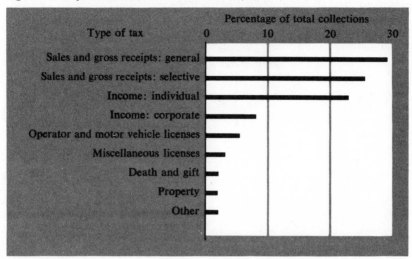

Source: Table 2-7.

Table 2-8. Income and Sales Tax Pattern of State Governments,
1928, 1941, 1951, and 1973

	Number of states[a]			
Type of tax	1928	1941	1951	1973
General sales tax only	0	8	13	9
Individual income tax only	12	14	12	4
Both	0	16	19	36[b]
Neither	38	12	6	1

Sources: Advisory Commission on Intergovernmental Relations, *State and Local Taxes, Significant Features, 1968* (GPO, 1968), pp. 12–13; and table A-10.
a. Hawaii and Alaska included.
b. Does not include New Hampshire and Tennessee, which levied taxes on interest and dividend income only, New Jersey, which levied on nonresident income only, and Connecticut, which levied on capital gains only.

only one state (New Hampshire) failed to utilize either a general sales tax or an individual income tax. The table indicates also that the number in this group has shrunk sharply over time. In 1973 thirty-six states utilized both taxes; over time, the number in this group has grown and it is likely to continue to grow.

In 1973 thirty-eight states secured half or more of their tax revenues from all taxes on sales and gross receipts (see table 2-9). In only five of the states (Oregon, Delaware, Massachusetts, Montana, and Alaska) that taxed individual income did this tax yield a larger

Table 2-9. Distribution of States by Percentage of Total State Tax Revenue Collected from Selected State Taxes, 1973

Percentage of total state revenue	Number of states taxing		
	All sales and gross receipts	General sales and gross receipts	Individual income
80–90	1 ⎫	0	. . .
70–80	9 ⎬ 38	0	. . .
60–70	14 ⎪	0	. . .
50–60	14 ⎭	1	1
40–50	6	8	2
30–40	3	21	8
20–30	3	11	16
10–20	0	4	12
Less than 10	0	0	5[a]
Total	50	45	44

Source: Derived from table A-10.
a. Includes New Hampshire, 4.9 percent; Tennessee, 1.5 percent; New Jersey, 1.3 percent; Connecticut, 4.4 percent.

slice of tax revenue than sales and gross receipts. If a comparison is made of percentage tax receipts from individual income tax and general sales tax in the thirty-six states that, in 1973, levied both, it appears that the yield of the latter was larger in twenty-eight states.

Conclusion

This brief survey indicates that the levels of state-local expenditure per capita are quite diverse from state to state. Even when the force of differences in the level of state income is excluded, the functional patterns remain diverse, except for expenditure on local schools and housekeeping functions.

Is a "satisfactory" level of governmental services being provided in "poor" states, and if not, how can it be provided? One may believe that a poor state should make an above average fiscal effort to achieve a satisfactory level. But if, despite such an effort, the level of state-local services remains unsatisfactory, should financial aid be provided by the federal government? If so, in what form?

With respect to revenues, the plight of many local governments is well known. Despite strong incentives and vigorous efforts, they have been unable to diversify, and they need more help from the state level. State governments have more revenue flexibility. Most of them have found taxation of consumption both suitable and responsive to their needs, but forty tax individual income, forty-five tax corporate income, and all but one levy death and gift taxes. Several minor taxes are limited to a few states. Severance taxes, now important only for Texas and Louisiana, can be utilized only by states with significant mineral extraction. Document and stock transfer taxes can raise important revenue only for states like New York and Florida that have a heavy volume of transfers of intangible property.

The major sources of revenue, state and local, are examined in detail in the chapters that follow. The fact that all or most state governments utilize a tax does not mean that they utilize it in the same fashion. Diversity of practices is the rule, and diversity may be on the increase. Diversity among the states in their efforts to secure a "fair" share of the tax base of interstate business creates interstate conflict and has an adverse economic impact on the nation. Federal intervention by legislation to specify the ground rules that state governments must observe has already occurred, and may be enlarged. And within states, intervention by state governments to reform the property tax, especially local diversities in assessment, seems indicated.

For many decades neither the state nor local governments have depended wholly on revenue derived from their own sources. Annual intergovernmental transfers have been made, principally through grants-in-aid. The grants, discussed in detail in chapter 3, have served a multitude of purposes, not all of them harmonious. This growth nonetheless appears to indicate a strong legislative belief in their merits.

CHAPTER THREE

Federal Intergovernmental Transfers

A VERY IMPORTANT development during the past forty years has been the proliferation of intergovernmental transfers, especially in the form of grants and shared taxes. These transfers of funds originate either with the federal government, flowing to the states and, in a smaller volume, to local governments; or with state governments, flowing to local governments.[1] In 1973, federal payments totaled $43,121 million, and state payments totaled $40,822 million. The likelihood is that the scope of both flows will be enlarged both absolutely and relatively.

Transfers to State Governments

The history of federal aid for certain functions, notably road construction and education, is quite old. In 1802, when Ohio was admitted as a state, Congress declared that 5 percent of the proceeds from the sale of public lands in the state should be applied to the construction of roads, and this precedent was followed for other west-

1. A modest flow from local to state governments—$802 million in 1973—is not examined here.

ern states. In 1818 Congress provided that states be given 5 percent of the net proceeds of land sales within their boundaries with the stipulation that 3 percent be used "for the encouragement of learning, of which one-sixth part shall be exclusively bestowed on a college or university."[2] Thereafter, Congress ceded millions of acres as an endowment for public schools, and, by the Morrill Acts, gave both land and money to establish colleges in every state. These early grants were outright donations with no matching requirement and no federal supervision. Not until 1887, when the Hatch Act made grants to each state to establish agricultural experiment stations, did Congress impose the modest condition that a financial report be submitted annually, and not until 1911, by the Weeks Act, which offered grants for forest fire protection, did Congress impose advance federal approval of state plans and federal supervision of performance. Several other federal grants—highways (1916), vocational education (1917), and so forth—were provided in the next two decades.

A great upsurge in federal grants began in the 1930s. After a temporary subsidence during World War II, growth continued, at first slowly and then explosively, in the 1960s and 1970s. The number of grants was 181 in 1963 and some 500 in 1973. The amount of expenditure for grants was $8,324 million ($44 per capita) in 1963 and $43,121 million ($204 per capita) in 1973. A better indication of the explosion is given by relating per capita grants to per capita state-local tax collections. Collections rose at a remarkable rate— from $234 per capita in 1963 to $577 in 1973—an increase of 147 percent (9.5 percent per year). But grants increased by 361 percent (16.5 percent per year). Grants were 18.9 percent of state-local taxes in 1963, and 32.6 percent in 1973. This growth in numbers and in amount of spending does not adequately mirror the growth in complexity of the grants. As a result a reaction developed in the late 1960s to which the Nixon administration was responsive. It proposed two broad changes: general revenue sharing, and special revenue sharing. By the first of these a general-purpose grant, without federal conditions, was to be provided to state and local governments. By the second, many existing specific-purpose grants were to be bundled into a limited number of categories.

Table 3-1 shows the shifts in the pattern of grants over the postwar

2. 3 Stat. 430.

Table 3-1. Federal Grants, 1948, 1963, and 1973

Purpose	Total, in millions of dollars			Percentage distribution		
	1948	1963	1973	1948	1963	1973
Public assistance	718	2,580	7,296	45.4	31.0	20.0
Health	55	442	5,668	3.5	5.3	15.5
Education	120	558	4,348	7.6	6.7	11.9
Economic opportunity	...	334	3,635	...	4.0	10.0
Miscellaneous social welfare	335	912	5,635	21.2	11.0	15.4
Highways	318	3,023	4,724	20.1	36.3	12.9
Other	33	477	5,179	2.1	5.7	14.2
Total	1,581	8,324	36,486[a]	100.0	100.0	100.0
General revenue sharing	...	...	6,636			
Total	1,581	8,324	43,121			
	Per capita, in dollars					
All purposes	11.01	44.39	204.04			

Sources: Sophie R. Dales, "Federal Grants to State and Local Governments, Fiscal Year 1973," *Social Security Bulletin*, vol. 37 (October 1974), pp. 27 and 32; *Annual Report of the Secretary of the Treasury on the State of the Finances for the Fiscal Year Ended June 30, 1963*, p. 675; U.S. Department of the Treasury, *Federal Aid to States, Fiscal Year 1973*, p. 10; and official U.S. Census Bureau population data. In all tables, years are fiscal unless otherwise noted. Figures are rounded. Dales reports on federal grants, the Census Bureau on federal intergovernmental payments. The Dales total of $43,121 million for 1973 includes $3,067 million allocated for food stamps, adjustments, Puerto Rico, Virgin Islands, and Samoa, Guam, and Trust Territory of the Pacific, which the Census total excludes, while the Census total of $41,666 million includes $1,612 million in shared revenues and miscellaneous items that Dales excludes.

a. In 1973, grants-in-aid accounted for over 80 percent of total federal intergovernmental transfers. Small amounts are in the form of shared revenues (most of which go to the states with large federal acreage), and net loans and repayable advances.

years. Two dominant categories at the outset—public assistance and highways—lost ground relatively after 1963. On the other hand, grants for public health and education grew steadily in relative and absolute amounts. A few of the major grants are described briefly here in order to bring out characteristics of the grant program as a whole.[3]

Public Assistance

Grants for public assistance began with the Social Security Act of 1935 when the federal government gave grants to the states to provide for three categories of needy unemployables—the aged, dependent children, and the blind. The grants reimbursed the states for one-half of their payments to the aged and the blind up to a $30 monthly ceiling, and one-third of their payments for children up to a ceiling of

3. A more detailed description is given in James A. Maxwell, *Specific Purpose Grants in the United States: Recent Developments*, Research Monograph 12 (Canberra: Australian National University, 1975).

$18 for the first child and $12 for each of the others. As conditions of eligibility, the federal legislation specified citizenship, residency, and age (sixty-five years for old-age assistance, and sixteen years for child dependency). The major responsibility, however, for determining what persons should be put on the welfare rolls was left to the states. And the grants were open-ended—payments to eligible recipients by the states, whatever their amount, created a federal liability to match or nearly match them. Since determination of eligibility was, in the main, left to the states, and since the criteria applied were not uniform, severe problems arose.

The program was rapidly accepted. Soon more liberal federal grants were provided and the format was altered. New categories were added—the permanently and totally disabled in 1950, and medical assistance to the aged, the blind, and the disabled in 1960 and 1962—and the coverage of families with dependent children was enlarged in 1961. The grants were made variable by providing that the federal contribution would be a larger fraction of a low payment than of a high one, and that payments by "poor" states (those with a low per capita personal income) would receive a larger reimbursement than those by "rich" states. For example, in 1969 the grant in a poor state for a family with dependent children was five-sixths of the first $18 paid monthly for the first child, plus 65 percent of the remainder up to a maximum of $32, that is, $24.10 as a grant for a payment of $32. The grant for a similar payment in a rich state was $22 (five-sixths of $18, plus 50 percent of $14).

Very early in the life of public assistance it became clear that interstate differences in standards of eligibility existed that arose out of state differences in definition and appraisal of need, as well as from differences in need itself. It became clear also that limiting grants to specific categories of public assistance had induced states—especially poor states—to load ineligible recipients on the eligible categories in order to minimize their expenditure for general assistance. General assistance, which received no federal grants, was a catchall program covering unemployables under sixty-five years of age and not blind, retired persons not in receipt of adequate retirement pensions, or employables not covered by unemployment insurance or not in receipt of adequate benefits.

For the first two decades after 1935, grants for old-age assistance absorbed more than half the grants for public assistance and had by

far the largest number of recipients. In 1950, however, the number of
recipients reached a peak and thereafter began a slow decline. The
main reason was that old-age insurance came to provide for more retired workers. At about the same time the number of recipients of
aid to families with dependent children (AFDC) turned upward: the
number of recipients was 2,486,000 in 1958 and 10,814,000 in
1973. The AFDC program became the dominant and the most con-
troversial category of public assistance. In 1973 almost 64 percent of
the money payments for public assistance ($7,212 million out of
$11,349 million) were for AFDC.

What brought the upsurge? The causes were multiple: the greater
frequency of divorce, separation, and illegitimacy enlarged the base;
an increased awareness of what the law allowed (because of the remarkable spread of legal assistance), and a liberalization of eligibility
rules[4] brought a substantial increase in applications.

In August 1969 President Nixon sent to Congress the family assistance plan (FAP) which proposed sweeping changes, most notably a federally administered program to replace AFDC. Under the
FAP, families with children and with income below a stipulated
amount would be eligible for benefits. The annual benefits were to be
$500 per person for the first two members of the family and $300
per person for each additional member. The family could earn $720
per year without loss of benefits. For each dollar of earnings in excess
of $720 per year, however, benefits were to be reduced by half a
dollar.[5]

The FAP was vigorously debated in the Congress for more than
two years, only to die in the Senate Finance Committee. Congress did,
however, make important changes in the federal welfare program by
"nationalizing" aid to the needy aged, the blind, and the disabled.
Under the Supplemental Security Income Act of 1972 (SSI), uniform eligibility criteria, benefit standards, and administration were

4. Two Supreme Court decisions helped this liberalization. In *King* v. *Smith*,
392 U.S. 309 (1968), the Court held that states could not declare families ineligible
because of the presence of a man in the house who was not married to the mother
of the family. In *Shapiro* v. *Thompson*, 394 U.S. 618 (1969), the Court eliminated
eligibility requirements based on the length of the residence period.

5. For further discussion of the FAP and other welfare reform proposals, see
Dorothy S. Projector, "Children's Allowance and Welfare Reform Proposals: Costs
and Redistributive Effects," in *National Tax Association, Proceedings of the Sixty-
second Annual Conference on Taxation* (1970), pp. 303–28.

provided for these three categories. Eligibility was assumed when the monthly income of an individual was less than $130, or less than $195 for an individual with an eligible spouse (raised to $146 and $219 by 1974). Earned income of $65 monthly was to be disregarded, plus half of any excess.

Highways

Grants for construction of highways began in 1916 under a formula that allocated funds among the states according to three factors: population, area, and rural delivery and star route mileage. Equal matching with state funds was required. A system of federal aid mileage was marked out in the 1920s and a plan of federal supervision was developed. The highway grants became the most orderly part of the whole program of grants.

During World War II plans were made for expansion and reform —expansion because a great postwar increase in traffic was certain, and reform in order to give more attention to urban roads. The plans came to fruition in the Federal-Aid Highway Act of 1956 which provided (among other things) for construction of a national system of interstate and defense highways of 41,000 miles (since raised to 42,500 miles), 90 percent of the cost to be paid by federal grants. A Federal Highway Trust Fund was established into which revenue from federal excises on motor fuel, tires, trucks, buses, parts, and so forth, is deposited and earmarked for the purposes of highway construction and maintenance. Annual receipts have ranged from $2 billion to almost $7 billion and the largest slice—70 percent in the early years—has gone for the interstate system. The share of each state is determined on a needs basis by computing the cost of constructing the mileage of a state in relation to total cost. The system, originally scheduled for completion in 1972 at a cost of $27.6 billion, was rescheduled for completion in 1990 at a cost of $98 billion.

In the 1970s, besides the interstate system, federal aid of approximately $1 billion annually has gone to the so-called ABC program under which the primary highway mileage received 45 percent, the secondary mileage 30 percent, and urban extension mileage 25 percent. For these, equal matching by the state was required until, in 1973, the federal share was lifted to 70 percent.

In recent years annual receipts of the Trust Fund ($6,675 million in 1974) have so greatly exceeded expenditures ($4,576 million) that a surplus has accumulated. The opinion has gained popularity that urban mass transit and high-speed rail transportation deserve federal aid, and that some part of the income of the Highway Trust Fund should be used for nonhighway purposes. The Federal-Aid Highway Act of 1973 permitted cities, beginning in 1976, to use annually $800 million of highway grant money either for highways, or for purchase of equipment, or for improvement and construction of mass transit projects. In 1974 a larger step was taken when Congress promised subsidies of $11.3 billion over a period of six years for urban mass transit and $0.5 billion for rural mass transit capital assistance.

Public Health

After precarious beginnings in the years after World War I, a new and broader support program for health services was set up in 1935 when grants were provided for public health work, maternal and child health services, and so on. In 1946 another aid program was added. By the federal Hospital Survey and Construction Act (Hill-Burton), the states were given grants to inventory their existing facilities in order to determine hospital needs, and grants were provided to construct both public and nonpublic facilities. Appropriations started at $75 million a year and were soon enlarged in annual amount and scope. Allocation to the states was according to population and a variant of per capita income.

The large program in the health area, however, is medicaid. Its beginnings can be traced to 1950 when Congress broadened the definition of public assistance to include vendor payments: direct payments by government to doctors and others for services rendered to persons on welfare rolls. A further step along the road of recognizing the medical needs of welfare recipients was taken in 1960 when the Kerr-Mills act established a new category of public assistance—medical assistance to the aged (MAA), offering to reimburse the states for 50–80 percent of the cost of state programs to provide medical care for "medically indigent" aged persons. The indigent who were blind, and the disabled, were added in 1962. The federal matching ratios (ranging from 50 percent to 80 percent) were to be inverse to state per capita income.

The grants proved attractive mostly to governments of rich states, and this fault induced Congress, in 1965, to create medicaid which extended the benefits of medical care to all recipients in federal-state public assistance programs, and also to the "medically indigent." The matching provisions of Kerr-Mills were, in general, carried over to medicaid.

Medicaid was rapidly accepted and, very soon, the grant payments, open-ended in type, rose at a rate much beyond the estimates. By 1973 these expenses amounted to $4.8 billion. Part of the explanation was that medicaid (and medicare) expanded demand more rapidly than the capacity of the health care system to deliver services. Another part was that the delivery system was inefficient and was sometimes used fraudulently by the providers of services and the recipients. Despite a matching formula that provided a higher rate of reimbursement by grants to low-income than to high-income states, the high-income states have expanded their coverage and their services more rapidly than low-income states. In 1974, for example, two states—New York and California—with 18.5 percent of the population of the nation received over 30 percent of the grants.

Education

Education was the first state-local service to receive federal grants. The early grants were in the form of land and the proceeds of land sales to be used to build roads and to endow public schools and colleges. In 1887 money grants were given to establish agricultural experiment stations, and in 1914 to create the agricultural extension service. In 1917 and again in 1940 Congress voted grants for vocational education, and in 1951 grant programs to help schools in federally impacted areas were approved by Congress. Eligibility of a school district for impacted area grants depended on such factors as a substantial increase in enrollment of children because of nearby federal projects, or federal acquisition of real property that impaired the revenue sources of local governments. The initial justification of federal aid in these circumstances is clear, and so also is continuance of aid in a limited number of cases. But Congress has not been selective; it has converted the program into a fairly general subsidy which sometimes goes to school districts suffering no adverse federal impact. The federal grants for these and all other education programs amounted in 1963 to $558 million, the largest single component being for federally affected areas.

Over the decades numerous efforts had been made to provide

grants for elementary and secondary education. But at all times the impediments to legislation were severe. The church-state issue was one impediment. If, as was widely believed, federal grants could go, for constitutional reasons, only to public schools, the relative position of nonpublic schools would worsen. On the other hand, an attempt to include nonpublic schools, even if it overcame the constitutional hurdle, would alienate many Protestants. In the 1950s and early 1960s both Catholics and non-Catholics locked themselves in un-yielding positions. Another impediment was the fact that need for federal grants seemed greatest in the South, and equalizing grants would be, in effect, for the relief of the southern states. The public school systems of these states rested on segregation, and even after it had been struck down by the Supreme Court, the belief lingered that deliberate speed in desegregation might be slowed by provision of grants.

It was therefore a legislative miracle when, in 1965, President Johnson proposed and secured enactment of a measure providing large grants for elementary and secondary education. How explain the miracle? One factor was the overwhelming political victory of the President in the 1964 election. His great prestige, coupled with political skill, enhanced the prospect of success for any measure he chose to endorse. Another factor was the accelerated pace of the movement for civil rights, and particularly passage of the Civil Rights Act of 1964 which required governmental recipients of fed-eral aid to demonstrate that no discrimination was being practiced in programs for which aid was being received. This step assuaged the fear that education grants would slow desegregation. Still another factor was the rediscovery of poverty. Poverty was not confined to poor states; it was present in all city slums adjacent to wealthy sub-urbs.

The Elementary and Secondary Education Act (ESEA) of 1965 offered grants to provide or strengthen programs for educationally disadvantaged children. The formula for allocating the grants to school districts depended on the number of children from families with incomes below $2,000 according to the decennial census plus the number from families receiving AFDC payments of more than $2,000. The AFDC figures were to serve as an updating factor since the census figures were collected only every ten years, and they were to include only children from families receiving in excess of $2,000 yearly in order to avoid double counting. The basic grant for a school district was calculated from the number of eligible children multiplied by one-half the average per pupil expenditure in the state or one-half the national per pupil expenditure.[6] Data for the calculations proved to be faulty, for the 1960 census was out of date, and the figures of eligibility for AFDC were capricious and heterogeneous.

In 1974 when Congress got around to extending and revising the formula,[7] it found that the relative weight of the AFDC figures had increased markedly since 1965. This shift had been unfavorable to the poorer states which were often less generous than rich states in placing families on the welfare rolls and sometimes had no AFDC families with incomes in excess of $2,000 on the rolls. As a consequence, no updating of the census numbers took place in these states.

The formula for grants devised in 1974 depended on the number of children from families officially defined as poor according to the new Orshansky index of poverty,[8] plus two-thirds of the number of AFDC children from families receiving payments in excess of the official definition. The new formula, therefore, decreased the importance of the AFDC count both because of the new definition of poverty and because only two-thirds of the number of AFDC children in excess of the poverty definition were reckoned. The payment rate was also altered. If the average per pupil expenditure of a state was less than 80 percent of the national average expenditure, school districts there would be entitled to 40 percent of 80 percent of the national average per pupil expenditure; if a state's average was in excess of 120 percent of the national average, school districts there would be entitled to 40 percent of 120 percent of the national average per pupil expenditure. Thus, a ceiling was set on the maximum payment rate.

The changes had the effect of reducing the ESEA grants to rich states such as New York and New Jersey. But this reduction was cushioned by a "hold-harmless" clause which provided that no school district should receive less in any fiscal year than 85 percent of the

6. The latter alternative was provided by amendment to the act in 1966.
7. Public Law 93-380.
8. The index measures poverty according to the number of children in the family, the sex of the head of the household, and the farm or nonfarm status of the family, in addition to family income. See Mollie Orshansky, "Counting the Poor: Another Look at the Poverty Profile," *Social Security Bulletin*, vol. 28 (January 1965), pp. 3–29.

amount it had received in the preceding fiscal year. Nonetheless, the rich states faced cuts, and this created dissent. The dissenters argued that the changes would take away grants from school districts with large concentrations of poverty children—particularly in urban areas. The dissent was, however, overridden.

Transfers to Local Governments

For many decades federal grants went wholly or predominantly to state governments. But this has changed and, in 1973, $11,067 million (more than one-quarter of the total) went to local governments (see table 3-2). Direct federal-local aid originated during the depression of the 1930s, and was administered by ad hoc agencies (the Federal Emergency Relief Administration, the Public Works Administration, the Works Progress Administration). Early in World War II these agencies were liquidated and the grants ceased. But in the postwar years a different set of grants, often representing community development, emerged.

Housing and Community Development

In the Housing Act of 1949 a program of urban renewal was started, the aim being to improve the physical condition of the cities. A local government submits a project for community improvement to a federal authority. After eligibility for federal aid is obtained, the locality acquires real property in the renewal area; it clears the land and disposes of it to a redeveloper. The federal government approves the plans, lends working capital, and provides grants up to two-thirds of the net project cost.

Progress of the program was slow and critics declared that too much emphasis was put on downtown commercial redevelopment, that too much construction favored middle-income housing units, and that relocation was disruptive and costly for poor displaced households. In one of many efforts to meet the criticisms, a model cities program was added in 1966, allowing selected communities to focus attention on specific blighted areas within their boundaries. Supplementary grants up to 80 percent of costs were provided to carry out approved plans. The model cities program, too, was over-regulated and underfunded.

This was the background when, on March 5, 1971, President

Table 3-2. Federal Intergovernmental Transfers to Local Governments, 1968 and 1973
Millions of dollars

Purpose	1968	1973
Education (school operation and construction in federally affected areas)	694	1,400
Housing and community development	784	2,025
Model cities	...	653
Airport construction	57	232
Waste treatment and water facilities	284	837
Urban mass transit	...	275
Other	453	1,221
Total	2,272	6,643
General revenue sharing	...	4,424
Total	2,272	11,067

Source: Census Bureau, *Governmental Finances in 1967–68*, table 6, and *in 1972–73*, table 6.

Nixon proposed special revenue sharing[9] for urban community development—the better communities bill. It aimed at remedying the two basic problems afflicting the existing system: excessive fragmentation of aid, and excessive federal controls on spending. Decisions had been biased toward federal viewpoints that often did not reflect the variety of local preferences and needs. In pursuit of the national interest in meeting urban problems, the error had been to assume that this interest required more uniformity in programs and more federal controls than was the case. Since the effects of the programs were largely local in character, local governments were in the best position to make efficient decisions concerning them.

When Congress in 1973–74 got around to consideration of the better communities bill, it was of two minds. While receptive to consolidation of grants and the notion of increasing the discretionary power of recipient governments, Congress was unwilling to give up requirements for prior planning reports to the Department of Housing and Urban Development, performance statements, and matching. Some congressmen worried also that block grants might not target the grants adequately toward low-income people, and that communities in the existing categorical programs would suffer from reduced grants if the number of recipients was expanded. By miracles of compromise, however, a new measure, the Housing and Community

9. Special revenue sharing was a form of block grant. The administration in January 1973 suspended homeownership assistance, rental assistance, and low-rent public housing.

Development Act of 1974, was framed and passed. While not special revenue sharing, the act did consolidate the major categorical programs of HUD—urban renewal, neighborhood development programs, rehabilitation loans, neighborhood facilities, open space land, basic water and sewer facilities, model cities—into a block grant, allocated by formula. The new grant authorized $8.4 billion to be distributed over three fiscal years, 1975–77; 80 percent was designated for standard metropolitan statistical areas and 20 percent for nonmetropolitan areas. The formula for distribution of the grants had three determinants: population, poverty (double-weighted), and the extent of housing overcrowding. All cities with populations of 50,000 and over, central cities of SMSAs, and urban counties were entitled to formula funds. No matching was required.

Distribution of the funds by formula was, however, complicated by extensive hold-harmless provisions. If an eligible recipient had received categorical grants that amounted to less than it was entitled to as a basic grant under the new formula, the recipient was to be "phased in" to its full formula level over a three-year period. But if a recipient's receipts for prior programs had exceeded the new formula entitlement, the recipient was to be held harmless for the first three years—it was to get grants equal to the prior level of receipts. In the next three years, by a "phase down," the payment was to be reduced by thirds to the formula level. As a further protection against shock, Congress was to review the application of the formula three years after it went into effect in order to be assured of its equity.

The community development program, on its face, moved strongly toward decentralization. A formula grant replaces ten categorical project grants; allocation, application, and administration are simplified. The number of applicants is enlarged with reduction of the opportunity for grantsmanship by applicants. The federal role becomes mainly one of review and monitoring of community programs; detailed approval and supervision of projects are discarded.

Waste Treatment and Water Facilities

The problem of pollution became an important public issue in the 1960s and 1970s. It seemed that an increasing standard of living was being accompanied by increasing environmental deterioration. As part of its response to this danger, Congress provided a great variety of grant programs to encourage state and local planning, research, demonstration, and construction. The obstacles to action were numerous. Planning and action concerning water pollution by single communities, or even states, were often ineffective because the appropriate unit was a river basin. Construction of municipal waste treatment facilities was ineffective unless action could be taken with respect to industrial pollution. Federal standards of water quality applied only to interstate waters, and application of such standards elsewhere encountered many problems, legal and economic.[10]

Federal programs to control water pollution stem from the Federal Water Pollution Control Act of 1956 (which has frequently been amended). The federal government began to make grants that would reimburse up to 55 percent of the construction costs of waste treatment plants. Allocation to the states was according to population and per capita income.

In 1970 and 1972 Congress passed acts committing the nation to an ambitious set of goals with respect to clean air and water, relying on regulation and on subsidies for construction of facilities to implement its new policy. The most significant shift in policy was to order limitation, and eventually elimination, of effluent discharges into water and air.[11] The grant provisions raised the authorization and lifted the federal share of cost for construction of facilities from 55 percent to 75 percent. Allocation of grants to the states is based on need as determined by the Environmental Protection Agency (EPA), which has since 1970 been responsible for administering most antipollution programs. The water pollution and clean air acts provide for retroactive reimbursement to communities that had earlier constructed facilities without federal grants. Eighty percent of the federal funds for control and abatement of pollution are aimed at water pollution, and by far the largest share is for construction of municipal waste treatment facilities.

10. For brief examinations of the problems and proposed remedies, see Charles L. Schultze and others, *Setting National Priorities: The 1972 Budget* (Brookings Institution, 1971), chap. 12; ibid.: *The 1973 Budget* (1972), chap. 11.

11. Allen V. Kneese and Charles L. Schultze, *Pollution, Prices, and Public Policy* (Brookings Institution, 1975), are very critical of this policy. They present "an alternative strategy with two central components: a set of national effluent and emission charges . . . and the creation of a set of regional authorities, under federal guidelines, to undertake the large-scale planning and public works construction needed for effective control of pollution in entire river basins or in the air above whole regions" (pp. vii–viii).

Bypassing State Governments

It is plausible to argue that direct federal grants to local governments are not compatible with the logic of federalism and are, moreover, administratively awkward. To work through fifty states would
appear to be better than to work through thousands of local governments. But difficult cases have operated to impair this general position. For instance, when the federal government, by extensive construction and operation of defense facilities in small geographic
areas, swells the school enrollment while not adding to taxable local
real property, federal grants to construct and operate schools seem
justifiable. Debate over whether or not the state government should
be the intermediary seems academic.

On their face the other types of grants to local governments (listed
in table 3-2) offer less plausible grounds for such direct action. But
the fact is that most state governments have not been interested in
urban renewal, low-rent public housing, airport construction, and
urban mass transit; most state governments have no such problems.
If national action was to be taken, it had to be by establishing a direct
federal-local relationship, federal aid being provided on a contractual
basis to numerous local agencies without an intervening state authority. The interests of the state in the activity, as well as its responsibility to its local governments, were sidetracked.

The problems, as well as the solution favored by Congress, are
illustrated by the debate in 1946 over the law authorizing federal
grants for airport construction. The enabling legislation specified
that any "public agency" (usually a municipality) could request federal aid for airport construction.[12] At issue was whether the state
governments should be required to establish state aviation agencies
through which the request was to be channeled. Should the federal
aid itself be channeled through state agencies? Such requirements in
the federal aid program for highway construction had worked well
for many decades. With respect to airports, however, the fact was
that many states had no agency and appeared uninterested. In 1946
the airport bill passed by the House did not, and the Senate bill did,
require channeling. A compromise position emerged: if states chose

12. 60 Stat. 170. It defined a public agency as the U.S. government or a state
or an agency thereof, or a municipality or other political subdivision, or a tax-
supported organization.

to require the channeling of requests and federal aid through a state agency, they could; if states did not wish to require such channeling, direct federal-local dealing was permitted.

This remains federal policy. Congress prefers to operate grants through a state program and will defer to state opinion, but it recognizes also that an overstrict and doctrinaire position would impair or destroy some desirable programs. Moreover, many city officials want direct federal grants, and they are supported by some interested federal administrators. When, in 1964, the Advisory Commission on Intergovernmental Relations (ACIR) recommended that federal grants for urban development programs be channeled through the states, minority dissent was expressed by Robert C. Weaver, administrator of the Housing and Home Finance Agency; by three city mayors; and by Senator Edmund Muskie.[13] The desire to bypass the states found full expression in many of the programs of the Office of Economic Opportunity.

Project Grants

Project grants are distinct from formula grants under which federal money is allocated among all eligible recipients according to a scheme established by law or regulation.[14] The allotment for a project grant remains in the hands of a federal administrator. Eligible recipients, whose projects have been approved by the administrator in a review and evaluation process, may compete to draw down funds in the grant allotment. Some allotments are made to state governments according to a formula and thereafter can be drawn on piecemeal by submission of projects to the appropriate federal administra-

13. *Impact of Federal Urban Development Programs on Local Government Organization and Planning,* prepared in cooperation with the Subcommittee on Intergovernmental Relations of the Senate Committee on Government Operations by the Advisory Commission on Intergovernmental Relations, 88:2 (GPO, 1964), p. 30.

14. The greatest users of project grants have been the Department of Health, Education, and Welfare (especially the Public Health Service and the Office of Education), and the Departments of Housing and Urban Development and Interior. Typical are grants for construction of community mental health centers, hospital staff development, mental health research, community development training, neighborhood facilities, urban beautification and improvement, urban planning research and development, coal mine health safety, outdoor recreation, and water pollution control.

tor for review. However, they should be regarded as formula grants that use the project technique for allocating funds. Highway grants, for example, are definite sums allotted to state governments which can be drawn down, bit by bit, through project applications. The important distinction is that decisionmaking on project grants is centralized in Washington, whereas for formula grants it is shifted out of federal control, usually to state governments.[15]

Project grants can, and should, be targeted at objectives that are closely defined. They should not, therefore, be simply supportive, that is, they should not simply lift from the grantees part of the financial burden of providing services or facilities (as is the case with a pure general-purpose grant). Project grants should be made for services that are new in type; besides, appraisal and evaluation of their achievement should be provided for.

The rapid growth of project grants in the 1960s was a matter of concern in some quarters. The Advisory Commission on Intergovernmental Relations, in 1967, noted:

The increasing reliance on project grants has important implications for the grant-in-aid system. It tends to diminish the National Government's certainty that Federal funds are being applied most effectively to meet nationally determined minimum requirements throughout the country. First, Congress leaves it to administrators to apply such distribution formulas, sometimes pursuant to legislative guidelines, imposing heavy pressure on administrators to weigh both program and political considerations in their decisions. Second, it places a premium upon the ability of applicants to know what aids are available, to prepare persuasive applications, and to expend the necessary efforts in following through to see that grants are forthcoming. By and large, this means that the state and local governments that are well organized and staffed will win the project grants. Yet they may have a relatively low index of need for the projects, or have a relatively high index of fiscal capacity with which to meet the need.[16]

Project grants are criticized chiefly because their proliferation has brought complexity, because they are seen as a threat to federalism,

15. The centralization of decisionmaking for project grants is imperfect since it often is diffused among many federal administrators so that even within an agency (such as HEW) overall coordination is loose. This impairs the advantage of better targeting which is expected to accrue through use of project grants.

16. *Fiscal Balance in the American Federal System* (GPO, 1967), vol. 1, p. 155. Total grant authorizations in 1966 numbered 379, of which formula grants numbered 99 and project grants 280 (ibid., p. 151).

and because they infringe horizontal equity (equal treatment of equals by government). The most commonly voiced, and well documented, complaint is that their number and variety are so great that a premium is placed on the ability of potential applicants to know what is available, how to prepare applications, and how to lobby them to funding. This ability and these skills are unlikely to be correlated with governmental needs, with the result that poor governments, and citizens for whom they have responsibility, are neglected. Multiplication of project grants, and the resultant problems of administration and delivery, have created other perversions. The flexibility of project grants has become a license for federal administrators to frame inconsistent patterns and to impose capricious rules. It is neither an excuse nor a vindication that these mistakes have been inadvertent. Selection and funding of projects has, to an appreciable extent, been politically motivated as a type of pork barrel spending.

The most philosophical—and most fundamental—criticism of the current chaos of project grants is that the basis and logic of federalism have been threatened. Programs have been put in operation that conflicted with the desires of responsible state and local officials. In such case, rational priorities to demands on limited community resources are difficult to frame; the decisionmaking function at state and local levels is eroded; achievement of uniform standards of provision of governmental services across the nation is defeated.

The rationale for project grants is that each is transient in its time period, self-limiting in scope, and so framed as to be capable of evaluation. However, continuance, year after year, when a project grant has fulfilled its purpose of demonstration, or experimentation, or innovation, infringes the principle of horizontal equity. Certain governmental services are, through the grant, rendered to people in certain geographical areas and not rendered to similarly situated people in other areas. Equals are not treated equally; instead, the federal government, through the grant, is being indefensibly discriminatory. The argument that it is better to render benefits to a limited clientele than not to render them at all is unacceptable. It assumes that no substitute exists on which the money spent for a particular project could be used, and this is nonsense.

Grants are an essential mechanism for federalism. Through them many governmental programs will be operated by state and local governments with some federal guidance and financial assistance. The grants should, predominantly, be of the formula type. Experience shows, however, that categorical programs require periodic appraisal and modification if they are to be responsive to changing public needs. Sometimes the programs should be broadened into block grants, and even converted into general-purpose grants. But sometimes the programs should be reshaped, and a principal instrument for accomplishing that is the project grant. It can be used to probe behind the facade of established methods and to expose the inertia of some state and local programs.

Another use of project grants is to detect unmet public needs and to design programs by which these needs can best be met. A project grant, so long as its coverage and scope are modest, can be targeted and tailored with precision; it can be framed so as to secure an evaluation of output. Not only will these features make for efficiency, they will also serve as safeguards when evaluation indicates that the project should be scratched.

The future of the project grant should, therefore, be as an instrument of cautious federal leadership in renovating and reshaping its intergovernmental grant programs.

Problems Raised by Grants

The proliferation of grants, piecemeal, has raised problems that until recently were not perceived by Congress. Once put into operation, grants live on, even though their original national purposes have altered or been achieved. Over the decades, an unforeseen and unjustifiable diversity has grown up in specific conditions to be met by the states—in mode of apportionment, in the basis for matching, in administrative rules, and so forth. Moreover, federal grants have altered the financial decisions of state governments; the bait of federal money has led state legislatures to spend in directions chosen by federal authority. The theory was that, in the national interest, performance of specific services by state and local governments needed stimulus which federal grants would provide. The possibility that matching requirements of federal grants might not reflect the relative federal versus the state-local benefits to be derived from the expenditure was overlooked. Nor did Congress appreciate that state legislatures, in order to finance the services eligible for grants, would sometimes divert state money from services not eligible for grants.

A notable illustration is found in expenditure for public assistance. State and local expenditures for four categories of public assistance

—old age, families with dependent children, the blind, and the permanently and totally disabled—were eligible for, and received, substantial federal grants; expenditure for general assistance, a catch-all group covering needy persons not in the four categories, was ineligible. Beyond question, state and local expenditure on general assistance has been skimped, especially in the poor states. Some idea of the contrast in provision of public assistance among the states in 1972 is given in these ratios of payments for old-age assistance to payments for general assistance in poor and rich states:[17]

Poor states	Ratio	Rich states	Ratio
Alabama	5,406:1	Delaware	1.68:1
Mississippi	222:1	New Jersey	1.08:1
Oklahoma	138:1	New York	0.75:1

The ratio was very much higher in the poor states than in the rich. For every dollar spent on general assistance in Mississippi, $222 was spent on relief to the aged.

Decisions Relevant to a Grant

A federal specific-purpose grant should be regarded as a payment to a state or local government for acting as federal agent in achieving a level or quality of a particular service that seems desirable in the national interest, care being taken to prevent substitution of grant money for existing state or local expenditures. The grant could be provided as a percentage of eligible expenditure. If the calculation of the amount of the appropriate federal and the appropriate state-local shares is accurate, state-local spending is not distorted by the grant. The federal expenditure, through the grant, is (indirectly) spending for national purposes; the state-local spending is (directly) for state-local purposes.[18]

17. U.S. Social Security Administration, *Social Security Bulletin: Annual Statistical Supplement, 1972*, p. 148.

18. The rationale for grants offered by George F. Break, *Intergovernmental Fiscal Relations in the United States* (Brookings Institution, 1967), chap. 3, is based on a calculation of spillovers or externalities. Benefits from some state services do not stop at state boundaries. Spillovers exist, and they induce states to supply less than would be in the national interest. The indicated technique for reaching the desired level is federal intervention through provision to pay for the increase in the supply or quality. The explanatory merit of this rationale is limited. Many federal grants do not fit into the spillover rationale. For example, public assistance grants are to be justified on broad humanitarian grounds—the federal responsibility to see that needy disadvantaged people are able to achieve a minimum standard of living.

In setting up a federal specific-purpose grant, the federal government should decide what, in the national interest, is the desirable level of provision and therefore the aggregate expenditure on the service, and what should be the federal share. Suppose the grant is to be provided for an established service, on which the state governments are making substantial expenditures on their own volition out of their own revenue sources. The federal government offers a grant because it believes that, in the national interest, the supply is inadequate in amount or deficient in quality. If the estimated aggregate required annual expenditure is 200, if the existing state expenditure is 100, and if the federal government offers 100 in grants, state expenditure will not be stimulated or distorted. The federal government will impose a maintenance-of-effort requirement. This requires no increase of state spending, no reduction of state spending for other purposes, and no undermining of state freedom of choice in expenditure patterns.

When a grant is to be made for a new service—one on which state-local expenditure is insignificant—any matching requirement would call for either provision of additional state revenue or a reduction of other expenditure. This may or may not distort state priorities. Sometimes state governments have refrained from providing a desired service—concealed their preferences—for fear of the economic impact on their competitive positions. Each state holds the others back. Provision of a federal grant serves to break the restraint and to remedy an existing distortion in state priorities. Careful prior investigation, including federal consultation with state officials, will enable the right choice for "new" grants to be made. The danger to be avoided is covert coercion of state governments, especially by a faulty matching ratio.

Open-ended versus Closed Grants

When the federal government indicates the annual amount of its grant, and this decision automatically determines the matching ratio, the grant is assumed to be closed. Most federal grants have been closed, but some—notably public assistance and medicaid—have been open-ended—the federal government has promised to share "whatever program costs the grantee wishes to incur and not limit its support to some fixed amount each year."[19] The federal govern-

19. Ibid., p. 78.

ment, in such case, simply responds to state-local spending decisions; it gives up control over the amount of its spending for the open-ended grants. This major fault in federal grants has, for decades, annoyed both the Congress and the executive.

Two major assumptions behind the open-ended grant—that the services eligible to earn grants can be defined with fair precision and that policing is not difficult—are seldom correct. Regularly, the content of an eligible service has been, and can be, enlarged beyond what Congress intended or desired because grants often go to segments of a state-local service, the boundaries of which are imprecise. Public assistance grants, for example, went to categories of needy people, with some categories excluded. The evidence is that many states placed ineligible people in the grant categories, thereby cutting back on state spending from own sources. This substitution is a second major fault of the open-ended grant. Moreover, even if the substitution is detected, it is not easy to eliminate because the persons affected are needy (though ineligible).

Open-ended grants should be confined to services for which objective methods of testing eligibility can readily be framed and utilized; these are rare. Closed grants also have a practical fault, in that they require review by the executive and the Congress. Because governmental priorities and preferences change, the annual allocation and the time period of each closed grant should be appropriate to that grant.

To assure that federal spending brings state as well as federal benefits, specific-purpose grants should contain matching requirements. And the requirements should reflect the ratio of estimated benefits, federal and state, to be derived from the spending. Specific-purpose grants also should contain provisions for federal supervision in order to achieve the federal objectives that are the justification of the grants.

Equalization

Equalization through grants is accomplished by the redistribution of income among the states. The equalizing effect is produced by two sets of forces. One is tax equalization, the process by which money that is eventually spent as grants is collected through the federal tax system.[20] The other is formula equalization which Congress provides by its allocation of grants and by the matching requirements it sets. By using variables that take account of relative capacity as a determinant in allocating grants, or in setting matching requirements, explicit recognition is given to differences in the fiscal capacity of states. A variable commonly used is the inverse of per capita income; grant allocation is larger, or matching ratio smaller, when per capita income is low than when it is high.

Measurement of the Redistribution

A rough measurement of the redistribution by states requires the use of estimates of state-by-state federal tax incidence. These estimates rest on assumptions that are disputable, and therefore the results are approximations. Verification is not feasible, since the different results depend on the different sets of assumptions. The figures of tax incidence in table 3-3, calculated by the Tax Foundation,[21] infer that when the federal government collected $1 in taxes from the average resident of the nation, it collected $1.43 from the average resident of Connecticut and only $0.55 in Mississippi.

The ratios of state tax incidence to the average U.S. incidence can be used to arrive at a measure of the redistributive effect of federal grants to states and of federal taxes collected from states to pay for these grants. In fiscal 1973 the federal government distributed $205 per capita in grants to state and local governments; in order to provide the grants, it collected this amount from the average resident of the nation. Thus, residents of Connecticut paid an estimated $293 per capita ($205 × 1.43); in fiscal 1973 Connecticut received $179 per capita in federal grants. The negative differential between the two

20. Grants are often criticized for simply taking money away from individual residents of states, bringing it to Washington, and then redistributing the money among the states (after deducting "freight charges"). One implication is that the freight charges are an unnecessary cost. In fact, federal costs of collection are much less than state costs would be. Another implication is that what the federal government collects to provide grants belongs to the state in which it was raised. This misconstrues the purpose of grants. Grant expenditure, like any other federal expenditure, is aimed at national objectives; it should, therefore, be allocated to achieve these objectives.

21. Tax Foundation, *Facts and Figures on Government Finance, 1973* (New York: Tax Foundation, 1973), p. 123. The method is discussed in Tax Foundation, *Allocating the Federal Tax Burden by State,* research aid no. 3 (rev. ed.; Tax Foundation, 1964).

Table 3-3. Estimated Per Capita Incidence of Federal Taxes for the United States and Selected States, 1972

State	Per capita tax incidence, in dollars	Ratio of state incidence to U.S. incidence
United States	934	1.00
Connecticut	1,338	1.43
Nevada	1,216	1.30
Arkansas	595	0.64
Mississippi	511	0.55

Source: Table A-12.

Table 3-4. Per Capita Redistribution of Income Attributable to Federal Grant Formulas and Tax Incidence in Connecticut and Mississippi, 1973

State	Grant formula	Tax incidence	Total
	Redistribution, in dollars		
Connecticut	−26	−88	−114
Mississippi	+93	+92	+185
	Percentage distribution		
Connecticut	23	77	100
Mississippi	50	50	100

Source: Table A-13.

amounts ($293 and $179) was, therefore, $114 per capita. Mississippi, with the lowest per capita incidence of federal taxes—$113 ($205 × 0.55)—received $298 per capita in grants in fiscal 1973; its positive differential was thus $185 per capita ($298 − $113).

How divide the total redistribution into that attributable to the grant formulas and to tax incidence? Assuming a neutral formula that allocates grants according to population, Connecticut and Mississippi would both have received in fiscal 1973 per capita grants of $205. In fact, their grants were, respectively, $179 and $298. Therefore, the formulas gave Connecticut a negative differential of $26 per capita, and Mississippi a positive one of $93. When these differentials are subtracted from the total redistribution, the part attributable to federal taxes alone gave Connecticut a negative differential of $88 and Mississippi a positive one of $92. As table 3-4 shows, the relative redistribution accomplished by federal taxes was considerably greater than that accomplished by grants for Connecticut, a rich state. Scrutiny of figures for all the states (see table A-13) indicates the greater weight of tax equalization, especially for the richer states. But exceptions are frequent because so many of the variables used to determine the distribution of grants to the states are not equalizing.

The interstate redistribution through taxes is wholly an accidental by-product, since Congress shapes the tax system without considera-tion of any particular grant or of grants in the aggregate. Nonethe-less, the knowledge that tax redistribution takes place does limit the willingness of Congress to provide much additional redistribution through grants.

One other aspect of federal grants is their service as an alternative to federal assumption of responsibility for an activity. Use of grants means that some part of the cost of the activity remains with state and local governments, and they provide this part through a regres-sive tax system. Such a procedure brings about less interstate redistri-bution of income than would complete federal assumption of the activity.

The allocation of a specific-purpose grant should rest on estimates of what would be required to achieve acceptable levels of provision of a particular state-local service, state by state, over the nation. If, for example, the specific service is construction of an interstate high-way system, then estimates should be made of eligible mileage and construction costs, state by state, of highways that meet national stan-dards of traffic needs and of defense. Two states equal in population, personal income, and area would be allotted different mileages and different amounts of estimated expenditure accordingly as their ter-rain and traffic needs were different. The equality or inequality of the two with respect to per capita income should not affect the allocation of grants to them. What if the specific service were of a welfare type? Again the question to be answered is: What is required, in the aggre-gate and state by state, to provide an acceptable level over the nation? The allocation to a poor state would be greater than that of a rich state because the number of its eligible recipients would be greater, and not simply because it is poor. The allocation would be equalizing, that is, redistributional in terms of the states as units. But this is not the direct objective; it is a by-product.[22] The objective is to achieve a

22. The redistribution is, in fact, very modest, as these Spearman coefficients of rank correlation by states between state per capita income, 1970–72, and federal specific-purpose grants, 1973, indicate: education, −0.5496; economic opportunity and manpower, −0.0397; public assistance, +0.0416; health, −0.1990; highways,

level of provision of the particular service, through cooperative effort, that is acceptable to the nation in every state.

What should be the matching ratio? If a nation has a system of general-purpose grants aimed directly at revenue equalization of governments in the different states (as is the case in Canada), then variable matching is inappropriate. The ratio for each specific-purpose grant should be uniform at, say, 50–50 when, in the aggregate, federal-state interests (and benefits) are equal, or say, 75–25, when this is the estimate of relative benefits. The United States has no such system of equalizing grants; specific-purpose grants with variable matching ratios have been utilized as an inadequate substitute.

Revenue Sharing

Revenue sharing is an approximate synonym for an unconditional or general-purpose grant. By such a grant the donor government does not manifest an interest in specific functions of the recipient government; rather it provides grants that the recipients may use as they choose. The logic of such a grant is that the federal government has an interest in enabling all standard state and local functions to be performed at a foundation (or average) level, and has an ability superior to that of state and local governments to raise revenue. With respect to many services, federal conditions and supervision would not be appropriate and efficient because they could not take account of the diversity and heterogeneity of state and local needs. The rationale of an unconditional grant is to enable governments in all states, by exerting an average fiscal effort, to provide an average level of services for their residents.

In the fall of 1964 a Task Force on Intergovernmental Fiscal Cooperation, created by President Johnson, recommended federal provision of unconditional grants to state governments.[23] Although President Johnson did not accept the plan, many political figures did, among them Richard M. Nixon, the Republican candidate for the presidency. In August 1969, as President, he made a formal proposal

---

−0.1740; miscellaneous social welfare, −0.5067; other, −0.1224; all specific-purpose grants, −0.2521.

23. This step was inspired by Walter W. Heller, chairman of the Council of Economic Advisers. The task force was headed by Joseph A. Pechman. The proposal came to be known as the Heller-Pechman plan.

of revenue sharing to the Congress. His proposal, markedly altered by the Ways and Means Committee (chaired by Wilbur D. Mills), passed the House of Representatives on June 22, 1972. In the Senate the Finance Commitee, while favoring revenue sharing, made several amendments to the House bill, of which the most important was a change in the allocation formula. By the House bill, allocation to the states had five determinants: population, per capita income (inversely), urbanized population, tax effort, and 15 percent of revenue from personal income taxation. By the Senate bill, allocation had three determinants: population, per capita income (inversely), and tax effort. The House formula was favorable to highly populated and rich states, the Senate one to rural and poor states. The House bill had a list of priority-expenditure categories on which revenue-sharing grants to localities were to be made, whereas the Senate bill had none.

The conference committee managed to produce a bill that became law late in October as the State and Local Fiscal Assistance Act of 1972. This provided general-purpose grants of $30,236 million for five years (January 1, 1972 to December 31, 1976), one-third going to the state governments and two-thirds to general-purpose local governments (numbering 38,552 at the beginning of 1972). Each state would be assigned its entitlement under the allocation formula that gave it the larger amount. This step would, of course, raise the total allotment. As a remedy, the allotment for each state was cut by the percentage excess of the total (8.4 percent for the first year). The allocation to thirty-one states was, therefore, based on the Senate formula, and that to nineteen states and the District of Columbia on the House formula. Within each state the formula for allocating funds to general-purpose local governments was, in general, based on three factors: population, per capita income (inversely), and tax effort.[24] A list of priority-expenditure categories included in the House bill was so expanded in the conference bill that it was ineffective as a directive.[25]

24. Tax effort for a state area is calculated as the ratio of total state and local tax revenue to personal income of the residents of the state. For local governments, tax revenues are adjusted to exclude revenue used to finance education (to get around the awkward fact that, while some general-purpose local governments have the responsibility for financing education, in other areas independent school districts have the responsibility).

25. The first version of the House bill had a maintenance-of-effort provision which required local governments to spend on the priority categories, from their

The complexity of the allocation formulas mirrors the variety of purposes that proponents of revenue sharing wished to meet. Heller and Pechman were interested in combating "fiscal drag" in the economy of the nation and in "equalizing" the fiscal positions of rich and poor governments;[26] others desired governmental decentralization, or slowing down the growth of specific-purpose grants, or reduction in state and local taxes, or helping local governments (especially the large cities). While the revenue-sharing bill was being framed, a great many different formulas were tried out on the computers, and the quantitative results with respect to each state or congressional district affected the attitudes of members of Congress.[27] Very obviously the determinants in the formulas do not pull in the same direction. And the remarkable fact that two sets of formulas are in operation confounds rationality; it creates a dualism without parallel in any other federal fiscal measure.

The formula allocations to local governments are subject to two ceilings and one floor. No county area or city or township can receive per capita more than 145 percent or less than 20 percent of the state-wide per capita amount available for local distribution. No local government can receive annually more than 50 percent of the amount it received from (nonschool) taxes and intergovernmental receipts.

Since the revenue-sharing act is limited to a five-year period, the question of replacement is a live issue.[28] What uses have been made

---

own sources, as much as they had spent in the two preceding years. When this requirement was deleted, most of the effect of the priority categories was destroyed. A local government could assign revenue-sharing grants to the priority categories, diverting revenue from its own sources to other purposes.

26. The value of the Spearman coefficient for state per capita income in relation to revenue-sharing grants is −0.393, indicating a slight negative correlation. Some rich states—New York, Hawaii, Massachusetts, Delaware—receive high grants, and some poor states—Oklahoma, Georgia—receive low ones. The spread between low and high grants is modest.

27. Chairman Mills, during the debate on the bill, told the House that the Ways and Means Committee "ran through computers every conceivable suggestion that could be made by any and all members," seeking results that would be supported by a majority of the members (*Congressional Record,* vol. 118, pt. 17 [1972], p. 21705).

28. Three studies of the act deserve mention: Richard P. Nathan, Allen D. Manvel, Susannah E. Calkins, and associates, *Monitoring Revenue Sharing* (Brookings Institution, 1975); Advisory Commission on Intergovernmental Relations, *General Revenue Sharing: An ACIR Re-evaluation* (GPO, 1974); and Wallace E. Oates, ed., *Financing the New Federalism: Revenue Sharing, Conditional Grants, and Taxation* (Johns Hopkins University Press for Resources for the Future, 1975).

of the grants? According to one study, local jurisdictions used 57.5 percent for "new" purposes, and 42.5 percent for substitution (such as tax reduction, or tax stabilization, or avoidance of borrowing); state governments used 35.7 percent for "new" purposes, and 64.3 percent for substitution.[29]

What are the main suggestions made for alteration in the act? Abolition or modification of the 145 percent ceiling and the 20 percent floor is stressed by the Brookings analysts. The 145 percent ceiling had served to reduce the allocations of large municipalities, notably of several large cities. Its elimination would "benefit the most hard-pressed local jurisdictions, curtail the law's bias in favor of multilayered local government, simplify its administration, and make the resulting allocations far more understandable to concerned officials and the public." The 20 percent floor had a "strong tendency to shore up marginal jurisdictions." This study also advises replacement of per capita income as a measure of relative fiscal capacity for state areas by a measure of "potential tax capacity," and for individual municipalities, townships, and county areas by a measure of "equalized taxable property values." The provision of the law that mandates that two-thirds of the total grants go to localities would be altered so that the state-local proportion "would vary from state to state according to the relative fiscal roles of the two levels of government." A uniform split (one-third, two-thirds) is unfair because it fails to take account of the marked variations in the division of state-local fiscal responsibilities from state to state.[30]

The reevaluation of revenue sharing by the ACIR led to a recommendation for renewal, with a shift to permanent trust fund financing which would be provided by a constant percentage of the federal personal income tax base. Retention of the present distribution formula is advised.[31]

Appraisal of Grants

In spite of faults, the device of federal grants has been strongly endorsed. The Hoover Commission in 1949 declared that, "in addition to decreasing inequalities of service, [grants had] raised the level

29. Nathan, Manvel, Calkins, and associates, *Monitoring Revenue Sharing.*
30. Ibid., pp. 168 and 169.
31. ACIR, *General Revenue Sharing*, pp. 26 and 30.

of all aided services, without transferring functions entirely to the National Government."[32] The Kestnbaum Commission declared that "the grant has become a fully matured device of cooperative government."[33] Differences of opinion exist, however, over the merits of specific-purpose and block grants. The former allow fairly precise application of federal conditions and controls in order to guide the performance of recipient governments. Unfortunately, this procedure brings administrative difficulties as the number of grants multiplies, and it may induce state and local governments to spend more on the segments of the aided activity than is warranted.

The enormous growth in the number and variety of specific-purpose grants in the 1960s brought a new awareness of their faults. As a result, a formidable information gap was created because state and local officials could not know what was available; "grantsmanship" was stimulated, and this enabled the alert rather than the deserving government to secure federal money.[34] The certainty is, moreover, that the federal government, misled by its superior fiscal power and by a lack of appreciation of the limitations of specific-purpose grants, had sometimes substituted federal preferences for those of the states. It had often failed to appraise practicalities by imposing controls that were too detailed, as well as inappropriate to the diversity of state-local needs. It had, in short, centralized decisionmaking beyond the limits of effective federalism.

Among the remedies proposed, the most popular was that related specific-purpose grants should be bundled into blocks. But application proved to be very difficult because of the opposition of federal and state bureaucracies, interest groups who wanted earmarked

32. Commission on Organization of the Executive Branch of the Government, *Overseas Administration; Federal-State Relations; Federal Research*, a report to the Congress (GPO, 1949), p. 30.

33. U.S. Commission on Intergovernmental Relations, *A Report to the President* (The Commission, 1955), p. 120.

34. Problems that bothered state and local governments were: different matching requirements; different procedures to process grant applications; the growth of project grants and the administration of them by different levels of federal officials even within a department. Efforts were made by federal agencies (notably the Office of Economic Opportunity and the Department of Health, Education, and Welfare) to catalog the grants. But the catalogs themselves were bulky and intricate, and they became obsolete with great speed. Other efforts have been made such as briefing sessions for state and local officials, and creation of federal task forces and interagency committees to simplify administrative procedures. All of these, however, are similar to the labors of Sisyphus.

grants, segmented congressional committees, and fragmented program administration. In 1971 the Nixon administration came up with the proposal of special revenue sharing. Some one hundred and thirty specific-purpose grants were to be bundled into six packages— law enforcement, manpower training, urban community development, transportation, rural community development, and education. The proposals went beyond block grants because special revenue sharing would require no matching, no maintenance of effort, and no prior project approval. Within each of the six broad areas, recipient governments would have the authority to spend the federal money on programs of the highest priority to them.

Over the next four years Congress considered and responded to the proposals for special revenue sharing. With some hesitation, it was receptive to consolidation of grants and the notion of increasing the discretionary power of recipient governments. But it was not willing to give up requirements for matching, and for planning and performance reports to the appropriate federal agency. The new system of grants provided in the Crime Control Act of 1973, the Housing and Community Development Act of 1974, the Comprehensive Employment and Training Act of 1973, and the National Mass Transportation Assistance Act of 1974 indicated that the drive behind special revenue sharing had force and appeal, even though certain of its features were unacceptable.

CHAPTER FOUR

State Intergovernmental Transfers

A SECOND BROAD STREAM of intergovernmental transfers flows from state to local governments. Local governments, constitutionally, are the creatures of the states, and the states have spawned a large progeny. When the first count was made, for the early 1930s, the total number of all types of governmental units in the United States was approximately 175,000. By 1967 it had fallen to 81,299 and by 1972 to 78,269 as a result of a steep decline in the number of school districts (see table 4-1). Undoubtedly, in many parts of the United States the number of governmental units is still excessive.

Structure of Local Governments

An important characteristic of many local governments is the overlapping of three or four—and occasionally seven or eight—layers of governmental units in the same geographic area. There may be school districts, sanitary districts, counties, soil conservation districts, drainage districts, and so on. In terms of public finance, the diversity and proliferation seldom make sense. In rural areas, small and overlapping units often lack the resources to perform any function

Table 4-1. Number and Type of Governmental Units in the United States, 1957, 1967, and 1972

	Number of units			Change in number	
Unit of government	1957	1967	1972	1957–67	1957–72
National	1	1	1	...	...
State	48	50	50	+2	+2
County	3,047	3,049	3,044	+2	−3
Municipality	17,183	18,048	18,517	+865	+1,334
Township and town	17,198	17,105	16,991	−93	−207
School district[a]	50,446	21,782	15,781	−28,664	−34,665
Special district	14,405	21,264	23,885	+6,859	+9,480
Total	102,328	81,299	78,269	−21,029	−24,059

Sources: U.S. Census Bureau, *Census of Governments, 1957*, vol. 1, no. 1, *Governments in the United States*, p. 1; and *1972*, vol. 1, *Governmental Organization*, p. 1. In all tables and figures, years are fiscal unless otherwise noted.

a. This counts only the so-called independent school districts. In 1972 dependent school districts numbered 1,457.

efficiently. State governments have an important responsibility for these situations; certainly they should be careful not to waste resources and perpetuate inefficiency by grants to archaic governmental units. In urban areas, governmental units of very unequal financial strength cannot provide a uniform level of service; the infirm ones cannot even provide the minimum level needed for the whole of the urban community.

The problems are most acute and intractable in metropolitan areas, which are composed of a central city or cities and a variety of suburban units. In 1972 the 264 standard metropolitan statistical areas of the nation contained about 70 percent of the total population; they had 22,185 local governments—more than one-fourth of all local governments in the nation. The Chicago metropolitan area alone contained 1,172 units, including 6 counties, 113 townships, 256 municipalities, 327 school districts, and 470 special districts.[1] While unification is understandably difficult and may not be wise, problems of sanitation, water supply, police, and transportation do need coordination. Sometimes, functional intergovernmental schemes which do not change the existing governmental structure have been put into operation—for example, the Metropolitan Water District of Southern California. But more complete structural integration is

1. U.S. Census Bureau, *Census of Governments, 1972*, vol. 1, *Governmental Organization*, p. 152.

often desirable even though annexation, the technique favored a few decades ago, has been halted in many states by the opposition of suburban areas.

In recent years the growth of the special district has been remarkable. These districts have peculiar features: they are created usually to perform a single function; they overlap geographically; except for school districts, most of them do not depend on taxation. While most of the blame for the excessive amount of local government fragmentation is to be placed on the states, which have often placed inflexible restrictions on the power of localities to handle public services, the federal government must bear a share because a good many special districts have been created through its "direct advocacy."[2] Specialists in the Department of Agriculture prefer to deal with officials of soil conservation districts (2,561 in 1972) rather than with county officers. Federal specialists in housing prefer to deal with officials of housing and urban renewal districts (2,271 in 1972) rather than with city officers. The pragmatic tendency of federal agencies to develop local counterparts has complicated local government structure and encouraged isolation of units within urban areas. Against the short-run convenience of special-purpose districts must be set the long-run confusion arising out of uncoordinated area development.

The organization of local governments is not, to be sure, merely a matter of administrative and fiscal efficiency. In a democracy a wide variation in performance is—and should be—tolerated. The present variation, however, exceeds acceptable limits. The obstacles to change here are patent and powerful: local loyalties, vested interests, urban-rural antagonisms, the inertia of the status quo. States have often made change difficult by constitutional and statutory provisions. Some state constitutions, for instance, prescribe a pattern of local government. Debt and tax limits for local governments are widespread, and their operation sometimes reinforces the maintenance of overlapping units because the pyramided separate limits of all the units in a given geographic area add up to more than the electorate might allow in consolidated government.

Yet the record of recent years proves that, given the will, much can be done—witness the great decline in the number of school dis-

2. John C. Bollens, *Special District Governments in the United States* (University of California Press, 1957), p. 250.

tricts over the past twenty years.[3] A forward step would be for the states to remove the self-imposed constitutional and statutory inflexibilities that stand in the way of governmental reorganization. Another would be for them to make enlargement of financial aid to local governments conditional on progress in structural reorganization. More efficient local governments would allow a larger measure of local financial responsibility in provision of local services. And it is a truth, as well as a truism, that only when local governments are strong does democracy flourish.

Transfers to Local Governments

There are two basic types of intergovernmental transfers from state to local governments: grants, or appropriated funds, and shared taxes, that is, portions of tax yields. State grants to local governments are straightforward transfers of funds. In the case of shared taxes, one level of government—the one most fitted to make efficient collection—assigns all or part of the collections on some basis to the government that gives up the tax. For example, a state government might assume the sole right to tax the income from intangible property, promising to distribute all or some share of the proceeds to local governments according to the place of residence of the owners; or it might assume the sole right to tax motor vehicles as property, promising distribution of the proceeds to local governments according to where the vehicles were principally garaged.

Shared taxes frequently began when a state government withdrew from the base of the general property tax some types of property that could not be efficiently or equitably taxed by local governments. A quid pro quo as revenue was assigned to local governments to make the move palatable. In the first instance the states tended to use such criteria as location of the property, prior assessed value of the property, and prior local revenue from the property. Quite frequently it turned out that because of the greater efficiency of state administration, the amounts collected by the state were much in excess of the prior collections of the local governments. Moreover, distribution

3. See table 4-1. An emphatic warning against assuming that "fragmentation of authority and overlapping jurisdictions are the primary causes of urban ills," and that consolidation is the remedy, is given by Robert L. Bish and Vincent Ostrom, *Understanding Urban Government* (Washington: American Enterprise Institute for Public Policy Research, 1973), p. 1.

according to origin of the revenue favored rich localities. Accordingly, the basis for sharing was shifted, usually toward some measure of local government need, and specific directions for use of the revenue were added. A variety of formulas was framed, the particular outcome depending on the tug and pull between those local governments wanting to retain a favorable allocation and those wanting a change appropriate to their needs. As a result, the original basis for tax sharing has been overlaid by numerous modifications that usually tend to allocate the proceeds according to some measure of local need, and to commit them to designated purposes.

In these two respects the original logic of the shared tax has been impaired and shared taxes, as now used, have come to resemble conditional grants. An important difference is, however, that the annual amount shared depends on the amount collected. It is therefore unstable, being larger in boom and smaller in recession years. This is awkward for local governments, since their spending has the opposite variation. Moreover, in many states the criteria for sharing different taxes are varied and complicated. They have grown ad hoc over the decades. At the very least it would make sense to pool the state collections, to distribute them according to a single formula, and to reduce earmarking. In such case the shared taxes would become an unconditional grant whose annual amount would depend on collections, whereas the amount of a grant would depend on an annual legislative decision.

The distinction between shared taxes and grants has become so blurred that the Bureau of the Census does not provide separate figures for them. Instead, figures for state payments to local governments are split into two categories, those for general local government support and those in support of specific functions such as education, highways, and welfare. In terms of the amount of revenue, state sharing is important for income taxes, liquor store profits, motor vehicle licenses and registration fees, gasoline taxes, sales taxes, tobacco taxes, and pari-mutuel taxes.

Table 4-2 and figure 4-1 show that from 1948 until the mid-1960s, state and local governments ran neck and neck in terms of overall tax collections. Since then state collections have outpaced local, and the likelihood is that the spread will increase. And yet, as table 4-3 and figure 4-2 show, in terms of expenditure, local governments have always outstripped the state governments.

Table 4-2. Tax Collections of State and Local Governments, 1948–73

Millions of dollars

	Tax collections				Tax collections		
Year	State	Local	Total	Year	State	Local	Total
1948	6.7	6.6	13.3	1962	20.6	21.0	41.6
1950	7.9	8.0	15.9	1964	24.2	23.5	47.8
1952	9.9	9.5	19.3	1966	29.4	27.4	56.7
1954	11.1	11.0	22.1	1968	36.4	31.2	67.6
1956	13.4	13.0	26.4	1970	48.0	38.8	86.8
1958	14.9	15.5	30.4	1972	59.9	48.9	108.8
1960	18.0	18.1	36.1	1973	68.1	53.0	121.1

Sources: Census Bureau, *Historical Statistics of the United States: Colonial Times to 1957* (GPO, 1960), pp. 727 and 729; and Census Bureau, *Governmental Finances*, annual issues. Figures are rounded.

Figure 4-1. Tax Collections of State and Local Governments, 1948–73

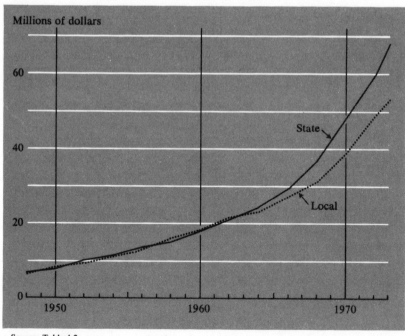

Source: Table 4-2.

Table 4-3. Direct General Expenditure of State and Local Governments, 1948–73
Millions of dollars

	Expenditure				Expenditure		
Year	State	Local	Total	Year	State	Local	Total
1948	6.2	11.5	17.7	1962	20.4	39.3	59.7
1950	8.0	14.8	22.8	1964	24.3	45.0	69.3
1952	8.7	17.4	26.1	1966	29.2	53.7	82.8
1954	10.1	20.6	30.7	1968	38.4	64.0	102.4
1956	12.3	24.4	36.7	1970	48.7	82.6	131.3
1958	15.6	29.3	44.9	1972	62.1	104.8	166.9
1960	17.9	33.9	51.9	1973	67.3	113.8	181.1

Sources: *Historical Statistics*, pp. 728 and 730; and *Governmental Finances*, annual issues. Figures are rounded.

The explanation is to be found in two sets of forces: state governments have taken over from local governments more responsibility for operation and finance of certain functions—welfare, highways, education, and so forth; and state governments have provided larger intergovernmental transfers for the support of certain local functions, the performance of which is left in local hands, and the federal government has enlarged its provision of grants to local governments.[4] Table 4-4 shows the total amount and breakdown by function of state transfers to local governments in 1973.

Intergovernmental expenditure by states on a significant scale is a phenomenon of the 1930s, although a structure had been built up earlier. In 1902, the first year for which the Bureau of the Census supplies figures, this state intergovernmental expenditure was $52 million. It is a mark of the limited scope of state governmental activities that $52 million amounted to 38.8 percent of total state direct general expenditure (see table 4-5). Local governments were then relatively much more important, and the $52 million received by them from state governments amounted to only 6.1 percent of their general revenue. By 1927, state intergovernmental payments had risen to $596 million—totaling 43.2 percent of total state expenditures and 10.1 percent of local general revenue. The 1930s and the postwar period brought further absolute increases. In recent years

4. Figures of federal payments to local governments are given in table 3-2.

Figure 4-2. General Expenditure of State and Local Governments, 1948–73

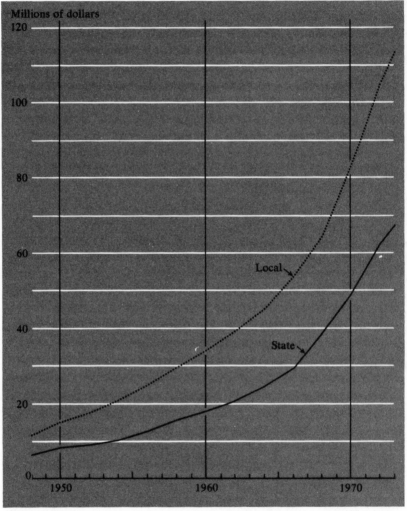

state intergovernmental expenditure has been more than half of state direct general expenditure and over 30 percent of local general revenue.

Significant changes have taken place, over the decades, in the functional distribution of state aid (see figure 4-3). In 1902 education was the major recipient—86 percent of the total; in 1973 it was still

Table 4-4. State Intergovernmental Payments, by Purpose, 1973

	Transfer payments	
Purpose	*Millions of dollars*	*Percentage of total*
Specific		
Education	23,316	57.1
Public welfare	7,532	18.5
Highways	2,953	7.2
Other	2,742	6.7
Total	36,542	89.5
General	4,280	10.5
Total	40,822	100.0

Source: Census Bureau, *State Government Finances in 1973*, p. 38. Figures are rounded.

Table 4-5. State Intergovernmental Expenditure, State Direct General Expenditure, and Local General Revenue, 1902, 1927, 1938, 1948, and 1973

Item	1902	1927	1938	1948	1973
	Millions of dollars				
State intergovernmental expenditure	52	596	1,516	3,283	40,822
State direct general expenditure	134	1,380	2,576	6,186	67,264
Local general revenue	854	5,903	6,651	11,373	118,355
	Percentage				
State intergovernmental expenditure as a percentage of state direct general expenditure	38.8	43.2	58.9	53.1	60.7
State intergovernmental expenditure as a percentage of local general revenue	6.1	10.1	22.8	28.9	34.5

Sources: *Historical Statistics*, pp. 728–29; and *Governmental Finances in 1972–73*, pp. 20–21.

the function receiving by far the largest slice—57 percent. But public welfare began to secure important state aid in the 1930s and by 1973 accounted for 18 percent of total state aid.

These developments mean, of course, a great increase in state-local collaboration. Figure 4-4 shows that state governments now provide a good slice of the finance of important functions of local government

Figure 4-3. Percentage Distribution of State Intergovernmental Expenditure, by Function, 1902, 1927, 1938, 1948, and 1973

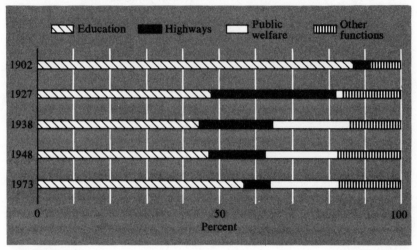

Source: Table A-14.

—nearly four-fifths of public welfare and over two-fifths of education and highways—and they give a good deal of direction as well. Some states have gone further, assuming complete control of a function.

Education

The per pupil expenditure by states for public education varies widely—from $590 to $1,584 in 1972–73—a major factor being the relative affluence of a state. State governments differ greatly in their direct assumption of responsibility for elementary and secondary education (see table 4-6). At one end of the spectrum is Hawaii, where the state government has assumed complete responsibility for financing and operating public schools. The other state governments merely provide financial assistance in the form of grants. In New Hampshire and Nebraska, the state grants are small and a heavy burden falls on local revenue sources, especially the property tax.

State aid for education is equalizing—the grants take account of differences among localities in their ability to support elementary and secondary education by providing greater aid to poorer school districts. In short, account is taken of need (per pupil or per teacher) in relation to fiscal resources. Most states guarantee a minimum or foundation level of spending per pupil. If a required property tax

Figure 4-4. State Intergovernmental Expenditure as a Percentage of Local Expenditure, by Function, 1902, 1927, 1938, 1948, and 1973

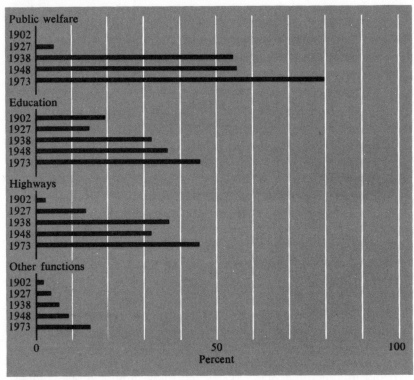

Source: Table A-15.

Table 4-6. Distribution of States by Per Capita Aid to Local Governments for Education, 1973

Aid, in dollars	Number of states
Under 50	3[a]
50– 69	2
70– 89	10
90–109	17
110–129	10
130–149	3
150–169	1
170–189	2
Over 190	2[b]

Source: Census Bureau, *State Government Finances in 1973*, p. 13.
a. Hawaii nil; New Hampshire $23.71; Nebraska $46.65.
b. Delaware $192.10; Alaska $293.82.

ratio fails to raise enough revenue to meet the foundation level, the state government pays the difference. For example, if the foundation level is $500 per pupil and the required property tax rate is 10 mills, a school district with 2,000 pupils and taxable value of $60,000,000 would only be able to raise $600,000 while the minimum required would be $1,000,000. The state government would make up the $400,000 difference.

How far should equalization be carried, and what should be the method of implementation? Should the grants be sufficient to enable every jurisdiction to spend a uniform amount per pupil, or to spend an amount per pupil that will provide a foundation program? In practice, simpler measures of needs and resources have been refined to take account of the fact that a dollar in grants has an unequal value from one school district to another. Educational costs differ for a pupil in an elementary school as compared with one in a high school; handicapped pupils are more costly to educate than normal pupils; salaries of teachers with the same qualifications are unequal from area to area. Complicated formulas have been developed to allow for differences in the costs of educating some pupils as compared with others. In addition, property valuations have to be adjusted to secure comparability in measurement of local fiscal resources.

The aid formulas have also been modified to take account of fiscal "effort," and to encourage local initiative in providing new programs or better qualified teachers. Very often these modifications conflict with and reduce the equalization effects because a wealthy school district can, and a poor one cannot, exercise initiative that calls for raising more revenue.

In several states the system of financing public primary and secondary education has recently been challenged in the courts as violating the Fourteenth Amendment to the federal Constitution and identical provisions in state constitutions. In the case with the greatest impact, *Serrano* v. *Priest,*[5] the supreme court of California held that the method of financing public schools was discriminatory against children in poor school districts. In general, about one-half of school revenue came from the property tax, and a poor district could not raise through it what a rich one could. The implication of the decision seemed to be that the state government should either more

5. *Serrano* v. *Priest,* 938254, L.A. California Supreme Court, 29820 (1971).

nearly equalize the revenues of school districts, or itself assume directly all or much of the cost of public education. In a Texas case that it accepted for review, the Supreme Court of the United States held that the state method of financing education did not violate the federal Constitution.[6] Although this decision cooled some of the fears concerning the necessity for startling changes in educational finance, it seems that many states must review and revise their methods.[7] The share of the state governments in finance will increase and so also will their responsibility for performing the educational function.

Public Welfare

The federal government since 1935 has taken a growing responsibility for financing public welfare. In 1972 it was the source of funds for 52.2 percent of the total expended, the state share being 36.3 percent and the local 11.5 percent.[8]

Federal leadership also induced an increase in state administration of public welfare and, in recent years, many state governments have provided direct state financing rather than grants. In 1973 the per capita grant expenditure exceeded the direct state expenditure in only nine states (California, Colorado, Maryland, Minnesota, New Jersey, New York, North Carolina, Virginia, and Wisconsin). In all the others, the main responsibility for finance and administration had been shifted to the state governments, the aim being to secure a broader jurisdictional reach and more consistency in standards.

The "nationalization" in 1972 of the public assistance programs for the needy aged, blind, and disabled was a further move toward centralization. Along with this trend has come one toward proliferation of programs aimed at meeting the needs of particular welfare groups.

Highways

A similar trend away from state aid to local governments for highways and toward direct expenditure has been evident for decades. In

6. *San Antonio Independent School District* v. *Rodriguez*, 411 U.S. 1 (1973).

7. For a summary of the issues see Advisory Commission on Intergovernmental Relations, *Financing Schools and Property Tax Relief—A State Responsibility* (Washington: ACIR, 1973), chaps. 9 and 10.

8. ACIR, *Federal-State-Local Finances: Significant Features of Fiscal Federalism, 1973–74 Edition* (GPO, 1974), table 77.

Table 4-7. Distribution of States by General-Purpose Grants Per Capita to Local Governments, 1973

Grants, in dollars	Number of states
Nil	4
Under 5	11
5– 9	7
10–14	7
15–19	2
20–24	7
25–29	0
30–34	2
35–39	5
40 and over	5[a]

Source: *State Government Finances in 1973*, pp. 37 and 50.
a. Wisconsin $113; Minnesota $74; Arizona $43; New Mexico $41; New York $41.

1973 direct expenditure of state governments for this function was $58 per capita while grant expenditure was $14. The local governments do, however, retain responsibility for street construction and maintenance; their direct general expenditure for highways in 1973 was $6,543 million.

Other Functions

The state governments also make grants to localities for health and hospitals, natural resources, housing and urban renewal, and air transport. This aid is not now important and is unlikely to show much growth. Federal aid for these services is important, and it goes directly to localities.

General Support

As table 4-4 shows, general-purpose aid in 1973 amounted to $4,280 million (10.5 percent of all state intergovernmental payments). This type of aid has grown relatively in recent years. Here again a wide variation prevails in state practice. As table 4-7 shows, four states gave no general-purpose grants, while at the other end of the range, Wisconsin and Minnesota gave $113 and $73 per capita, respectively. The source of these grants is almost always shared taxes.[9]

9. For details see ibid., tables 53–56, pp. 74–81.

Conclusion

Sometimes states through intergovernmental transfers to existing local governmental organizations have perpetuated the lives of inefficient units and placed barriers in the way of desirable reforms. State governments should be alert to couple aid with reorganization whenever reorganization has merit. The aid in such cases serves as an alternative to state assumption of full responsibility for the particular service. Centralization at the state level is often not the best move. State aid offers a middle course: it leaves performance of the specific governmental activity in local hands, while providing state financial assistance and a modicum of overall direction.

But the present clutter of grants and shared taxes that make up state intergovernmental payments is an untidy accumulation that should be consolidated. The shared taxes in each state should be converted into state revenues, with payment of equivalent or appropriate amounts as outright grants. No set pattern for the conversion can be prescribed that would be suitable for all states; diversity is appropriate. In states that are compact in size and homogeneous in economic structure, a centralizing program with a bias toward direct state performance of services and collection of revenues is feasible and desirable. In large states, on the other hand, strengthening of local governments is likely to be a better alternative, and here state grants are a useful instrument. Many specific-purpose grants now in use have faulty distribution formulas. They should be reshaped by precise definition of the services for which they provide support. In addition, the local ability to finance a foundation program for a service should be defined and measured. Adequate and objective evidence on which to base a quantification of need and ability is not easy to secure. State governments can, however, make greater use of general-purpose grants, for they can serve to equalize the revenue capacities of similar types of local governments.

CHAPTER FIVE

State Taxes on Individual Income and Sales

Whoe'er expects a faultless tax to see
Expects what neither is, nor was, nor e'er shall be.

John Ramsay McCulloch

BEFORE THE TWENTIETH century, taxation of individual incomes by the states had a long and unsuccessful history. So marked was the failure that many eminent students of public finance expressed the opinion that failure was inevitable. The key to the failure was ineffective administration. One economist, T. S. Adams, believed that "past failure did not preclude future success," and his faith was justified by the marked success of the Wisconsin tax of 1911. This success rested on "two administrative innovations": centralized administration and use of information-at-source returns.[1] And the Wisconsin tax, be it noted, antedated the Sixteenth Amendment to the Constitution which made a federal income tax possible.

Taxes on Individual Incomes

Despite the enactment of a federal tax on individual incomes in 1913 and the remarkable extension of federal coverage and rates

1. Clara Penniman and Walter W. Heller, *State Income Tax Administration* (Chicago: Public Administration Service, 1959), pp. 5–6.

during World War I, state income taxes at this time experienced a wave of popularity. By 1920, nine states and Hawaii were levying the tax. In the next decade five more states were added; by 1937 the total was twenty-nine states plus Hawaii. In the next two decades only Alaska (1949) joined the ranks. But in the 1960s six states (West Virginia in 1961, Indiana in 1963, Michigan and Nebraska in 1967, Illinois and Maine in 1969), and in the 1970s three states (Ohio, Pennsylvania, and Rhode Island) levied the tax. The total as of January 1975 was, therefore, forty states.[2]

A simple count of the states using the individual income tax overstates its importance as a source of state revenue (see chapter 2). In the 1920s it was never better than fifth among the major sources of state tax revenue. In the 1950s, however, it rose to third place, and in the 1960s and 1970s to second place. In 1973 it produced 22.9 percent of state tax collections. The improvement is due partly to higher rates, broadened base, and improved administration (especially through adoption of withholding), and partly to the great responsiveness of the tax to a rise in gross national product (GNP). According to ACIR calculations, every 1.0 percent rise in GNP increases the yield of state individual income taxes by 1.75 percent.[3] But the high elasticity of the individual income tax has a two-way stretch, so that collections decline sharply when GNP declines. As a trend, GNP may confidently be expected to rise, but it will rise and fall cyclically. This instability is a worry to state governments because their ability to finance operating deficits by borrowing is limited.

Diversity in State Yields

Although the aggregate yield of the state individual income taxes is unimpressive, the yield in some states is striking. For Oregon in 1973 it was 50 percent of all tax collections and, as table 5-1 shows,

---

2. Plus the District of Columbia, which enacted an income tax in 1939. In addition, New Hampshire and Tennessee levy a tax on interest and dividends, New Jersey one on the income of nonresident commuters, and Connecticut one on capital gains. Six other states (Florida, Nevada, South Dakota, Texas, Washington, and Wyoming) have no income tax. See Advisory Commission on Intergovernmental Relations, *Federal-State-Local Finances: Significant Features of Fiscal Federalism, 1973–74 Edition* (GPO, 1974), p. 159.

3. This is an average of estimates calculated for three states in ibid., p. 320; the ACIR report contains the most up-to-date estimates of the income elasticities of the major state and local taxes.

Table 5-1. State Individual Income Tax Collections, Highest and Lowest Seven States, 1973

Individual income tax	Percent of state's total tax revenue	Individual income tax	Amount, in dollars
As source of revenue		Collection per capita	
Highest states		Highest states	
Oregon	50	New York	176
Massachusetts	43	Hawaii	162
Montana	41	Wisconsin	159
Alaska	40	Delaware	156
New York	39	Massachusetts	151
Wisconsin	39	Minnesota	150
Minnesota	36	Oregon	135
Lowest states[a]		Lowest states[a]	
Louisiana	9	Louisiana	29
Maine	10	Maine	30
Mississippi	11	Mississippi	31
New Mexico	13	Ohio	35
Ohio	14	Oklahoma	39
North Dakota	15	Alabama	40
Oklahoma	15	North Dakota	43

Source: Tables A-10 and A-16. In all tables and figures, years are fiscal unless otherwise noted.
a. Excludes New Hampshire, Tennessee, New Jersey, and Connecticut, where income taxes were limited in scope.

it was 39 percent or more for five other states. On the other hand, for some states the yield was very modest.

This same diversity is displayed by per capita figures (table 5-1). Per capita collections for the highest state, New York, were more than six times those of the lowest state, Louisiana. The seven states with the highest per capita collections accounted for 35 percent of total collections although their population was only 21 percent of the total population of the forty states that have a general income tax. Per capita figures do not, of course, take account of the inequality of the states in tax base, rate structures, exemptions, deductions, and so on.

In ten states (Pennsylvania, Wisconsin, Ohio, Delaware, Kansas, Montana, Virginia, West Virginia, New York, and Oregon) the personal exemption is lower than that of the federal tax ($750), and in eleven the same. In all but six of the nineteen states with a higher exemption, dependents have a lower personal exemption than a single person has. For example, the personal exemptions for a single person and a married couple in Georgia in 1973 were $1,500 and $3,000, respectively, while the exemption for each dependent was $700.

Excluding states with a limited income tax, thirty-three (and the District of Columbia) allow an additional exemption on account of age, and thirty-five (and the District of Columbia) on account of blindness. Seven states—Arkansas, California, Iowa, Kentucky, Louisiana, Minnesota, and Wisconsin—provide the personal exemption by a tax credit. For example, in Wisconsin, a single person has a tax credit of $15. Since the rate of tax on the first $1,000 of net income is 3.1 percent, this tax credit is equivalent, for the first bracket, to a personal exemption of $484. A $15 tax credit for a spouse is equivalent to an additional personal exemption of $484—a total of $968.

The variety of personal exemptions can be explained partly on the basis of history. States, when they first enacted their tax, would adopt an exemption acceptable at the time. Thereafter, different sets of forces and needs would operate on them and on the federal government, making for diversity.

The statutory rates of the state taxes are graduated[4] to a modest level, the highest being 18 percent (Delaware). About half have five to seven brackets, the top one including a wide range of income —for example, in North Dakota, "over $8,000," in Oregon, "over $5,000." The lower brackets are, therefore, narrow (often with $1,000 intervals) and the effective rates of progression, at first quite steep, flatten out or turn down for incomes that are above $15,000.[5]

4. Except in Illinois, Indiana, Michigan, and Pennsylvania, where a flat rate is used, and in Massachusetts, where a higher rate is applied to investment income. The effect in Massachusetts is to produce rough progression because larger incomes usually contain more investment income than small. A good many small incomes, nonetheless, are chiefly or wholly from investment, and a few large incomes are chiefly "earned." Alaska, Nebraska, Rhode Island, and Vermont impose flat rates based on taxpayers' modified federal tax liability.

5. ACIR, *Significant Features, 1973–74 Edition,* table 139, p. 259, indicates that for 1971 the effective median rate of state tax for a married couple with two dependents and an adjusted gross income of $5,000 would be 0.5 percent; with an adjusted gross income of $25,000, the rate would be 3.2 percent. In fourteen states some deductibility of federal tax payments is allowed in calculating the state liability. The effect is to reduce progression of the state taxes in the lower brackets and to bring about regression in the higher ones. See Emanuel Melichar, *State Individual Income Taxes: Impact of Alternative Provisions on Burdens, Progression, and Yields* (University of Connecticut, Storrs Agricultural Experiment Station, 1963), pp. 207–17.

A good many federal practices find their way, with a considerable lag, into the state laws. Thus, in 1973, thirty-two states (and the District of Columbia) allowed a variety of standard deductions as an alternative to itemizing; twenty-three (and the District of Columbia) provided an optional tax table; thirty-nine (and the District of Columbia) had adopted withholding and most of them complemented it with declarations of estimated tax. Withholding was pioneered by Oregon in 1948 and now only North Dakota is without it. In all adopting states the increase in collections was strong in the first year because of the transition to current payment coupled with nonforgiveness, so that the taxpayer was liable for any overlap between what was due for the previous year and the current year.[6] Withholding serves to locate taxpayers who otherwise might not file; it reduces delinquency by keeping taxpayers current; it collects without lag from a growing tax base. Recently, compliance has been eased in thirty-one states by adoption of the federal tax base (with modifications). Starting with adjusted gross income from the federal return, the taxpayer will deduct interest on federal securities (since, constitutionally, this is not taxable by a state), and add interest on securities of other states and of local governments in other states. Before 1963–64, the state tax in Alaska was approximately a flat 16 percent, and in West Virginia 6 percent, of the federal tax liability.[7] The federal tax cut of 1964 caused a change. But West Virginia established a rate schedule of its own designed to yield the same revenue as would have resulted if no federal tax cut had been made. Alaska made the 16 percent applicable to the federal tax payable at rates in effect on December 31, 1963. Nebraska, when it adopted an individual income tax in 1967, based its rate on the taxpayer's federal liability before credits; the rate for 1973 was 13 percent.

The moves toward conformity with the federal law should not be overstressed.[8] Important differences exist between the federal and the state definitions of taxable income, of which the most difficult arise out of the allocation of interstate income and definition of residence.

6. Only three states (New York, Minnesota, and Wisconsin) and the District of Columbia provided any significant forgiveness.

7. Technical qualifications of this statement are disregarded.

8. The ACIR reports that, in 1973, virtually complete conformity of state personal income tax to the federal personal income tax base had been achieved by four states, and substantial conformance by seven more. *Significant Features, 1973–74 Edition*, table 145, p. 275.

Less vital differences occur with respect to income splitting, dividend credits, capital gains, and variation in allowed deductions. Much of the variation rests on no better basis than inertia; some is an expression of state experimentation; some, especially with respect to income arising outside the state, grows out of the insoluble problem of state boundaries and a desire to define taxable income so as to tax nonresidents. The inconvenience to the taxpayer receives slight consideration.

Residence and Origin of Income

The question of residence arises for the federal tax only with respect to foreign income, since the federal definition of income applies over the nation. But for the states the question is important. The classic solution, proposed in the model plan of the National Tax Association in 1919, was that residence of the taxpayer should govern; individuals should be taxed on their entire net incomes by their home state.[9] Nonresidents would not be taxed on income earned within the state, nor residents on income earned outside the state. The other approach, pioneered by Wisconsin, was to levy a tax on all income arising in the state whether earned by residents or nonresidents; income accruing to residents from outside the state was not taxed. Either plan would eliminate most discriminatory taxation of individual income, the former favoring states whose residents had large investments outside the state, the latter those in the opposite situation.

In law and in practice neither approach has been accepted. In law, most states claim the right to tax the total income of a resident, whatever its origin, and also to tax income originating in the state and going to nonresidents. In practice, the states, while casting a wide net, have moderated the discrimination inherent in their laws through crediting and reciprocity provisions by which they allow a credit for income taxes paid by their residents to other states or exempt, on a reciprocal basis, each others' residents.[10]

9. National Tax Association, *Proceedings of the Twelfth Annual Conference on Taxation* (1920), pp. 401–03, and *Twenty-sixth Conference* (1934), pp. 365–74.
10. ACIR, *Significant Features, 1973–74 Edition*, table 144, pp. 273–74. Crediting for residents is offered by all forty states with personal income taxes, for nonresidents by twelve states. Thirteen states require reciprocity from the other state before credit is allowed to either residents or nonresidents.

As indicated in chapter 2, ten states have not enacted broad-based taxes on individual incomes, and some of the forty utilizing such taxes have employed them sparingly. Most states have chosen to cultivate other sources of revenue, especially taxation of consumption.

Taxes on Sales

Taxation of consumption has taken the form of taxes on particular commodities (selective sales), and on general sales, mostly imposed at the retail level.

Selective Sales Taxes

Selective sales, or excise, taxes are predominantly of two types: benefit taxes, notably those on motor fuel, and sumptuary taxes, for example, those on liquor, tobacco, and pari-mutuels. The rationale of benefit taxes is that they are a quid pro quo for public services that yield particular and measurable benefits to individuals. Failure to levy them would be to allow receipt of particular services without particular payments; the cost of such services would then be borne by the community as a whole through general taxes (this subject is examined in greater detail in chapter 8). The rationale of sumptuary taxes on liquor, tobacco, and pari-mutuels is more illusive. The taxes penalize consumption of these things and should fulfill the sumptuary purpose of diminishing their consumption. In fact, in an affluent society the taxes are pushed not hard enough to secure much diminution but hard enough to secure a large revenue. The compromise rationale seems to be that if particular consumers care to pay a penalty tax, the proceeds to be used for collective purposes, they may continue to consume.

Table 5-2 shows state revenue in 1973 from selective sales taxes. Taxation of motor fuel is common to all the state governments, and so is taxation of liquor, cigarettes, and insurance. Twenty-nine states tax pari-mutuels and forty tax public utilities by excises, although only a few secure a substantial revenue thereby.

MOTOR FUEL. The first taxes on commodities widely used by the states were on gasoline and tobacco products (especially cigarettes). In 1919 Oregon imposed a gasoline tax, and so productive and acceptable did it prove that by 1929 it was used by every state in the

Table 5-2. State Revenue from Selective Sales Taxes, 1973

Tax	Amount, in millions of dollars	Percentage of total selective sales tax collections
Motor fuel	8,058	46.5
Alcoholic beverages	1,817	10.5
Tobacco products	3,112	18.0
Insurance	1,607	9.3
Public utilities	1,347	7.8
Pari-mutuels	590	3.4
Other	798	4.6
Total	17,330	100.0

Source: U.S. Census Bureau, *State Government Finances in 1973*, p. 6. Figures are rounded.

union. During the 1930s and early 1940s it was the most important tax source of state governments, yielding one-quarter or more of their tax revenues (see chapter 2). Gasoline rationing during World War II cut the yield, and taxes on general sales became the leading revenue producer, a position that they have not relinquished.

The rates at which the states tax motor fuel are fairly diverse, as shown in the following distribution of states by their gasoline tax rates on July 1, 1973:[11]

Cents per gallon	Number of states
Under 7	4
7	18
7½	3
8	10
8½	4
9	10
10	1

There is, moreover, diversity concerning exemptions and refunds. In three states (Hawaii, Mississippi, and Nevada) local gasoline taxes are levied at rates of 1–5 cents per gallon.[12]

Federal use of the gasoline tax began in 1932 amid strong state protest at federal trespass. This time the protest rang true: the states had made vigorous use of the tax; their administration of it was reasonably efficient and had brought no significant jurisdictional conflicts. The issue of federal trespass was therefore a real one, and state

11. Ibid., p. 310.
12. Ibid., table 59, pp. 84–89.

pressure for federal withdrawal had merit. The issue was, however, sidetracked when Congress, in 1956, not only enlarged federal aid to highway construction but also provided that, for sixteen years, large slices of revenue from the federal motor fuel tax (as well as from other highway user taxes) be placed in the new Highway Trust Fund and spent for an expanded program of highway construction.

TOBACCO. In 1921 Iowa enacted a cigarette tax, and by 1929 seven other states had followed suit. The depression of the 1930s accelerated adoption of this tax (or a tax on tobacco products). By 1961 all the states and the District of Columbia taxed cigarettes. In 1973 twenty-one imposed excises on other tobacco products. In ten states some local governments tax tobacco and tobacco products.[13]

In taxing cigarettes the states encountered important administrative difficulties because they had to collect from wholesalers and jobbers within their jurisdiction rather than—as does the federal Treasury—from a small number of manufacturers. State taxes could be evaded either by smuggling, or by purchase in interstate commerce. An early device to defeat evasion was enactment of a state use tax, a levy on commodities purchased outside a state but brought into it for use. Applied first to the gasoline tax and then extended to other commodities, the tax gave tax administrators a legal base for enforcement, leaving unsolved the task of finding the commodities on which the tax had not been paid.

The states turned to interstate cooperation, especially by providing lists of consignees to tax administrators in states to which cigarettes were shipped. The device was useless, however, when sales came from states that did not tax these items, since no basis for reciprocity existed. Moreover, cigarettes could be shipped by parcel post (as gasoline could not), and dealers, protected by the privacy of the United States mails, did not declare such shipments. The Post Office resisted schemes that would have required it to provide information to the states concerning shipments of tobacco products.

But after World War II, as the number of states imposing taxes on tobacco products grew, pressure for federal help mounted, and in 1949 Congress required sellers of cigarettes in interstate commerce to send to tax administrators copies of invoices of every tobacco shipment into their state. This effectively closed a major loophole.

13. Ibid., tables 162 and 163, pp. 308 and 309.

Table 5-3. Distribution of States by Percentage of Total Tax Revenue Collected from Tobacco Taxes, 1971

Percentage of total taxes	*Number of states*
0–2	3
2–4	12
4–6	23
6–8	9
8–10	2
10 and over	1[a]

Source: Advisory Commission on Intergovernmental Relations, *Federal-State-Local Finances: Significant Features of Fiscal Federalism, 1973–74 Edition* (GPO, 1974), table 15.
a. New Hampshire 14.4 percent.

Tobacco taxes in 1971 produced 4.9 percent of state tax revenue collections; table 5-3 shows the yield distribution by states.

ALCOHOLIC BEVERAGES. The third bundle of commodities subject to state excises is liquor. After repeal of Prohibition the states chose two different methods of controlling, and gathering revenue from, the liquor business. In 1973 thirty-three used the license system, raising revenue mostly from a gallonage excise and license charge; sixteen had chosen the monopoly system of state stores, raising revenue chiefly from profits. In 1973 the revenue from state excises on alcoholic beverages was $1,817 million; from licenses, $140 million; from state monopoly systems' net contribution to general funds, $402 million.[14] And local governments collected $78 million on alcoholic beverage sales.

The interstate tax conflict and trade barriers have raised intricate problems. The states used the freedom given them by the Twenty-first Amendment to the Constitution, which excluded alcoholic beverages from the protection given to interstate commerce, to levy liquor taxes and license charges as trade barriers in order to protect local producers and distributors. A counter-agitation developed against such practices which halted further growth of discrimination, although it did not remove that already in existence.

General Retail Sales Taxes

The success of selective excises (particularly on motor fuel) as revenue producers held back the development of state taxes on general retail sales. The states were, besides, afraid that taxation of sales

14. Details concerning state and local taxes are provided in ibid., tables 167–70, pp. 314–17.

might cause migration into tax-free states and they were conscious of the Supreme Court's zealousness in barring taxation of all transactions of an interstate character. Sales made by merchants to customers outside a taxing state, and sales made by merchants who were outside a taxing state to customers in a taxing state, could not be taxed. The effect of this strict Court interpretation was to discriminate in favor of interstate commerce.

The depression of the 1930s broke through some of the obstacles, and it turned out also that the Supreme Court relaxed its constitutional interpretation. The states perceived that a general sales tax was a source of revenue that, unlike income taxation, held up in bad times. Moreover, Congress indicated clearly in 1931–32 that a federal sales tax was unacceptable. The states, worried by the collapse of the property tax and the desperate plight of local governments, saw sales taxes as a means of financial salvation. Mississippi adopted a sales tax in 1932. In 1933 thirteen states enacted a general tax on retail sales,[15] and by the end of 1938 nine more states and Hawaii had followed suit. World War II halted the swing, but afterward, as states prepared to finance the backlog of demands bottled up during the war, there came a second wave of sales taxes. In 1944 the general retail sales tax became the most important tax source of state governments, and its lead has widened in the years since. By 1973 forty-five states (and the District of Columbia) imposed the tax, and it accounted for 29 percent of their tax collections.

Figure 5-1 and tables 5-4 and 5-5 give an indication of the interstate variation in the significance of the tax. In 1973, general sales taxes produced over $90 per capita in tax revenue for twenty-eight states; individual income tax produced this amount for fourteen states. The range of sales tax rates—from 2 percent to 7 percent—is shown in table 5-5.

Meanwhile, local governments have utilized the tax, following the examples of New York City in 1934 and New Orleans in 1938 (see chapter 8). After the war, local sales taxes spread and by July 1, 1973, were utilized in twenty-five states (although in six by only a few local governments).[16] About 4,460 local governments—most

15. Includes Indiana, which taxed gross income only but is usually included in tabulations of sales taxes.
16. Ibid., table 136, pp. 252–53.

Figure 5-1. **Distribution of States by General Sales Tax and Individual Income Tax Collections Per Capita, 1973**

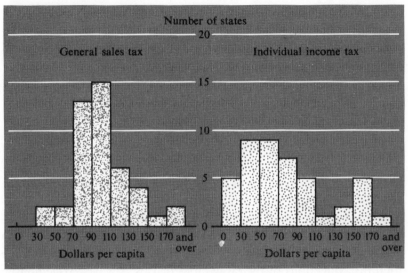

Source: Table 5-4.

Table 5-4. **Distribution of States by General Sales Tax and Individual Income Tax Collections Per Capita, 1973**

	Number of states	
Dollars per capita	*Sales tax*	*Income tax*
Under 30	0	5[a]
30– 49	2	9
50– 69	2	9
70– 89	13	7
90–109	15	5
110–129	6	1
130–149	4	2
150–169	1	5
170 and over	2[b]	1[c]

Source: Table A-16.
a. Includes Connecticut, New Hampshire, New Jersey, and Tennessee where taxes were applied to special kinds of income.
b. Hawaii $253.23; Washington $200.56.
c. New York $175.85.

Table 5-5. Distribution of States by General Sales Tax Rate, 1973

Tax rate, percent	Number of states
2	2
$2\frac{1}{2}$	1
3	16
$3\frac{1}{2}$	1
$3\frac{3}{4}$	1
4	16
$4\frac{1}{2}$	1
5	5
6	1
7	1

Source: ACIR, *Significant Features, 1973–74 Edition*, table 133.

notably in California, Illinois, Texas, and Washington—imposed the tax. In twenty-one of the states with local general sales taxes, administration was by the state (piggyback). While the aggregate revenue secured—$3,199 million or 6 percent of local tax revenue in 1973—may seem modest, the tax brings in 20–30 percent of the total tax collections of the large cities of Los Angeles, Washington, Dallas, Houston, and San Diego, and 40–60 percent to smaller cities such as Phoenix, Tulsa, and Denver.

Some Characteristics

The state (and local) governments chose retail sales as the base of their sales tax. Some states have few manufacturing concerns, and others many, that ship across state lines. A sales tax at the manufacturing level would burden these concerns compared with competitors outside the state; it would, besides, raise complications concerning interstate commerce. Taxing at the retail level avoids or limits these difficulties.[17] The tax as employed is, therefore, approximately a single-stage tax on retail sales. Sales for resale are excluded from the base; most sales to industrial customers are also excluded, either by an ingredient test or by a direct-use test. The ingredient test removes from the tax base property that becomes an ingredient of a product to be sold; the direct-use test removes property used directly in producing goods to be sold. But neither rule excludes completely from

17. Difficulties with respect to interstate commerce arising out of the levy of use taxes on commodities purchased outside a state, and brought into it for use, are examined in chapter 6 because the difficulties are similar to those in interstate apportionment of corporate income.

the tax base sales of supplies used in industrial processes. Sales of office supplies and of fuel, for example, are included in the base. Although complete exemption of goods that have an industrial consumption or production use would not be justified, the result of inclusion in the base is multiple taxation. The tax on goods used in production is shifted forward and becomes a cost of the relevant consumer goods which, in turn, are taxed when sold at the retail level. In addition to a tax at the retail level of 4 percent and 5 percent, respectively, Hawaii and Mississippi levy fractional rates on wholesale transactions; Hawaii levies a fractional rate at the manufacturing stage.[18]

A general retail sales tax should logically include services in the base. In fact, most services are excluded, and thereby a considerable slice of consumers' expenditures is not taxed. It is, however, common to include in the base admissions, transient lodging, meals served in restaurants, and some public utility services (sales of gas and electricity, telegraph, and telephone services). Some states, on grounds of equity, exclude specific categories of tangible consumer goods—in 1973, medical supplies were exempt in twenty-nine states and the District of Columbia, and expenditures on food for home consumption were not taxed in nineteen states and the District of Columbia. Less than half a dozen states exempt clothing. The Tax Foundation estimated in 1970 that "discretionary exemptions (i.e., goods and services considered suitable for taxation but exempt in some states) comprise fully one-half the volume of total taxable sales."[19]

In almost two-thirds of the states the tax rate is uniform (commonly 3 percent and 4 percent) for all taxable items. All the sales-tax states have supplementary use taxes, applicable to goods bought outside the state and brought into it for consumption. In 1937 the Supreme Court upheld the use tax, declaring that it was not a tax on interstate commerce, but on the privilege of use after commerce had ended.[20] Since then the constitutional basis of sales and use taxes has been so greatly broadened that serious concern is now expressed that the states will put discriminatory burdens on interstate trade.

Information concerning administrative and compliance costs of

18. See ibid., table 134, pp. 242–50, for state rates on services and nonretail businesses.
19. *State and Local Sales Taxes* (New York: Tax Foundation, 1970), p. 63.
20. *Henneford* v. *Silas Mason Co.,* 300 U.S. 577 (1937).

sales taxes is faulty. Compliance costs fall mostly on retailers, rather than on consumers, and studies in the fifties and sixties indicated that about half the states compensated them for their costs to the extent of 1–5 percent of the tax obligation; in the past, administrative costs reported by the states have run at less than $2 per $100 of sales tax revenue.[21] State governments spend too little in seeing that firms remit payment of tax at the required time. A more serious administrative weakness is inadequate audit. The size and technical training of audit staffs and the compensation paid them are usually inadequate.

The Charge of Inequity

Beyond question the most weighty criticism of the sales tax has been its inequity. The tax is on consumption, and since consumption must absorb a higher percentage of income for poor than for rich persons, a tax that rests on consumption is regressive. Its rate, as a percentage of income, is higher for the poor man than for the rich. The extent of the regression depends on the coverage of the sales tax. Exemption of food and medicine reduces regression simply because low-income persons spend a relatively high portion of their income for these items. But exemptions narrow the tax base and discriminate in favor of persons who consume relatively large amounts of the exempt items. This discrimination may accord with social policy, but it complicates administration and therefore induces or allows evasion of taxes. A firm that sells exempt and nonexempt articles must distinguish between them in its accounts. Besides, definition of food, medicine, and so on, raises borderline cases that require arbitrary decisions. In Massachusetts baby oil is nontaxable, but baby lotion is taxable; needles are taxable, but thread is not; batteries are nontaxable only when used for hearing aids; insulin is tax-exempt, but an insulin needle and syringe are taxable; work clothes are nontaxable, but safety clothing worn in hazardous occupations is taxable. Are candy, coffee, and Coca-Cola to be defined as "food"? Rulings here differ. Every exemption is, in effect, a subsidy to consumers of the untaxed product, and therefore requires justification.

Table 5-6 presents a rough estimate of the incidence of the general

---

21. See Clinton V. Oster, *State Retail Sales Taxation* (Ohio State University, 1957), pp. 160–62 and 188; John F. Due, *State Sales Tax Administration* (Chicago: Public Administration Service, 1963), pp. 225–30. Due provides a careful description and analysis of all aspects of administration.

Table 5-6. Estimated Burden of State and Local General Sales Taxes for a Family of Four, by Income Group, 1972

Family income, in dollars	Rate, percent
5,000	1.8
7,500	1.6
10,000	1.4
20,000	1.1
25,000	0.9
50,000	0.7

Source: ACIR, *Significant Features, 1973–74 Edition*, table 38, p. 53.

sales tax. General sales tax payments as a percentage of family income decline gradually but continuously as the level of income rises. The effective rate of the sales tax, however, has an unfortunate tendency to increase as the size of the family grows. The potential magnitude of these inequities is softened when food is exempt from the tax base.[22] Several states have provided a sales tax credit against income tax liability, and the plausible argument is advanced that such a credit is superior to an exemption on grounds of equity, revenue productivity, and compliance costs.[23] States with both an income tax and sales tax should, therefore, prefer the credit to exemption of food (and other) purchases.

Regression of sales taxes is concerned with vertical equity, measured usually by the relation of average tax payments of families by income classes. Variation in the characteristics of the family—horizontal equity, or equal treatment of equals—has been neglected. Horizontal equity may be measured by the standard deviation, "computed from the differences between the effective tax rate for each family [in an income class] and the average effective rate of each family" in an income class.[24] Tax credits so arranged as to take account of family

22. Reed R. Hansen, "An Empirical Analysis of the Retail Sales Tax with Policy Recommendations," *National Tax Journal*, vol. 15 (March 1962), pp. 1–13.

23. James A. Papke, "New Perspectives in Retail Sales Taxation," National Tax Association, *Proceedings of the Fifty-eighth Annual Conference on Taxation* (1966), pp. 258–70. "The credit can be fixed or variable. A variable one is phased out at higher income levels. Variable credits have created serious administration problems and have failed to benefit large numbers of potential recipients." Tax Foundation, *State and Local Sales Taxes*, p. 35.

24. James A. Papke and Timothy G. Shahen, "Optimal Consumption-Base Taxes: The Equity Effects of Tax Credits," *National Tax Journal*, vol. 25 (September 1972), p. 481.

characteristics, notably family size, improve horizontal equity; indeed, "for the majority of taxpayers, effective tax rate differentials result from differences in consumption patterns which are explained primarily by factors other than income."[25] The relative importance of mitigating regression in effective sales tax rates can therefore be questioned. For most taxpayers, horizontal inequities outweigh vertical, and horizontal inequities are "primarily a function of family characteristics and not of income."[26]

J. K. Galbraith in his widely read *The Affluent Society* argued that liberal opposition to a more extensive and intensive use of sales taxation was an instance of "conventional wisdom," irrelevant to problems of the present. In an affluent society where most spending by most persons is far above subsistence, moderate regression is unimportant.

A very different position was taken in the AFL-CIO booklet, *State and Local Taxes*, which declared that the most important standard of judgment in deciding on the goodness or badness of a tax is equity. By this standard "the most unfair taxes of all . . . are the sales taxes." Taxes "based on ability to pay and the progressive principle . . . are the only really desirable taxes."[27]

The equity argument, whatever weight is given to it, should be placed in perspective by relating the sales tax burden to the total tax burden borne by taxpayers. The fact that one tax is regressive or progressive has significance only with respect to its weight in the total system of taxes. The sophisticated and abstract argument that has been developed by economists concerning tax sacrifice among individuals assumes a summation of the sacrifices imposed by the whole system of taxes. For decisive practical reasons, local governments utilize regressive taxes. State governments have more freedom, but their choice concerning tax progression is narrowly limited because taxpayers subjected to high rates in one state can move to others

25. Ibid., p. 486.

26. Ibid. The study pays no attention to "the differential administrative costs of alternative exemption or sales tax credit provisions; nor was any attempt made to estimate the compliance costs and effectiveness of these provisions" (ibid., p. 487). The Tax Foundation study offers evidence that compliance and administrative costs are considerably greater for variable than for fixed credits, and that variable credits are not easily utilized by the taxpayers for whose relief they are provided (*State and Local Sales Taxes*, pp. 32–35).

27. AFL-CIO publication no. 80 (1958), pp. 10, 70, and 105.

Table 5-7. Effective Rates of Federal and State-Local Taxes under Most Progressive and Least Progressive Incidence Assumptions, by Income Class, 1966

Percent

Adjusted family income, in thousands of dollars	Most progressive assumptions[a]			Least progressive assumptions[b]		
	Federal	State-local	Total	Federal	State-local	Total
0–3	8.8	9.8	18.7	14.1	14.0	28.1
3–5	11.9	8.5	20.4	14.6	10.6	25.3
5–10	15.4	7.2	22.6	17.0	8.9	25.9
10–15	16.3	6.5	22.8	17.5	8.0	25.5
15–20	16.7	6.5	23.2	17.7	7.6	25.3
20–25	17.1	6.9	24.0	17.8	7.4	25.1
25–30	17.4	7.7	25.1	17.2	7.1	24.3
30–50	18.2	8.2	26.4	17.7	6.7	24.4
50–100	21.8	9.7	31.5	20.1	6.3	26.4
100–500	30.0	11.9	41.8	24.4	6.0	30.3
500–1,000	34.6	13.3	48.0	25.2	5.1	30.3
1,000 and over	35.5	13.8	49.3	24.8	4.2	29.0
All classes	17.6	7.6	25.2	17.9	8.0	25.9

Source: Joseph A. Pechman and Benjamin A. Okner, *Who Bears the Tax Burden?* (Brookings Institution, 1974), p. 62.
a. See description of variant 1c, ibid., pp. 37–38.
b. See description of variant 3b, ibid, pp. 38 and 39.

where the rates are lower. The national government has much greater freedom, since moving outside the national boundaries in order to avoid taxes imposes other costs, many of them nonmonetary, of great weight.

The relevant issue, then, is the incidence on individuals of total taxes—federal, state, and local. In terms of overall equity, the regressivity of particular taxes—notably sales taxes, or even the total taxes of state and local governments—is not very significant. In table 5-7, showing the results of Pechman and Okner's comprehensive study of tax incidence,[28] estimates of federal and state-local taxes under the most progressive set of incidence assumptions are contrasted with estimates based on the least progressive set of assumptions. Federal taxes appear progressive under both variants. They are more so under the most progressive assumptions, where the corporation income tax is assumed to fall on corporate owners and property income recipients; under the least progressive, half of the cor-

28. Joseph A. Pechman and Benjamin A. Okner, *Who Bears the Tax Burden?* (Brookings Institution, 1974), p. 62.

porate income tax is thought to be passed on to consumers. The distribution of state-local taxes is quite sensitive to the incidence assumptions used. Under the most progressive, where property taxes on improvements fall on property income, the distribution is progressive. Under the other set of assumptions, when the property tax on improvements is assumed to be passed on to consumers, state-local taxes exhibit a regressive pattern.

The potential degree of overall progressivity should not be exaggerated. According to Pechman and Okner, "regardless of the incidence assumptions, the tax system is virtually proportional for the vast majority of families in the United States. Under the most progressive set of assumptions examined in this study, taxes reduce income inequality by less than 5 percent; under the least progressive assumptions, income inequality is reduced by only about 0.25 percent."[29]

Some awkward, if abstruse, questions remain unanswered. Should it be assumed that Congress determines the progression of the federal tax system after consideration of the evidence concerning the incidence of state and local taxes? Does Congress use the federal tax system as an instrument to secure the right—the desired—total incidence? Evidence in support of the opinion that Congress does so act would be hard to produce, and yet no harder than evidence concerning how Congress resolves many major decisions concerning spending and taxing.

Another difficult, if more niggling, question is: How can Congress make an adjustment in the progression of federal taxes so as to fit the different tax systems of fifty states? A scale of federal progression suitable as an instrument of adjustment to the tax systems of states, where taxes on consumption are dominant, would be less suitable for states where they are not. Congress must, it seems, be assumed to aim at adjusting to a hypothetical average state and local tax system. This interpretation of the procedure adopted, of necessity, by Congress brings to light a fault of a markedly regressive (or progressive) state tax system. If Congress adjusts the progression of federal taxes to an average state system, citizens in a state with a system that diverges markedly from this average secure an imperfect adjustment.

29. Ibid., p. 64.

Sales Tax or Income Tax?

The equity argument over income and sales taxes interweaves with many of the other arguments about the relative merits of these taxes.

Revenue Productivity

Proponents say that sales taxation produces more revenue than income taxation. A 1959 Wisconsin study estimated that a typical sales tax at the rate of 2 percent would yield more annually than the existing normal income tax with rates running from 1 percent to 7 percent[30] and tax credits of $7 for a single person and $14 for a married couple. Opponents of sales taxation retort that the high revenue productivity grows out of a tax base that leaves no minimum of consumption free from tax. Spending by a worker out of unemployment compensation, or by a recipient of old-age assistance, is taxed. Only income that is saved, or perhaps spent on services, is not taxed. Opponents usually then extend the attack by declaring that all taxes, regardless of form, are paid out of income. Whatever tax revenue a state legislature wishes to raise could therefore be secured via an income tax that would gauge and allow for individual and family needs on a rational and aboveboard basis.

This logical rationale often fails to persuade the state legislature. An income tax structure that would be capable of producing a revenue equal to a sales tax seems likely to raise severe voter opposition and possibly to stimulate migration out of state. Opportunism concerning the form of taxation is bound to be a characteristic of legislatures, not because they are reactionary, but because they aim to minimize the adverse reactions of voters. Payments of sales tax are somewhat concealed, and even when overt and known, the payments are little by little. A taxpayer is always current and never in arrears; a large lump of sales tax is never due at deadlines. Withholding of income tax does, to be sure, capture some of this feature, but each bite is still sizable. The sensible opinion that tax burdens on

30. University of Wisconsin Tax Study Committee, *Wisconsin's State and Local Tax Burden* (University of Wisconsin, 1959), p. 96. A flat rate earnings tax with no exemptions, as is now levied by some large cities, would yield more than a retail sales tax at the same rate (see Robert A. Sigafoos, *The Municipal Income Tax: Its History and Problems* [Chicago: Public Administration Service, 1955], pp. 137–39).

citizens should be explicit, and that concealment is a fraud, seems overstrict to the legislator concerned with short-run responses.

Interstate Mobility and Federal Deductibility

A practical issue of some consequence is the comparative effect of sales and income taxes on interstate movement. A state income tax on top of a heavy and steeply progressive federal income tax may seem oppressive and even confiscatory to a high-income person. A shift in domicile to avoid the state tax might result. Proponents of state income taxes sometimes brush aside this possibility by demonstrating the ameliorative effect on progression and on total income tax of federal deductibility—payments of state income tax may be deducted from the base of the federal tax. In short, the base of federal tax is income after deduction of state income tax payments (and of many other deductible items). The federal Treasury, therefore, collects less federal tax from a taxpayer in an income tax state. If, for example, a married taxpayer in 1973 had a taxable income of $3,600 in a state with no income tax, his federal tax would be $552; but in a state that collected $35 in income tax from him, his federal tax would be reduced to $546 (the tax on $3,600 minus $35), and he therefore would pay only an additional $29 as a result of the state income tax. Similarly, a taxpayer with a taxable income of $27,600 would pay a federal tax of $6,956 in the former state, but only $6,249 in the latter where his state income tax of $1,965 would add only $1,258 to his total income taxes. In the face of this situation, why have states been reluctant to use progressive income taxes? Have they failed to appreciate the effects of deductibility?

This illustration, while valid, is defective and unrealistic. The state without an individual income tax must raise, from alternative taxes, a revenue equivalent to that of the state with an income tax. Moreover, the federal income tax law allows individuals to deduct state and local sales and most other taxes from adjusted gross income. Therefore, taxpayers in the state that had no income tax could reduce their federal income tax by deducting their state sales tax payments. The relevant comparison is between the aggregate tax levels (federal and state) of taxpayers in the two states. Is it favorable to one or the other?

It is easy to show that for two such states, with the same total revenue, a differential would exist that would be favorable at the bottom end of the scale to residents of the income tax state and at the upper end to residents of the sales tax state. Since income tax payments are progressive, and sales tax payments regressive, the deductible amounts in the sales tax state will be relatively large for low- and middle-income taxpayers, and relatively small for high-income taxpayers. Conversely, in the income tax state, deductible amounts will be relatively small for low- and middle-income taxpayers, and relatively large for high-income persons, those most likely to migrate for purposes of tax avoidance. Therefore, a state legislature might choose to enact a sales tax rather than an income tax: it might worry more about interstate migration than equity.

Other Considerations

With respect to costs of administration, probably the income tax has a modest advantage over the sales tax in costs as a percentage of receipts, where costs are 1½ to 2 percent of receipts. With respect to compliance, the income tax puts costs chiefly on the payers of the tax, while the sales tax puts them on retailers. Sales taxation has sometimes been favored because part of it can be shifted out of state —to tourists, visitors, and out-of-state buyers of the products of a state. But states also use the income tax to tap nonresidents, as when New York levies a tax on the income earned in the state by commuters from New Jersey and Connecticut. While some states have more ability than others to exact such tribute, the net amount of the tribute is probably exaggerated.

Sales tax and income tax differ significantly in revenue stability. The yield of a progressive income tax will vary more over the business cycle than that of a general sales tax, both because the base of the income tax is the more variable, and because its rates are progressive. State (and local) governments favor taxes with stable yields because, in recession, they cannot easily borrow to finance deficits. And yet an income tax with a high built-in revenue flexibility promotes national economic stabilization.

Current Trends

In the 1930s and the postwar years, when sales taxes were being adopted by many states, sales taxation and income taxation were widely regarded as alternatives. Debate over the two is still sometimes couched in these terms, even though it has come to be quite unrealistic. In 1973 only New Hampshire had neither a general retail sales tax nor an individual income tax, and therefore only it is free to make a choice (see chapter 2). Nine states eschew an individual income tax and have only a general sales tax; four have made the opposite choice and have only an individual income tax. State use of income tax might increase if decreased federal use of the tax took the form of credits to taxpayers for payments of state income tax.[31] Without some such push, state legislatures seem likely to favor sales tax for several reasons, not least because it is unutilized by the federal government. In 1973 thirty-six state governments utilized *both* income and sales taxes. The prospects are for additions to this number. Certainly it is unlikely that states with both taxes will drop one, or that states with one will shift to the other.

31. For an analysis of such a move, and of other federal credits, see James A. Maxwell, *Tax Credits and Intergovernmental Fiscal Relations* (Brookings Institution, 1962).

CHAPTER SIX

Other State Taxes

But you must confine yourself within the modest limits of order.
Twelfth Night

THE IMPERFECT RATIONALE for state taxation of business income is some version of a benefit theory. Business, it is held, owes taxes because of benefits received from the jurisdictions where business is carried on. The states have utilized this rationale to levy an amazing variety of taxes, most of them financially insignificant. Attention here is confined to income taxes on corporations,[1] in the form of either a direct tax on net income or an excise on the privilege of doing business and measured by or according to net income. Choice of one or the other depends on two legal considerations: a direct tax may, and an excise tax may not, be levied on an out-of-state corporation engaged solely in interstate commerce; an excise may, and a direct tax may not, include interest on federal securities in the net income used to measure the tax.

Corporation Income Tax

The modern version of a state tax on corporate income, like that on individual income, started with the Wisconsin tax of 1911.

1. Of the states that levy no corporation income tax, one (Texas) raises considerable sums by annual license taxes on corporations in general, and the others raise modest amounts using these taxes. Some states (Delaware, Alabama, Ohio, Pennsylvania, and New Jersey) with corporate income taxes raise significant additional amounts in a similar way.

115

Table 6–1. Adoption of State Corporation Income Taxes, 1910–73

Years	Number of states
1910–19	9[a]
1920–29	8
1930–39	15
1940–49	2
1950–59	2
1960–69	6
1970–73	3

Source: Advisory Commission on Intergovernmental Relations, *Federal-State-Local Finances: Significant Features of Fiscal Federalism, 1973–74 Edition* (GPO, 1974), table 96.
a. The Hawaii tax, enacted in 1901, is included here.

Thereafter, most states, when they enacted income taxes, taxed both individual and corporate income.[2] By 1973 forty-five states (and the District of Columbia) had a corporation income tax (see table 6-1). Thirty-two states (and the District of Columbia) use flat rates—4.0 percent to 12.0 percent—and thirteen graduated rates. These taxes in 1973 produced 8.0 percent of total state tax collections, while license taxes on corporations in general produced an additional 1.4 percent. As always, variation among the states was appreciable. The distribution of collections per capita by states for 1973 is shown in table 6-2. Indiana, West Virginia, and Nebraska were at the bottom; New York and Connecticut at the top.

According to the Advisory Commission on Intergovernmental Relations (ACIR), the states in 1964 were "moving toward greater reliance on the Federal tax base for State corporate income taxes as well as for individual income taxes."[3] The move has continued. In 1973 thirty-three used the federal base. The remaining states (and the District of Columbia) defined net income in a manner independent of the federal definition. This creates obvious problems of compliance, since the taxpayer has to consider not only the federal provisions, but also those of the state. The problems are compounded for the corporation that earns income in several states. The existing diversity is rooted in historical, constitutional, and policy reasons.

2. In 1973, however, five states—New Jersey, Connecticut, New Hampshire, Florida, and Tennessee—taxed corporate but not individual income (the New Jersey tax on commuter income, and the Tennessee tax on income from intangibles are not counted).

3. Advisory Commission on Intergovernmental Relations, *Tax Overlapping in the United States, 1964* (GPO, 1964), p. 142.

Table 6-2. Distribution of States by Collections Per Capita from State Corporation Income Taxes, 1973

Collections per capita, in dollars	Number of states
Under 10	4
10–15	5
15–20	11
20–25	13
25–30	3
30–35	2
35–40	0
40–45	5
45–50	2

Source: U.S. Census Bureau, *State Government Finances in 1973*, p. 11.

The weight of these reasons needs current appraisal because the advantages of uniformity, through approximate conformity to the federal definitions, are very strong. At present the level of compliance is poor when departures from the federal base are complex. Conformity means also that a state secures the benefits of federal enforcement with little or no state expense.[4]

All payments of state corporation income taxes are deductible by corporations in computing net income for federal corporation income tax purposes. The federal tax is, of course, much heavier than the combined state taxes; in 1973 the former yielded $36.2 billion and the latter $5.4 billion. Since the federal yield is so high and the rate so nearly proportional, tax differentials from corporate income taxation, state by state, are not large.

Interstate Allocation of Income

The most persistent and acute problem in state use of the corporate income tax concerns the allocation of interstate income. At present thousands of companies in the nation do business and earn income in more than one state. On what basis should states reckon their tax share of the net income base? Three rules for division are used: formula apportionment, specific allocation, and separate accounting. Separate accounting, while permitted by most states, has only lim-

4. *State Taxation of Interstate Commerce*, Report of the Special Subcommittee on State Taxation of Interstate Commerce of the House Judiciary Committee, 88:2 (GPO, 1964), vol. 1, chap. 17.

Table 6-3. Illustration of Inequities in Formula Allocation of Taxable Income of a Hypothetical Corporation with Interstate Property and Sales[a]

Location	Value of property, in dollars	Sales, in dollars	Proportional allocation formula		More favorable formula	
			Allocation fraction	Taxable income, in dollars	Allocation fraction	Taxable income, in dollars
State A	800	500	5/12	250	8/12	400
State B	300	1,500	3/8	225	1/2	300
State C	100	200	3/40	45	1/12	50
State D	0	800	2/15	80	4/15	160
Total	1,200	3,000		600		910

a. Property valued at $1,200, annual sales of $3,000, annual net income of $600.

ited application.[5] It assumes that the operations of a multistate business can be split into pieces; in fact, most such businesses are unitary. Specific allocation, provided by all except six states, means that some items of income are regarded as nonapportionable—for example, dividends and interest—and must be allocated wholly to one state or another. But the states differ on the kinds of income that are to be so allocated, and also on where a particular kind of income has its source.[6] Specific allocation, it should be appreciated, applies only to part of the income of a business; it is used mainly as an adjunct to formula apportionment.

FORMULA APPORTIONMENT. The states have devised many formulas for apportionment, and not infrequently the aim has been to secure a tax advantage for a state without consideration of what is fair for a corporation doing a national business. A simple hypothetical example will show how inequities may exist. Assume a corporation with an annual net income of $600, with property of $1,200 distributed in three states, and with sales of $3,000 distributed among four states (see table 6-3). Each of the states levies taxes on the basis of an allocation formula that represents the proportion that the corporation's sales and properties in its state bears to the corporation's total property and sales. Each state gives equal weight in the formula to property and sales. Thus, in State A the allocation fraction is $5/12$ (that is, $800/$1,200 plus $500/$3,000, divided by two) and its

5. Ibid., pp. 160–67.
6. Ibid., pp. 197–217.

share of income is $250 ($\frac{5}{12}$ of $600). The other states calculate
their tax base similarly. If, however, each state were to use either
property or sales alone, taking care to choose the one that is more
favorable to it, the results would be as shown in the last column of
table 6-3, where the aggregate tax base adds up to more than the
corporation's net income.

No easy way exists to show the diversity of state apportionment
of interstate corporate income.[7] However, the difficulties and costs
created for business by the differences in the treatment of interstate
corporate income are important. The Council of State Governments
has pointed out that the states pay an administrative penalty

due to the diversity among their corporate income tax laws. For example,
cooperative auditing by States of returns filed by multistate businesses
would appear to be desirable in the interests of efficient tax administration. But the States are largely foreclosed from using this device because
of the differences in their laws and the tax forms required. Exchange of
information among States and comparison of returns filed by taxpayers
can have only limited value under present conditions. Greater uniformity
among the States with respect to formulas and other key features of their
corporate tax laws would make interstate cooperation in this field more
feasible and thus increase the efficiency and effectiveness of State tax
administration.[8]

A UNIFORM FORMULA. A uniform apportionment formula would
make available for taxation 100 percent of the income of a corporation, assuming its use by all states in which the corporation did business. At present, since the states use different bases, selecting factors
favorable to them, the bases (and the income) add up to more than
100 percent.[9] Moreover, some states use catch-all sales factors that
require all sales destined to the state to be counted in a formula even
though some will later be shipped out to other states.

Three factors currently in use are worth notice: property, payroll,
and sales. The Massachusetts formula gives equal weight to each.

7. For a list of states that follow the uniform division of income for tax purposes act and those that have adopted the multistate tax compact, see ACIR, *Federal-State-Local Finances: Significant Features of Fiscal Federalism, 1973–74 Edition* (GPO, 1974), table 149, p. 290.

8. *State Income Taxation of Mercantile and Manufacturing Corporations*, Hearings before the Special Subcommittee on State Taxation of Interstate Commerce of
the House Judiciary Committee, 87:1 (GPO, 1962), p. 514.

9. Five states do not tax corporate income.

Two major variants exist, one defining sales according to origin, that is, the state in which the goods are produced, the other according to destination, that is, the state in which the goods are consumed or used. In recent years, the trend has been toward increased use of "destination of sales" as a revenue-raising measure by states that are —or think they are—net importers. In some states, however, use of the destination factor was meant to favor locally based firms that sold outside the state. The tax bill of such a firm in the home state would be lower when the sales factor is destination rather than origin. To be sure, the tax base apportioned out of the home state should be added to the tax base of the state of sales destination.

Substantial justice could be achieved by any one of several formulas, provided only that the states could agree. Fractional allocation might then be based on factors that are easy to ascertain, enabling both the taxpayer and the tax administrator to respond promptly in an economical and equitable manner. At one time the Massachusetts formula was used quite widely. But in postwar years, encouraged by laissez-faire decisions of the Supreme Court, some of the states displayed anarchical tendencies, and the feeling arose that Congress should intervene.

In 1959 the Supreme Court upheld a Minnesota tax on a corporation that solicited orders in Minnesota but owned no real estate and warehoused no merchandise there. Three justices dissented, and one, Justice Felix Frankfurter, declared forcibly that a situation was emerging that required congressional remedy. As a result of the decision, he argued, state governments would place new burdens on interstate commerce. Many small corporations would become subject to a separate income tax in each state. They would "have to keep books, make returns, store records, and engage legal counsel, all to meet the divers and variegated tax laws of forty-nine States, with their different times for filing returns, different tax structures, different modes for determining 'net income,' and, different, often conflicting, formulas of apportionment."[10] The courts could not provide a remedy; indeed, reliance on them "only aggravates the difficulties and retards proper legislative solution. . . . The solution . . . ought not to rest on the self-serving determination of the States of what they

10. *Northwestern States Portland Cement Co.* v. *Minnesota,* 358 U.S. 450, 474 (1959).

are entitled to out of the Nation's resources. Congress alone can formulate policies founded upon economic realities."[11]

Congress did act. Public Law 86-272, which was enacted on September 14, 1959, restricted the authority of the states to impose taxes on interstate commerce. Income taxation of a corporation was not allowable if the only activity of a corporation within the state was the solicitation of orders. Such an activity did not constitute doing business in a state. The law left uncertainties concerning what was or was not proscribed. But it was meant to be temporary, since it ordered Congress to study and propose legislation concerning the taxation of interstate commerce. The first results of the study, dealing with corporation income taxes, were released in June 1964.[12]

THE ECONOMIC LOGIC. On economic grounds, which formula is to be favored? The nub of the argument here concerns where income is earned, that is, where is the location of the factors that create income? C. Lowell Harriss argues as follows:

Income is created by human and material resources. The resources utilized by a business as a whole in producing its income can be measured reasonably well by what is paid for them. Moreover, the places where the resources have been producing during a year can be determined on a consistent, though not completely unambiguous, basis.[13]

Property and payrolls should count. Opinions differ on what property should be included and what standard of valuation should be used, as well as on the composition of payrolls, and the state in which payrolls are located. But these issues can be resolved without great difficulty.

A workable formula would not give sales a separate or distinct

11. Ibid., 476–77.

12. *State Taxation of Interstate Commerce,* Report of the Special Subcommittee, vols. 1 and 2. When the Supreme Court in *Scripto, Inc.* v. *Carson,* 362 U.S. 207 (1960), extended the reach of the states in taxing interstate sales, Congress passed legislation (P.L. 87-17 [April 7, 1961]) ordering the study of all interstate and local taxes.

13. "Interstate Apportionment of Business Income," *American Economic Review,* vol. 49 (June 1959), p. 400. A very similar argument is spelled out in more detail by Charles E. Ratliff, Jr., *Interstate Apportionment of Business Income for State Income Tax Purposes* (University of North Carolina Press, 1962), chap. 5. A very different basis would be to measure the relative extent to which a multistate company "has caused the various States to incur governmental costs." For a discussion of this method of allocation, see *State Taxation of Interstate Commerce,* Report of the Special Subcommittee, vol. 1, pp. 158–59.

place. Sales effort would be represented merely by the cost of the economic resources used in selling; it would not be represented by the value of sales made in a state. Proponents of the value of sales destination as a separate component argue that selling effort is an essential part of the economic process, and that without sales no income would be created; they argue also that out-of-state sellers "exploit" the market of a state. The first argument leads only to the conclusion that the cost of sales effort should count to the extent that it is a part of cost. To imply that since sales are necessary, they should count in their totality is a fallacy. Property is necessary; so are management, materials, and skilled and unskilled labor. Each factor and subfactor makes a contribution appropriately measured by its cost, and no economic justification exists for overweighting one type of cost. The second argument assumes that selling is exploitation of a market. This also is a fallacy unless important monopoly features are present. In a free market neither buyer nor seller is exploited; exchange is a two-sided and mutually beneficial process. If, indeed, important monopoly features are present, exploitation may exist. But surely inclusion of a sales destination factor in a formula has no logical bearing on such a situation.[14]

REVENUE PRODUCTIVITY. A major practical difficulty in changing to a uniform formula is the possibility that the revenue of some states will decrease. Attempts to measure the potential revenue effects indicate that most states greatly exaggerate the revenue advantages to them of their particular formulas.[15] The study made for the Special Subcommittee of the House Committee on the Judiciary in 1964

14. Dissent from these opinions (see particularly Jerome R. Hellerstein, "Allocation and Nexus in State Taxation of Interstate Businesses," in *State and Local Taxes on Business,* symposium conducted by the Tax Institute of America [Tax Institute, 1965]) emphasizes, first, that the federal government in income taxation regards income as arising where the sale is effected, and second, that a sales destination factor is the major way by which a significant share in the tax base can be allocated to "market" states. While deploring the present disorder, the opinion is advanced that a federal prescription of uniformity of methods of dividing interstate income would go a long way toward simplifying compliance and administration, especially if a quantitative minimum limit (for example $100,000 of receipts from sales in a state) were set for establishment of nexus (jurisdiction to tax).

15. See, for example, Council of State Governments, "Report of Survey of Effects on State Revenues of Various Proposed Uniform Apportionment Formulas" (Chicago: Council of State Governments, 1956; processed); other surveys are reported in *State Income Taxation of Mercantile and Manufacturing Corporations, Hearings.*

provided definitive answers. It measured the comparative revenue effects of three uniform formulas: a two-factor formula including only property and payrolls, a three-factor one in which a sales-origin factor is added, and a three-factor one in which a sales-distribution factor is added. The revenue consequences to the states of a change-over to any one of the three formulas would be modest:

For only two States do the staff's estimates indicate that changeover to any of the three formulas studied could produce a loss in total tax revenues of as much as 1 percent; for two States a gain of more than 1 percent of total tax revenues could be produced. The vast majority of the income tax States could adopt any of the three uniform formulas studied with either a gain in revenue, no change in revenue, or a loss of less than one-half of 1 percent of total tax revenues. Even these estimates are based on the assumption that the States are able today to collect all revenues as-signed to them by the relentless application of the formulas currently in use, and thus take no account of the limitations imposed by jurisdictional rules and enforcement problems. If it may be assumed that any uniform system for division of income would be designed in a fashion to mitigate these problems, the losses would certainly be smaller in fact, and in some cases a revenue gain might be produced even though the staff's estimates suggest a loss.

In short, as a factor to be weighed in choosing among alternative uniform schemes for the division of income for tax purposes, revenue consid-erations are very minor.[16]

COMPLIANCE COSTS. What other considerations come to mind? One is "the cost to taxpayers of remitting their State income tax pay-ments." A large compliance cost is inefficient in itself, and it also impairs the quality of compliance. Computation of a property factor is, the Judiciary study finds, "relatively simple if property is valued either at original cost or at adjusted basis for Federal tax purposes," and computation of payroll factors is "generally quite simple." But a sales factor, especially for smaller companies, is costly to compute and these compliance costs are "wholly disproportionate to the tax liabilities involved."[17] Indeed, any formula that attributes income to a large number of states—as a sales destination factor must often do —is bound to bring either high costs of compliance, or else noncom-pliance.

16. *State Taxation of Interstate Commerce,* Report of the Special Subcommittee, vol. 1, p. 562.
17. Ibid., pp. 562–63.

Many companies involved in interstate commerce are quite small, and most of them, even though their markets are spread over many states, have a place of business in only one state. The recent tendency of state governments to demand that tax returns be filed by a company wherever it has a sales office, or inventories, or itinerant employees, has induced a low level of compliance. The picture that emerges is of a tax system "which works badly for both business and the States. It is the picture of a system in which the States are reaching farther and farther to impose smaller and smaller liabilities on more and more companies. It is the picture of a system which calls upon tax administrators to enforce the unenforceable, and the taxpayer to comply with the uncompliable."[18] The legal requirements and the world of facts are far apart. Broad assertions of jurisdiction, even when constitutionally valid, have not been accompanied by fulfillment.

The likelihood is that formulas with a sales destination factor more often lead to under- than to over-taxation. A company that makes shipments into states where it has no business location is permitted by the formula to reduce its tax base in the states where it has places of business. The company will, however, often fail to report this base in states where it makes the sales. In short, jurisdictional rules bring about a shrinkage of the base in the home state, while actual compliance does not bring this income into the base in the sales destination states.

The Need for Federal Intervention

The erection of unreasonable tax obstacles to interstate trade in this country is a serious matter. Commerce should flow freely because, more than ever before, the United States is economically one nation. The jurisdiction of the state governments in taxing commerce should stop at state lines, and reasonable rules are available to define the proper tax base of each state in the net earnings of a multistate business. But many of the states have been unwilling to accept the

18. Ibid., p. 598. "Thus among 819 instances studied in which companies had salesmen soliciting and accepting orders, returns were filed in 21 cases. Among 130 instances in which companies maintained sales offices, only 44 returns were filed. And among 234 instances in which companies owned goods in public warehouses, only 91 returns were filed. In each of these cases, the States involved required filing on the basis of the activity considered." Ibid., p. 597.

rules, and the result has been discrimination, excessive costs of tax administration, multiplication of litigation, costly compliance and victimization of exposed businesses—and noncompliance by other businesses. These costs are not easily perceived by the public, but are serious in their effect on the national economy.

Efforts to persuade the states to adopt a uniform rule for division of corporate income have been made for decades. The results have been negligible, and no hope can be affirmed of better progress in the future.[19] Rather would realism predict a worsening situation as the upward trend of state tax rates continues. Congressional intervention seems, therefore, to be an indicated and desirable step. How the income of a multistate company should be divided, for tax purposes, among the states is a question that demands one answer. The diversity of present answers provided by state laws is a perversion for which no rationale can be found in the theory of federalism.

TAX CREDIT OR TAX SHARING. Other and much less satisfactory forms of congressional intervention would be provisions for tax credit or tax sharing. By the former, Congress might declare that some defined part of a state income tax payment could be credited by a corporation against its federal income tax payment in states that tax corporations according to conditions specified by Congress. Such a step would, in effect, force the five states that have no corporation income tax to enact one; it would, besides, favor the richer and more industrialized states in which most corporation income is created. Neither of these results is appealing. Tax sharing would require state withdrawal from taxation of corporate income in return for receipt of some predetermined slice of federal collections. On what basis should the share of each state be determined? State-by-state federal collections now reflect where the federal return was filed and the federal tax paid. Usually a single federal return is made at the principal place of business of the company. Therefore the figures of federal collections by states give no accurate report of where income was earned; they overstate the income earned in the states where corporations have their headquarters. State governments attempt to tax all corporate income derived within their own borders, and the nonindustrial states therefore collect much of their revenue from

19. By July 1973, nineteen states followed neither the multistate tax compact nor the uniform division of income for tax purposes act.

corporations that report their income for federal tax purposes from other states.

As a result, if state-by-state collections of revenue from corporate income tax are expressed as percentages of the federal collections reported by the commissioner of internal revenue, the percentages are usually high for the less industrialized states. Thus, substitution of federal-state sharing of tax collections for the present situation would provide a generous share to states like Mississippi and Arkansas. Any sharing based on origin of income is sure to favor the richer states; sharing based on other criteria—origin of sales, destination of sales, payrolls, and so forth—might be more favorable to the poorer and less industrialized states. But so long as the economic criterion of origin of income is utilized, such sharing will be advantageous to the richer states.[20] Moreover, sharing is a centralizing step that should have a much stronger justification than is provided by the need for a uniform apportionment formula.

The Use Tax

The use tax is a state levy on commodities purchased outside a state, but brought into it for use. As state retail sales taxes grew in number, the strong protection given by the Supreme Court in the 1920s and 1930s to interstate commerce was annoying to tax administrators and to retailers in sales tax states. These states discovered a remedy in the form of the use tax which, in 1937, the Supreme Court held to be constitutional. Designed merely as a supplement to the sales tax, its rates, application, and so forth, are identical.

A major problem with the use tax has been enforcement. Application to residents' out-of-state purchases is obviously awkward except where, as in the case of automobiles, the article must be registered. More and more the states have ordered out-of-state sellers to collect the use tax for them. In 1941 the Supreme Court upheld the right of Iowa to require a mail-order house to collect a use tax on its sales to residents of the state. Since then the Supreme Court has liberalized its interpretation, the culmination coming in 1960 with *Scripto, Inc.* v. *Carson.* A Georgia corporation with no office or place of business in Florida shipped goods there pursuant to orders from jobbers. The

20. See James A. Maxwell, *Tax Credits and Intergovernmental Fiscal Relations* (Brookings Institution, 1962), pp. 145–47.

Court held that Florida was within its rights in requiring the Georgia corporation to be responsible for the collection of a use tax on products shipped to Florida. Thereafter many states were prompt to impose use tax collection on out-of-state manufacturers and vendors, and soon agitation developed to place some restrictions on the states parallel to those of P.L. 86-272 restricting states' authority to impose taxes on interstate commerce.

One line of argument was that sellers who had no office or place of business in a taxing state should not be required to collect the state's use tax on sales in the state. Compliance here, so ran the contention, was even more complex than in the case of state income taxes because the bases of state sales and use taxes were more complex and subject to frequent change. State officials argued, in rebuttal, that collection through out-of-state sellers was essential to enforcement, and that exemptions patterned on the P.L. 86-272 restrictions would bring a serious reduction in state revenue.

The fact is, then, that interstate sales currently raise serious problems not only with respect to corporation income taxes, but also state sales and use taxes. The Supreme Court in 1967 refused to sanction collection of a use tax, imposed by Illinois, on sales by a mail-order house entirely through catalogs, declaring that "it is difficult to conceive of commercial transactions more exclusively interstate in character."[21]

Death and Gift Taxes

Death and gift taxes are not an important source of state tax revenue—in 1973 they provided only 2.1 percent of total state tax collections. Most of the states levy inheritance rather than estate taxes, although no summary description of the variety is accurate. Sixteen states levy taxes on gifts as complements to death taxes.

There is, of course, a marked variation in yield among the states, as table 6-4 shows. For twenty-two states death and gift taxes in 1973 provided less than $4 per capita of tax revenue, but for Connecticut, Massachusetts, and California, they supplied over $12 per capita.

21. *National Bellas Hess, Inc.* v. *Department of Revenue of the State of Illinois,* 386 U.S. 759 (1967). Three justices dissented.

Table 6-4. Distribution of States by Dollars Per Capita Collected from Death and Gift Taxes, 1973

Dollars per capita	Number of states
Less than 2	10
2– 4	12
4– 6	6
6– 8	8
8–10	5
10–12	5
Over 12	3[a]

Source: *State Government Finances in 1973*, p. 11. Nevada had no death or gift taxes.
a. California and Massachusetts $13, Connecticut $21.

The Federal Tax Credit

The state governments have used death taxes much longer than the federal government. On three occasions before 1916 a federal tax was used as an emergency device—1798–1802, 1861–70, and 1898–1902—and repealed when the emergency need had passed. A few state governments levied inheritance taxes early in the nineteenth century, but by 1891 less than ten states were using these taxes, all of them with low flat rates. Thereafter the need for revenue and an agitation against concentration of wealth combined to popularize the tax. By 1916 forty-two states were levying it (all but Florida, Mississippi, New Mexico, Nebraska, South Carolina, and Alabama), usually at low progressive rates, raising $30.7 million or 8.4 percent of their tax revenue. Almost all of the taxes were on inheritances, that is, on the portions of a decedent's estate passing to each individual heir.

In 1916 the federal government imposed an estate tax, that is, one on the entire net estate left by a decedent. The state governments, by virtue of long prior occupancy, regarded death taxation as their preserve, and they resented federal intrusion. Further, the states advanced the legal theory that they—and not the federal government —had the right to regulate the descent and distribution of property at death. In the 1920s, when federal finances eased and those of the state governments tightened, agitation for federal repeal mounted. In 1924, a curious compromise emerged. Congress raised the rates of the federal estate tax, but it also provided for a credit of up to 25 percent against the federal tax for death taxes paid to the states. If, for example, the federal tax on an estate was $100 and the state tax $25, the total tax, after credit, would be $100 rather than $125.

At this time (1924) three states—Florida, Nevada, and Alabama —were without a death tax. Florida had never had such a tax, but in November 1924, by constitutional amendment, it forbade enactment of either inheritance or income taxes. The purpose of this move was only too apparent: by supplementing the attractions of its climate with the establishment of a tax haven, Florida hoped that rich people would domicile themselves within its borders. Since domicile for the purpose of taxation was easy to establish, the other states had reason to fear the migration of estates beyond their jurisdiction. Nevada promptly met the threat, or rather imitated Florida, by passing a similar constitutional amendment in July 1925; California, which had up to this time been the natural competitor of Florida as a domicile for retired millionaires, discussed the need for parallel action.

Nothing more was needed to bring home the realization that the future of death taxes as a source of state revenue was in serious jeopardy. At the very time when many state officers were urging federal withdrawal from the field, here were signal illustrations of the inability of the states to use a system of death taxation with success. And the most casual survey indicated that there were other weaknesses in the state taxes. Rates, exemptions, definitions, and administrative practices were diverse. While complete uniformity in these matters was not to be hoped for, the existing variation was beyond reason. Even more dangerous were the discriminatory practices that had grown up, particularly in the taxation of nonresident decedents.

Some attempt to clean house was imperative, and at the meeting of the National Tax Association in September 1924, a resolution was adopted recommending that the association assemble a conference of federal as well as state representatives to consider remedies for the existing difficulties over death taxation. In February 1925 the conference met at Washington. Delegates appointed by the governors attended from twenty-five states, and President Calvin Coolidge, addressing the conference, promised his "cordial cooperation." After thorough discussion it was voted that the chairman, Dr. T. W. Page, should appoint a committee of investigation to report recommendations to a second national conference. A committee of nine members was named with F. A. Delano as chairman, and it reported in November 1925.

The committee had a twofold objective. It wished to stifle the anarchistic moves of Florida and Nevada, and also to apply some pressure on the states generally to reform their taxes. Accordingly it recommended increase of the federal tax credit from 25 percent to 80 percent, and repeal of the federal tax in six years if, meanwhile, the states had cleaned house. At this same time, in 1926, the Ways and Means Committee of the House of Representatives was holding hearings on revenue revision. It decided to accept one of the recommendations of the Delano committee—enlargement of the federal credit to 80 percent. By this step the tax advantages sought by Florida and Nevada were largely canceled out, since the estate of a decedent in those states would pay the full federal tax.

This was the turning point of the movement for repeal of the federal tax. Many state officials were, on the one hand, pacified by the 80 percent credit, and on the other hand, timid about the prospect of federal withdrawal. For a few years progress toward reform was made.[22] In 1931 federal credits for state taxes offset, on the average, 75.6 percent of the federal tax liability; the number of states using the estate tax only had risen from two in 1925 to seven in 1932, and the number using estate and inheritance taxes jointly had risen from three to twenty-seven.

But in 1931–32 all such progress stopped because of the depression. Congress underscored this retreat when, in 1932, it enacted a supplementary estate tax (with an exemption of $50,000) against which no credit for state taxes was provided. The provisions were retained, including the 80 percent credit, but the idea of repeal was no longer contemplated. On several later occasions Congress increased the federal rates and altered the exemptions in order to increase federal collections. As a result, the federal tax credit, which in 1931 came to nearly 76 percent of the federal tax liability, had declined by 1942 to 10 percent. The aim of providing the states with a larger share of death tax revenue was sidetracked.

So also was the aim of tax coordination. Disintegration of state death taxation through interstate tax competition was indeed averted and as of 1973 only Nevada had no death tax. But in other respects coordination has not been achieved. State governments differ in type of tax, definitions, rates, exemptions, deductions, exclusions, and ad-

22. The reform came through decisions of the Supreme Court which limited the situs of intangibles to the domicile of the decedent, and through adoption of reciprocity (that is, State A would exempt intangibles of nonresident decedents provided that State B reciprocated).

ministrative practices. The Advisory Commission on Intergovernmental Relations in 1960 found many types of state taxes.[23] In 1973 six states (Alabama, Alaska, Arkansas, Florida, Georgia, and New Mexico) had pure "pick-up" taxes modeled on the federal statute and designed to impose a tax liability equal to the maximum allowable credit. For example, if the federal tax on an estate under the 1926 provisions was $100 and the credit $80, the state tax would be $80 to pick up the total available credit. Two states (Mississippi and North Dakota) had estate taxes only; seven had estate and pick-up taxes; two had inheritance only; thirty-one had inheritance taxes with pick-up taxes as supplements in order to secure "unused" federal credits. Effective rates are quite divergent.

Federal-State Coordination

The ACIR in 1961 recommended that Congress increase and modify the federal credit in order to spur the states toward coordination and to provide a modest increase in state revenues. In place of a flat percentage, a two-bracket graduated credit was proposed that would make available a relatively larger share in the lower tax brackets and a smaller share in the higher brackets. For example, a credit of 80 percent of the gross federal tax liability might be allowed on the first $250,000 of taxable estates, and 20 percent on the balance. Such a change would provide a substantial increase in the value of the aggregate credit; it would also be somewhat more favorable to the nonindustrialized states, and would provide a more stable revenue. The commission recommended, however, that two conditions be attached to the new credit: revenue maintenance, and a shift to estate taxes.

State death taxes at the time averaged 2.8 times the amount credited under the 1926 law. Thus many estates paid state death taxes in excess of the amount that could be credited against the federal tax. If the maximum federal credit were to be increased, these estates could claim larger credits. For this reason the ACIR believed that "the immediate effect of an increase in the Federal credit, especially in the lower brackets, would be Federal tax reduction, not increased State collections."[24] Unless a state felt an urgent need for additional revenue, it might be loath to take action depriving its residents of the

23. *Coordination of State and Federal Inheritance, Estate, and Gift Taxes* (ACIR, 1961), p. 35.
24. Ibid., p. 76.

federal reduction. The commission felt strongly that it was no part of its duty to recommend a tax decrease (or increase). Accordingly, it declared that the new credit should be conditional on revenue maintenance, that is, "certification by the Governor to the Secretary of the Treasury that the estimated annual revenue level of his State's death taxes has been raised in an amount corresponding to the estimated aggregate increase in the tax credits on Federal estate returns filed from his State. This Commission further recommends that the States be required to maintain these higher tax rate levels for a period of five years."[25]

While the new credit, coupled with revenue maintenance, would provide the states with additional revenue, it would in itself do nothing to alleviate the complexity of death taxation, a complexity "due largely to the prevalence of inheritance type taxes among the States." Tax simplification was an important objective, and therefore the ACIR recommended "that the higher Federal estate tax credit . . . be limited to estate type State taxes, as distinguished from inheritance taxes."[26] So far Congress has not acted on the recommendations of the Advisory Commission.

Conclusion

The weight of the arguments in favor of federal withdrawal from death taxes has diminished over the decades. After nearly sixty years of unbroken federal occupancy, the historical plea of prior state occupancy seems unconvincing, and while property does pass at death under state law, the constitutional right of the federal government to tax transfer of property at death is now beyond dispute.

The argument that the fiscal need of the states exceeded that of the federal government was persuasive in the 1920s, and it has weight today. Here the question is whether or not death taxation is a logical or promising source of state revenue. Death tax revenue from its very nature is unstable for the nation as a whole. This instability increases when the taxing unit is a state because, in such case, the yearly number of returns is small and the composition of taxable estates is highly variable from state to state. Rates for this tax should not be significantly different from one state to another, because decisions concerning where to do business and where to reside should not be af-

25. Ibid., p. 18.
26. Ibid., p. 20.

fected by such factors. The sources of private wealth recognize no state lines, and the basis on which the states mainly rest their right to tax—domicile of the decedent—is often quite unrelated to the geographic origin of a decedent's wealth. In short, for most states the death tax is not now, and cannot be, a satisfactory revenue source. Uninhibited attempts to apply the tax, which overlook the national interest, may distort decisions concerning economic activity.

The Property Tax

A tax as ancient as that on property tends to become an institution and to accumulate fondly clinging traditions as it evolves over the years.
ACIR, *The Role of the States in Strengthening the Property Tax*

DURING MOST of the history of the nation, the property tax has been, by a wide margin, the most important tax revenue source. Table 7-1 shows that in 1902 it provided over 51 percent of total federal, state, and local tax collections. No other tax even approached it in importance. As late as 1940 the property tax provided nearly 35 percent of total tax collections; the second-ranking tax, on corporation income, provided 10 percent. With World War II, however, the property tax lost ground. By 1944 it provided only 9.4 percent of total collections, and was outranked by the revenue from taxes on individual and corporate income. The reason for the shift was, of course, the vast expansion of *federal* tax collections to which the property tax made no contribution, since it was, and always had been, wholly a source of state and local funds.[1] Recently the property tax has regained some ground and in 1973 it provided 15.8 percent of total tax collections.

Significance to State and Local Governments

The significance of the property tax as a source of state and local tax revenue is indicated in table 7-1. Completely dominant in 1902

1. The so-called direct tax levied by the federal government in 1798, 1814–19, and 1861 might be regarded as a property tax, since it was levied chiefly against

Table 7-1. Property Tax Collections in Relation to Total Federal, State, and Local Tax Collections, Selected Years, 1902–73

| Year | Total tax collections, in millions of dollars | | | Property tax collections as percentage of | |
	Federal, state, and local	State and local	Property tax	Federal, state, and local tax collections	State and local tax collections
1902	1,373	860	706	51.4	82.1
1913	2,271	1,609	1,332	58.7	82.8
1927	9,451	6,087	4,730	50.0	77.7
1938	12,949	7,605	4,440	34.3	58.4
1944	49,095	8,774	4,604	9.4	52.5
1948	51,218	13,342	6,126	12.0	45.9
1962	123,816	41,554	19,054	15.4	45.9
1966	160,836	56,741	24,670	15.3	43.5
1973	286,595	121,102	45,283	15.8	37.4

Sources: U.S. Census Bureau, *Historical Statistics of the United States: Colonial Times to 1957* (GPO, 1960), pp. 722 and 726; and Census Bureau, *Governmental Finances in 1964–65*, pp. 15 and 18, *in 1965–66*, p. 20, and *in 1972–73*, pp. 15 and 20. In all tables, years are fiscal unless otherwise noted.

and 1913, and only slightly less so in the 1920s, the property tax lost relative ground in the 1930s and during World War II. In 1973 property taxes provided 37 percent of the total state and local tax collections. The reason for the decline was that state governments replaced the property tax with other revenue sources.

States replaced the property tax because they found new and more attractive taxes, and because the administrative machinery of the property tax was local. State governments did not assess and collect property tax through state officers; instead they apportioned to their local governments yearly a sum that the local governments were instructed to secure and turn over to the state treasury. This procedure was not popular and when in the 1930s delinquency in property tax payments became large, the state tax was bitterly resented. As a measure of relief to local governments, many state governments discontinued their tax; collections, which were 23.0 percent of state taxes in 1927, fell to 6.8 percent in 1942. The downward trend has continued and, in 1974, the figure was 1.8 percent. The general property tax has become a local tax. The proposition that state and local

property. See Paul Studenski and Herman E. Krooss, *Financial History of the United States* (2d ed.; McGraw-Hill, 1963), pp. 50–51, 76–78, 92, and 141.

Table 7-2. **General Revenue of Local Governments, 1927 and 1973**

	Amount, in millions of dollars		Percentage of total	
Source of general revenue	1927	1973	1927	1973
Tax revenue				
Property tax	4,360	43,970	73.9	37.2
Other taxes	119	9,062	2.0	7.7
Nontax revenue				
State and federal aid	605	47,866	10.2	40.4
Charges and miscellaneous	819	17,456	13.9	14.7
Total	5,903	118,355	100.0	100.0

Sources: *Historical Statistics*, p. 729; and *Governmental Finances in 1972–73*, p. 30. Figures are rounded.

sources of taxation should be separate, rather than overlapping, found practical application here. In forty-five states, less than 5 percent of state tax revenue came from the general property tax in 1974. In four states the property tax contributed between 5 percent and 10 percent of the state total, and in Montana 10.2 percent of the total.[2]

Not only has the general property tax become local, in terms of revenue productivity it is almost the only local tax. In 1973 it provided 83 percent of local tax revenue. The efforts of local governments during the past thirty years to develop other taxes have borne fruit only in large cities (see chapter 8). Additional nontax revenues have, however, been found, notably state and federal aid and collection of charges. As table 7-2 shows, these nontax revenues provided about one-quarter of local funds in 1927; by 1973 they provided more than half. Therefore, if attention is concentrated on all general revenue, the importance of the property tax to local governments has diminished in recent decades.

Local governments are of many types, and the property tax is not of the same importance to all of them. As table 7-3 shows, the dependence of school districts on the property tax is nearly complete— it provides 98 percent of their tax revenue—and that of counties, townships, and special districts is almost as great. Municipalities, however, have managed to secure more than one-third of their tax revenue from other sources.

The extreme dependence of local governments on the property tax

2. Tax Foundation, *Facts and Figures on Government Finance, 1975* (New York: Tax Foundation, 1975).

Table 7-3. Local Government Property Tax, Tax Revenue, and General Revenue, by Type of Governmental Unit, 1973

				Property tax	
	Amount, in millions of dollars			*As per-centage of general*	*As per-centage of tax*
Governmental unit	*General revenue*	*Tax revenue*	*Property tax*	*revenue*	*revenue*
All units	118,355	53,032	43,970	37.2	82.9
Counties	28,427	11,029	9,257	32.6	83.9
Municipalities	37,993	18,477	11,879	31.3	64.3
School districts	41,732	19,545	19,140	45.9	97.9
Townships and special districts	10,203	3,982	3,694	36.2	92.8

Source: *Governmental Finances in 1972–73*, p. 30.

rests on one ineluctable fact—lack of option. No other tax is available for productive use. Local taxation of income, sales, or business would induce shrinkage in the tax base and, therefore, bring serious injury to the locality. But real property is quite immobile; differential taxes of some severity will not induce migration out of a local geographic area. Workers must reside close to their work; retail outlets must locate close to consumers; manufacturing establishments, once committed, tend to stay put, since even severe property taxes are a modest part of their total costs. In short, real property offers a base on which local governments can safely levy taxes.

The yield of the tax in postwar years has been quite elastic, responding well in the aggregate to increase in gross national product, as well as to increases of population. Jesse Burkhead concludes that, on the basis of its statistical record in the 1950s, "the property tax is a far better fiscal instrument than most of its critics have allowed. There is every reason to believe that it will continue to hold its relative fiscal importance in state-local public finance structures."[3]

Is the property tax administered with efficiency? Is it equitable in its incidence? Both questions must be answered with qualified negatives. Complaints against the tax have been voiced ever since the

3. *State and Local Taxes for Public Education* (Syracuse University Press, 1963), p. 70. In chap. 4 Burkhead reviews the measurement of property tax elasticity made by others and presents his own investigation of elasticity over time with special references to the state of New York. Less optimistic conclusions are offered by Benjamin Bridges, Jr., "Past and Future Growth of the Property Tax," in Richard W. Lindholm, ed., *Property Taxation—USA* (University of Wisconsin Press, 1967).

property tax began to be a significant burden. Proposals for reform have been advanced for nearly as long a period, and, while some of these proposals have passed into limbo, some are very current. The failure to apply remedies, despite reiterated complaints, must mean that remedies are difficult to implement.

Should a renewed effort at reform be made? Is the property tax worth refurbishment? An affirmative response must lean heavily on the belief that local governments should have a major source of revenue of their own.

Incidence and Economic Effects

How should the property tax be rated in terms of the principles of taxation? Does it conform to standards of equity? How does its incidence compare with that of other taxes? What are its economic effects? To make this appraisal, let it be assumed that administration of the property tax conforms to good current practice (now achieved in about one-half of all local areas). In particular, let the assumption be made that the assessment of real property (the mainstay of the tax) is quite uniform within each taxing jurisdiction and levied on the gross value of real property.

This definition itself brings into view some obvious problems. The base of the tax is gross value, rather than net, and this is characteristic of an impersonal tax that is levied against things. Against this gross value a proportional tax rate is levied. If equity is held to indicate that tax payments be proportional (not to say progressive) in relation to net wealth, the property tax is defective.

Incidence

One estimate of the incidence of the property tax, based on 1966 data, indicates that it is about as regressive with respect to income classes as are general sales and excise taxes. The estimates, developed by Joseph Pechman and Benjamin Okner according to the traditional or orthodox assumptions concerning the shifting and incidence of these taxes, are shown in table 7-4. General sales taxes and excise taxes are assumed to be shifted forward in the form of higher prices for goods and services. The property tax is treated as two separate taxes; one on land and the other on improvements. The shifting as-

Table 7-4. Estimated Effective Rates of Property and Sales Taxes under Two Sets of Incidence Assumptions, by Income Class, 1966

Adjusted family income, in thousands of dollars	Orthodox incidence assumptions[a]				Alternative incidence assumptions[b]	
	Tax rate, in percent		Rate relative[c]		Property tax rate, in percent	Property tax rate, relative[c]
	Property tax	Sales and excise taxes	Property tax	Sales and excise taxes		
0–3	6.5	9.2	191	184	2.5	83
3–5	4.8	7.1	141	142	2.7	90
5–10	3.6	6.4	106	128	2.0	67
10–15	3.2	5.6	94	112	1.7	57
15–20	3.2	5.1	94	102	2.0	67
20–25	3.1	4.6	91	92	2.6	87
25–30	3.1	4.0	91	80	3.7	123
30–50	3.0	3.5	88	70	4.5	150
50–100	2.8	2.4	82	48	6.2	207
100–500	2.4	1.7	71	34	8.2	273
500–1,000	1.7	1.4	50	28	9.6	320
1,000 and over	0.8	1.3	24	26	10.1	337
All classes	3.4	5.0	100	100	3.0	100

Source: Joseph A. Pechman and Benjamin A. Okner, *Who Bears the Tax Burden?* (Brookings Institution, 1974), p. 59.

a. The tax on land is borne by landowners and the tax on improvements is shifted in the form of higher prices of shelter and consumption.

b. The burden of property taxes on both land and improvements is apportioned according to property income.

c. The average tax rate is assigned a value of 100; the rate relative for each income class group is a percentage of the average.

sumptions are that the tax on land falls entirely on the landlord (that is, taxes are fully capitalized in the price of land) and that the tax on improvements is reflected in higher prices for shelter and other goods.

The rate relative figures in table 7-4 show the variation—in either direction—from the average tax rate for both property and sales taxes (the value of 100 is assigned to the average effective tax rate). Thus, the relatives for the property tax under the orthodox incidence assumptions range from 191 to 24 and for the sales and excise taxes from 184 to 26. The similarity of the two sets of figures provides the evidence for the standard conclusion that the property tax is just about as regressive with respect to income classes as is the general sales tax.

Critics of this approach point out that the use of current income rather than average or permanent income in the calculation of effective tax rates overstates the regressivity of the property tax.[4] They also suggest an alternative view of property tax incidence in which all owners of capital may be thought of as sharing the property tax. The argument goes as follows: If all capital is taxed and the supply of capital is unaffected by the tax, the tax burden falls on property income rather than being shifted forward to consumers in the form of higher prices for goods. If only some capital is taxed, the economic reaction will be for assets to move to more lightly taxed areas or uses. The reaction will continue until the rate of return on capital, net of taxes, is the same in all uses. The result of the adjustment process is that the burden of the tax is felt by all owners of capital and not simply those whose property is subject to direct taxation.[5]

This distribution of the tax burden is demonstrated in table 7-4 under the alternative incidence assumptions; the tax on both land and improvements is assumed to be absorbed by property income and not passed on in higher prices. The estimates indicate that the tax burden is more progressive than generally believed.

Which view, the traditional or alternative, provides the more accurate picture of property tax incidence? The answer lies somewhere between the two. The use of current rather than permanent income does overstate the regressive nature of the tax. The more crucial problem, however, is measuring the elasticity of the supply of capital. The traditional view assumes an elastic supply of capital, the alternative view an inelastic supply. Unfortunately the empirical evidence on this point is meager and therefore no answer to the question is possible.[6]

Some writers have argued that the property tax is not levied according to the ability-to-pay principle but rather according to the benefit principle; if so, the tax should be regarded as a payment by individuals for services rendered. This argument is most plausible

4. In any given year some people experience unusual gains and others unusual losses. Thus, two families with the same permanent income who perhaps consume the same amount of housing may have different amounts of current income. Dividing property tax payments by current income produces a regressive tax distribution. See Henry J. Aaron, *Who Pays the Property Tax? A New View* (Brookings Institution, 1975), pp. 27–32.

5. For a detailed description and analysis of the various views of property tax incidence, see George F. Break, "The Incidence and Economic Effects of Taxation," in Alan S. Blinder and others, *The Economics of Public Finance* (Brookings Institution, 1974), pp. 154–68; and Aaron, *Who Pays the Property Tax?* chap. 3.

6. Aaron, *Who Pays the Property Tax?* pp. 49–50.

with respect to such local governmental services as fire protection, street improvements, sewerage construction and operation, street lighting, and so forth. But even here general benefits, which spill over to the community, are present. And education expenditure, the most important component of local budgets, is not related in any meaningful sense to property taxes. The benefits from primary and secondary education spread far beyond the recipients, and assessment of property tax for it is, moreover, quite unrelated even to the direct benefits that accrue to recipients. The general property tax is, then, only partially a benefit tax. This benefit does, however, serve to leaven the nonprogressivity of the tax.

Economic Effects

What, finally, are the economic effects of the property tax? Since it is levied on ownership of property (especially real property), rather than on current economic effort, it does not adversely affect labor incentives. But the tax must discourage private spending for housing and thus reduce the housing supply by some unascertainable amount. Similarly, it has adverse effects on business investment in taxable property. In urban areas the property tax, combined with fragmentation of governmental units, has a distorting effect on land-use patterns. Heavy taxes on property in core cities induce business and people to move to the suburbs, and the migration of relatively wealthy individuals and on-going businesses from the core city increases the pressure on cities to raises taxes further.[7]

Judged, therefore, in terms of equity and economic effects, the property tax cannot be awarded a high position. As a source of state income, it has no attraction, because other broad-based and productive taxes are in successful use. But no alternative local taxes are in sight. For local governments the property tax provides a large, predictable, certain, and elastic revenue.

7. Burkhead suggests that "although imperfections remain, property tax resources do tend to be more uniformly distributed among the municipalities within a given metropolitan area over time" (*State and Local Taxes for Public Education*, p. 106). For a less optimistic view, see Dick Netzer, *Economics of the Property Tax* (Brookings Institution, 1966), pp. 67–85. For an analysis of how taxes and expenditures affect the distribution of population in metropolitan areas, see J. Richard Aronson and Eli Schwartz, "Financing Public Goods and the Distribution of Population in a System of Local Governments," *National Tax Journal*, vol. 26 (June 1973), pp. 137–60.

The Base of Property Taxation

During colonial times and the early years of the Republic, property was taxed selectively and at nonuniform rates. But with the nineteenth century a strong swing began toward inclusion of all property in the tax base, and toward taxation within each jurisdiction at a uniform rate. The two rules of universality and of uniformity were widely accepted and, indeed, often embodied as requirements in state constitutions. Governmental property was, however, exempt, and so also was the property of religious, charitable, and educational establishments. The main component in the tax base was real property —land and its improvements. But personal property—tangible and intangible—was another component. Tangible personal property includes machinery, inventory, livestock, motor vehicles, furniture, jewelry, and so on; here the significant split is between business property (including farms) and household effects. Intangible personal property consists of legal rights to valuable things—stocks, bonds, mortgages, bank deposits, and the like. Most of these are "representative" of real property or of tangible personal property; a few—such as patents and copyrights—are nonrepresentative; and sometimes intangibles are mixed. Inclusion in the tax base of both the representative property and the real property on which the representative property rests is clearly duplicative. Yet if the real property—a farm—is in one taxing jurisdiction and the mortgage is located in another jurisdiction, a problem arises concerning the relative rights of each jurisdiction to levy and collect the tax.

In the years before the Civil War, when property tax rates everywhere were low, personal property was a substantial part of the base. In Boston, for example, the tax rate in 1850 was $6.80 per $1,000, and personal property accounted for about 40 percent of total assessments. Although the amount of personal property in the form of intangibles is unknown, Charles J. Bullock concluded that at the time nondeclaration was not usual. But when, in the 1870s, the property tax rate in Massachusetts rose sharply, assessment of personal property diminished and real property came to be an increasingly large component in the tax base.[8] This was the pattern nearly everywhere.

8. "The Taxation of Property and Income in Massachusetts," in Charles J. Bullock, ed., *Selected Readings in Public Finance* (3d ed.; Ginn, 1924), pp. 307–08 and 315–16.

Table 7-5. Gross Assessed Value of Locally Assessed Property, 1956 and 1973

	Assessed value, in billions of dollars[a]		Percentage of total	
Type of property	1956	1973	1956	1973
Real[b]	209.8	704.6	81.3	86.6
Personal[c]	48.3	108.7	18.7	13.4
Total	258.0	813.2	100.0	100.0

Sources: Census Bureau, *Census of Governments, 1957*, vol. 5, *Taxable Property Values in the United States* (1959), p. 22; and Census Bureau, *Property Values Subject to Local General Property Taxation in the United States: 1973*, p. 32.
a. Value before exemptions.
b. The most important category is residential (nonfarm) property.
c. The most important category is commercial and industrial tangible property.

In some states the facts of the situation were recognized by legal enactment, and in others by administrative practice that disregarded the law.

Table 7-5 shows that in 1973, 87 percent of locally assessed property was real ($704.6 billion out of a total of $813.2 billion). Personal property was assessed at $108.7 billion, of which almost the whole was tangibles. Tangible personal property was legally exempt in four states (Delaware, Hawaii, New York, and Pennsylvania); general coverage prevailed in ten states, and partial coverage elsewhere. The disappearance from the assessment rolls of some kinds of tangible property, such as household effects, is notorious, even though state law has not always recognized this fact. Assessors cannot ascertain the existence of such property by acceptable administrative techniques, and they cannot accurately value it when ascertained. Commercial and industrial tangible personal property was legally taxable in forty-seven states, household personal property in twenty-seven states, and motor vehicles in twenty-two states. This listing exaggerates the taxation of household personal property, since many of the twenty-seven states provided partial exemptions. But it underestimates the taxation of motor vehicles, since ten states that exempt them from local general property tax apply a special property tax, and most of the remaining states apply some other form of taxation. Commercial and industrial property is generally the most important component of personal property. Valuation of this kind of property is often based on an agreement between owner and assessor, rather than on appraisal. Some states classify tangible personal property, taxing it at specified rates lower than the rate on real property, and sometimes—in Ohio, for example—this method works fairly well.

Two kinds of tangible personal property—one, machinery and equipment, the other, inventory—are used in business. The former has been a more satisfactory component of the property tax than the latter. Inventory is movable, its amount is often highly variable over the year, and its turnover is different from industry to industry (and even among firms in the same industry). Inventory can, therefore, be manipulated for the purpose of tax avoidance and its removal from the property tax base has considerable appeal.

Intangibles were legally part of the local general property tax base in fifteen states in 1972. From census data on five of them, it appears that intangibles represent an insignificant part of total assessed personal property.[9] (Louisiana had the highest proportion of intangible property to total personal property—12.4 percent.)

As this brief survey indicates, the base of the property tax is no longer general; intangibles have been legally or administratively removed. The reason is not, of course, their lack of relative value, for intangibles account for a large proportion of the value of all property. But because most intangibles are representative property, to tax them as property is obviously "double" taxation. And because intangibles are easy to conceal, they can elude the most persistent assessor, and they will do so unless the rate on them is very low.[10] Devices to detect ownership of intangibles have been suggested. None of them is feasible on a local, or even a state basis, because the location of intangibles can so easily be shifted. When, some decades ago, a classified property tax was in favor, the argument gained credence that the rate on intangibles in all localities should be $3 per $1,000, or approximately 5 percent of a yield of $60. A number of states chose to follow—and still do—this technique of taxing intangibles at a special low rate, uniform for the whole state.[11]

Compared with other types of property, discovery and assessment of real property is relatively easy. Adam Smith observed that "the

9. U.S. Census Bureau, *Census of Governments, 1972,* vol. 2, pt. 1, *Taxable and Other Property Values* (1973), p. 94.

10. See J. Richard Aronson, "Intangibles Taxes; A Wisely Neglected Revenue Source for States," *National Tax Journal,* vol. 19 (June 1966), pp. 184–86.

11. Usually property was classified as real estate, tangible personal property, and intangible personal property, with different rates applied to each of the three groups.

quantity and value of the land which any man possesses can never be a secret, and can always be ascertained with great exactness."[12] While the history of property taxation in the United States makes this generalization seem oversanguine, the fact remains that real property can more readily be discovered and assessed than other kinds of property. In this area, administrative abuse is least defensible; and here abuse must be rooted out if the property tax is to be retained as the mainstay of local revenues.

Assessment

The most publicized and the most serious administrative fault of the general property tax is inaccurate assessment. The inaccuracy may result either from underassessment or from deviation of individual property values from the general assessment ratio of the taxing jurisdiction.

Underassessment

The *Census of Governments* since 1957 has included incisive and cogent materials concerning the valuation of real property across the nation. The Census Bureau has developed extensive tabulations of assessment-to-sales-price ratios on this most important component of the general property tax. The numerator of the ratios is assessed value, "as shown on local tax records prior to the sale"; the denominator is "measurable sales," that is, the price paid for properties "changing hands on an ordinary market basis."[13] In 1971 the average assessed value of locally assessed taxable real property was 32.7 percent of market value as indicated by measurable sales (see table 7-6). The state ratios ranged from 3.8 percent in South Carolina to 83.9 percent in Kentucky. The actual level of assessment ratios is generally well below that prescribed by law. Twenty states called for assessment at full value, and even in those states that permit fractional assessment ratios the actual ratio is well below the legal standard.[14]

Undervaluation in itself is not inequitable. If all property were assessed at some uniform percentage of true value, the result would

12. *The Wealth of Nations,* bk. 5, chap. 2, pt. 2.
13. *Census of Governments, 1962,* vol. 2, *Taxable Property Values* (1963), p. 9.
14. See ACIR, *The Property Tax in a Changing Environment: Selected State Studies* (GPO, 1974), table 2, pp. 7–8.

Table 7-6. Distribution of States by Ratios of Assessed Value to Sales Price of Real Property, 1956, 1966, and 1971

Assessments as a percentage of sales	Number of states		
	1956	*1966*	*1971*
0– 9	2	1	5
10–19	16	17	11
20–29	16	10	9
30–39	4	7	10
40–49	7	6[a]	8[a]
50–59	2	6	4
60–69	1	2	1
Over 70	0	2	3
Average percentage	30.0	32.8	32.7

Sources: *Census of Governments, 1957*, vol. 5, *Taxable Property Values*, p. 81; *1967*, vol. 2, *Taxable Property Values* (1968), table 9, pp. 42–47; and *1972*, vol. 2, pt. 2, *Assessment-Sales Price Ratios and Tax Rates* (1973), table 2, pp. 34–39.
a. Includes the District of Columbia.

be simply a higher rate of tax. In practice, however, general under-valuation induces inequity in individual assessments; it also impairs or defeats the objectives of other state financial legislation.

Inequity in Individual Assessments

More than half a century ago, Bullock diagnosed the failure of uni-form and general undervaluation:

If the practice is to assess realty at its true value, the assessor has a defi-nite mark at which to aim, and the citizen a definite standard by which he can compare his assessment with his neighbor's; but when the opposite practice prevails, assessor and taxpayer alike are left in uncertainty. Abso-lute accuracy, of course, is not to be expected, but errors can be more readily detected if the standard is full valuation. If two buildings worth $100,000 each are assessed, the one for $20,000 and the other for $18,000, the discrepancy seems to be but $2,000; in reality it is $10,000, since it represents one-tenth part of the tax burden.[15]

Among the statistical evidence on the extent of undervaluation collected in the *Census of Governments* are assessment-to-sales ratios for 1956, 1966, and 1971 collected in over a thousand "se-lected areas" for nonfarm houses, a class of property that is large and

15. "The General Property Tax in the United States," in *Selected Readings in Public Finance*, p. 293.

Table 7-7. **Illustrative Calculation of a Coefficient of Dispersion for Nine Properties**

Property	Assessed value, in dollars	Assessment ratio	Deviation from median assessment ratio[a]
A	6,400	32.0	18.0
B	7,400	37.0	13.0
C	8,000	40.0	10.0
D	8,800	44.0	6.0
E	10,000	50.0	0.0
F	11,000	55.0	5.0
G	11,600	58.0	8.0
H	12,800	64.0	14.0
I	13,200	66.0	16.0
Total	...	...	90.0[b]

Source: Frederick L. Bird, *The General Property Tax: Findings of the 1957 Census of Governments* (Chicago: Public Administration Service, 1960), p. 54.
a. Negative signs are disregarded here.
b. Average deviation = 90.0/9 = 10.0. Coefficient of dispersion = (average deviation/median assessment ratio) × 100 = 20 percent.

relatively homogenous.[16] The Census reckoned a median ratio for each area. Individual ratios would, of course, differ from the median, and an average of the difference can be computed. In illustrative table 7-7, the median assessment ratio of the nine properties is 50.0, and the average deviation is 10.0. Another area with the same average deviation of 10.0 might have a much lower median ratio, however —say, 25.0. To secure comparability between the ratios in different areas, the deviation from the median ratios within an area should be expressed in relative—not absolute—terms. This is accomplished by dividing the average deviation by the median assessment ratio. This measure—the coefficient of dispersion—is 20 percent for the series of properties with a median assessment ratio of 50.0 and an average deviation of 10.0, and 40 percent for the properties with a median assessment ratio of 25.0 and the same average deviation. The relative dispersion in the latter instance is greater than in the first.

Table 7-8 shows the median assessment ratios for nonfarm houses and their coefficients of dispersion for selected local areas in 1956, 1966, and 1971. The general relationship has been inverse: as assessment ratios rise—that is, as assessments come closer to sales prices— the coefficients tend to decline—that is, relative deviation from the average diminishes. It seems, then, that severe undervaluation is un-

16. *Census of Governments, 1962*, vol. 2, table 15, p. 96; *1967*, vol. 2, *Taxable Property Values*, table 12, p. 75; and *1972*, vol. 2, pt. 2, table 6, p. 55.

Table 7-8. Coefficients of Intra-area Dispersion for Principal Median Assessment Ratios for Nonfarm Houses, Selected Local Areas, 1956, 1966, and 1971

Median assessment ratio	Coefficient of dispersion		
	1956	*1966*	*1971*
Under 20.0	37.3	26.1	27.2
20.0–29.9	32.0	20.7	21.3
30.0–39.9	25.1	18.7	21.4
40.0 or more	22.2	15.8	16.6

Source: *Census of Governments, 1957*, vol. 5, table 17, p. 86; *1967*, vol. 2, table 14, p. 76; and *1972*, vol. 2, pt. 2, table 7, p. 56.

likely to be uniform, and for this reason it engenders inequities in individual assessments.

Undervaluation has other faults. It obscures unequal assessments and thereby prevents a taxpayer from being aware that his assessment is out of line with that of other properties. He may suffer from an undervaluation illusion. Since the assessed value of his property is below market value, he may fondly believe that he is especially favored and therefore be silent. Even if he is under no illusion, he will have difficulty in securing a review of his assessment. When the law specifies full value, acceptable evidence of undervaluation in support of an appeal for adjustment is not easy to obtain.

Impairment of Other Financial Objectives

Assessed valuations carried out by local governmental units have often been incorporated into state financial legislation. In the days when state governments allotted local shares of a state general property tax according to local assessed valuation, local units perceived that an easy way to cut their shares was to reduce their valuation. Such a move was, of course, easily imitated, and a rash of competitive undervaluations resulted. Discontinuance of the state tax in most states eliminated this pressure for undervaluation, but the property tax continues to be allotted on the basis of assessed valuation to raise revenue for county governments and a miscellany of other units with no tax resources of their own. State governments have also distributed some grants-in-aid and some state-collected taxes to local governments, using assessed values as an indicator. For example, state governments in allocating educational grants have often assumed that a low assessed value per child of school age indicated a low financial ability. But unless interarea valuations are uniform, this is faulty evidence. In short, assessed value has been and is an elastic measuring stick.

State governments, perceiving these defects, have instituted state equalization of local assessments as a remedy. No attempt is made to value individual properties, but state officers estimate aggregate property values for each local unit, using these to secure a more equalized interarea standard for allocation. This technique, whatever its merits, does nothing to rectify inaccurate values of particular properties or to push localities toward full-value assessment. The two broad uses of assessed valuation by the state governments pull local governments in opposite directions. A locality is tempted to set a low valuation in order to reduce its share of county tax assessment and to set a high valuation in order to secure larger shares of state grants or of state distributions of taxes.

The state equalization process has often been crudely executed, resting on subjective and personalized decisions of a few state officers. In recent years, the sales-sampling technique has been developed. The ratios of sales price to assessed value are determined for a sample of recently sold properties, and these ratios constitute the basis for updating and equalizing the assessments of different localities. If the sample is adequate and representative, this method has merit.

State governments should recognize that a good central assessment is important not only to provide more accurate guidelines for distribution of state grants and tax collections for counties, but also as a foundation on which an effective state review of local assessment may be built.

Local assessed valuations have been used widely in state constitutions or in state legislation as the base for ceilings on local debt and property tax rates. Extensive and variable underassessment means that regulatory policy is determined by the assessor as well as the constitution or statute. For example, if assessment ratios decline while tax and debt limit ratios remain fixed, the effective taxing and borrowing power of a governmental unit is reduced.

Tax exemptions are another instance in which the apparent objective of state legislation is distorted by general undervaluation. The homestead and the veterans' exemptions—the two common types— are usually specified in dollars. Thus, the greater the degree of underassessment, the more valuable is the exemption. For example, a flat

$10,000 exemption is potentially twice as valuable to beneficiaries if the assessment ratio is 50 percent rather than 100 percent.

The remedy for the defects arising from underassessment is, in principle, quite obvious. Assessed values should be used only as the base for property taxes; constitutional and statutory requirements that they be used for other purposes should be abolished. A less sweeping remedy, assuming that state governments wish to continue partial property tax exemptions as well as local tax and debt limits, would be to specify that full value, rather than assessed value, should be the base.[17]

Uniformity of Intra-area Assessments

While deep underassessment appears to induce inequitable assessments, full value assessment is not a practicable goal. When taxpayers are uninformed concerning relative underassessment, they suffer from the illusion that underassessment of their property is a favor. But even when free of this illusion, taxpayers feel that full value assessment would not be accompanied by a proportional reduction in the nominal rate of the property tax. They suspect, instead, that it would bring an acceleration in expenditures. Assessors also are motivated to favor undervaluation. They are aware that it blunts objections from taxpayers. Assessors suspect also that current property values are inflated, and they fear that full valuation would, in the event of deflation, bring overvaluation. Modest undervaluation is a cushion against this possibility. Some assessors are also conscious of the power over local borrowing that undervaluation puts in their hands.

The goal should, therefore, be assessment uniformity within an area at some figure not much below fair value. Since perfection here is an aspiration only, the question arises: What standard of uniformity is achievable? What coefficient of dispersion is tolerable within each assessment area? Frederick L. Bird has suggested a figure of 20.0 percent.[18] The cumulative percentages in table 7-9 show that the

17. ACIR, *The Role of the States in Strengthening the Property Tax* (GPO, 1963), vol. 1, pp. 60–61.

18. *The General Property Tax: Findings of the 1957 Census of Governments* (Chicago: Public Administration Service, 1960), p. 54. The general property tax has the peculiarity that its base, and therefore the amount of the tax liability, is de-

Table 7-9. Distribution of Selected Local Areas by Coefficient of Intra-area Dispersion for Assessment Ratios of Nonfarm Houses, 1956, 1966, and 1971

Coefficient of dispersion	Percentage of areas			Cumulative percentage		
	1956	1966	1971	1956	1966	1971
Under 15	7.9	28.2	24.6	7.9	28.2	24.6
15.0–19.9	12.5	25.2	24.3	20.4	53.4	48.9
20.0–29.9	29.7	27.1	30.2	50.1	80.5	79.1
30.0–39.9	21.1	9.8	11.8	71.2	90.3	90.9
40.0 and over	28.7	9.8	9.1	100.0	100.0	100.0

Source: *Census of Governments, 1957*, vol. 5, table 19, p. 88; *1967*, vol. 2, table 16, p. 78; and *1972*, vol. 2, pt. 2, table 9, p. 58.

Table 7-10. Distribution of States by Coefficient of Intra-area Dispersion for Nonfarm Houses, 1956, 1966, and 1971

Median area coefficient of dispersion	Number of states		
	1956[a]	1966	1971
Under 15.0	1	5	5
15.0–19.9	2	19	13
20.0–24.9	5	14	14
25.0–29.9	10	10	14
30.0–34.9	11	2	2
35.0–39.9	11	0	1
40.0 and over	5	0	1

Source: Same as table 7-9.
a. Not computed for Arizona, Delaware, Nevada, Hawaii, and Alaska.

tolerable limit of coefficients of dispersion for nonfarm houses in 1956 was met by only 20.4 percent of the areas, in 1966 by 53.4 percent, and in 1971 by 48.9 percent. The marked improvement in assessment uniformity in the ten-year period from 1956 to 1966 was followed by a slight worsening in the degree of uniformity from 1966 to 1971. Table 7-10 shows the distribution of states by coefficients of intra-area dispersion. In 1966 two states had coefficients of dispersion

termined by administrative decision. Tax liability for retail sales tax or individual income tax is determined by the taxpayer, subject to the possibility of audit by administrators. Figures showing the results of state audits are rare and, for this reason, coefficients of dispersion for state retail sales and individual income taxes cannot be computed as they have been by the Bureau of the Census for assessments of nonfarm houses. Thus is it not possible to say whether such coefficients, if computed, would be larger or smaller than those presented above for nonfarm houses.

of over 30 percent. Again the trend appears to be marked improvement from 1956 to 1966 and then some regression during the period 1966–71.[19]

The Role of the States in Reform

What part should state governments play in improving assessment procedures, and, indeed, in reforming the property tax?

Five decades ago the theory in vogue was that separation of state and local sources of revenue would bring about the reform of the property tax, especially of assessment. State governments would withdraw from the property tax, leaving it wholly in the hands of local governments, and thereby remove the incentive for competitive undervaluation. E. R. A. Seligman argued also that real estate, the backbone of the tax, could "far better be valued by officials of the neighborhood who are cognizant of the local conditions."[20]

Some economists argued against separation. T. S. Adams declared that local desire to evade the state tax was a minor factor in inefficient assessment. Discontinuance of the state tax would, therefore, bring no improvement. Adams went on to predict that if state governments withdrew from use of the property tax, state supervision and guidance of local governments in assessment would diminish. It was, he believed, "idle and academic—in the worst sense—to say that we can have general or central supervision over local taxes without the central jurisdiction making active use of the same basis of taxation."[21]

The argument in favor of state withdrawal was strongly reinforced by the desire of local governments to gain full control of property tax revenue, and in the 1940s state withdrawal became a fact. The evidence is strong that harm resulted. Local governments, in sole possession of general property taxation, did not improve administration; instead, standards of equity and assessment deteriorated. More-

19. What can account for the lack of improvement in the period 1966–71? It may be that with inflation, property values in general were increasing more quickly and unevenly than in the previous decade. Thus, even if reassessments were being carried out more often than in 1956–66, the new increased rate of change in values might still be reflected in higher coefficients of dispersion.

20. *Essays in Taxation* (9th ed., Macmillan, 1921), p. 353.

21. "Separation of State and Local Revenues," *Annals of the American Academy of Political and Social Science,* vol. 58 (March 1915), pp. 134–35.

over, the property available to local units as a tax base did not match particular local needs for expenditure. State governments were persuaded to provide financial assistance to poor localities. But sometimes this aid was misdirected: it went to units with no rational basis for existence, or to units whose fiscal ability, measured by property valuation, was misjudged.

Recently a reform movement has developed that aims at rehabilitating the property tax; it assumes that state governments will be the prime movers. State governments are not to secure any revenues from the tax; their interest in reform is to be motivated by their interest in obtaining efficient and effective local government.

In what ways might greater state responsibility be displayed? One extreme is illustrated by Hawaii where a state agency assesses all real property, collects the revenues, and turns over the collections to the local governments. The four local units (counties) determine their tax rate. The record shows relative uniformity of assessments with a low degree of dispersion within and among the four counties.[22] The governmental organization of Hawaii, as well as its taxes, is highly centralized: public education, public health, and welfare functions are carried on and financed by the state government. This centralization, which differentiates Hawaii from the other states, makes centralization of assessment a natural phenomenon. Without such centralization, imitation of Hawaii is unlikely.[23]

State governments may, perhaps, press for reforms in three other directions:[24]

Local assessment districts should be reorganized. Each district should have adequate resources to provide professional assessment. In some states the county would be the appropriate unit to carry out assessments, but in states with many small counties the creation of regional assessment districts or assessment by state officers would be necessary.

Administration of assessment must be professionalized. Many

22. Y. S. Leong and Robert M. Kamins, "Property Taxation in the 50th State," *National Tax Journal*, vol. 14 (March 1961), pp. 59–69.

23. In 1973 Montana moved all assessing to the state level and Maryland began a three-year phasing-in period to do so. See ACIR, *The Property Tax in a Changing Environment*, p. 17.

24. *The Role of the States in Strengthening the Property Tax* spells out what state governments should do (vol. 1, pp. 13–25). For a tabulation of ACIR recommended reforms see ACIR, *The Property Tax in a Changing Environment*, p. 294.

cities and large counties have already taken this step. But over the nation the majority of assessors are elected, often for short terms, and often for part-time work.[25] Professionalization and the reorganization of assessment districts are obviously interrelated steps. Assessors qualified to do the difficult task of property valuation can only be secured when properly paid, and this, in turn, requires that each assessing unit have resources to support qualified officials.

A state agency devoted to supervising the administration of local property taxation must be established. This agency would also engage in assessing some classes of property. Over the decades state governments have provided or offered help to local governments. Most commonly state supervisors of local assessors have given technical instruction, kept an eye on local performance, heard complaints, ordered reassessment, and so on. But strong supervision has seldom been authorized or exercised. And unless the work is professionalized and districts reorganized, supervision cannot be effective. The ablest and most determined supervisor cannot operate through part-time, badly paid, and unprofessional local assessors; strong supervision can, however, promote professionalization of assessors and district reorganization.

An important technique in the exercise of supervision would be collection and analysis of assessment ratios, with public announcement of the results. Individual assessing areas would thereby become aware of their own performance; taxpayers would secure information by which the equity of their assessments might be judged; state legislatures would have at hand more accurate measures of local fiscal ability.

The ACIR organized and published twenty-nine recommendations for property tax reform more than a decade ago.[26] It is fair to say that since then numerous improvements have been made in property

25. "Local governments are accustomed to employing trained accountants, engineers, health officers, social workers, and school teachers, but they seem willing to elect as assessor any resident citizen who is old enough to vote and does not have a criminal record, and pay him less than the school janitor. Very fortunately this is not the universal procedure, but it is sufficiently widespread to explain in part why assessing is mediocre to poor in many areas." ACIR, *The Role of the States in Strengthening the Property Tax*, p. 104.

26. See ibid.; and ACIR, "The Property Tax—Reform and Relief—The Legislator's Guide" (ACIR, 1973; processed).

Table 7-11. Value of Totally Tax-exempt Property Reported by Sixteen States[a] **and the District of Columbia, by Type of Exemption, 1971**

Exemption	Amount, in millions of dollars	Percent of total value
Religious	9,089	10.4
Educational	10,618	12.1
Charitable	2,698	3.1
Governmental	51,296	58.5
Other or unallocable	13,944	15.9
Total	87,648[b]	100.0

Source: *Census of Governments, 1972*, vol. 2, pt. 1, table F, p. 14. Figures are rounded.

a. Arizona, California, Florida, Hawaii, Indiana, Kansas, Louisiana, Massachusetts, Minnesota, Nevada, New Jersey, New York, Ohio, Oregon, Rhode Island, South Dakota.

b. Includes $7,188 million in personal property not classified by type.

tax administration and assessment procedures.[27] Yet by the ACIR's own evaluation, "numerous reform measures are still required by most States to bring the property tax to an acceptable level of administration and equity."[28]

Erosion of the Tax Base

Reform of the property tax, so that it may become a more powerful source of local revenue, will require that erosion of the base of the property tax be halted and even reversed. This also is mainly a task for state governments. Some of the erosion is so long-established and so widespread as to be almost "impervious to question."[29] Exemption of the property of nonprofit religious, charitable, and educational institutions rests on the opinion that they render semigovernmental services and promote the public welfare. The total value of all such excluded property nationwide is unknown. However, state and local assessing officials for the first time reported values for excluded property for the *1972 Census of Governments*. The total and percentage breakdowns are shown in table 7-11. The most important category is the property holdings of governments themselves which account for more than half the reported total.

27. For a summary table see "State Progress in Strengthening the Property Tax, 1963–1973," ACIR, *The Property Tax in a Changing Environment*, pp. 4-5.

28. Ibid., p. 3.

29. ACIR, *The Role of the States in Strengthening the Property Tax*, p. 83.

Tax base erosion occurs because property values are either removed or excluded from the base. In general, property value removed from the base refers to portions of otherwise taxable value that are exempt from taxation.[30] The exemption of major classes of property —intangible and some types of tangible personal property—has often been undertaken as a step in the reform of the general property tax; this erosion is often justifiable. But erosion by state legislation to provide hidden subsidies to private persons or firms is highly questionable. The property tax is paid directly only by owners, and property tax concessions cannot, therefore, be assured for a veteran or an aged person who is not an owner-occupant of real property. A tax concession to a class of persons—the aged—assumes that all of them are in need, and this is not so.

Business Exemptions

Exemption of certain types of industrial property from the local property tax for a specified period has, intermittently, been tried in many states. The aim is to induce investment in the locality by new firms, and some states permit existing firms to share in the subsidy by exempting additions to plant and equipment. Quantitative evidence concerning the effects of the exemption is scanty and unsatisfactory, partly because administration is usually by local governments with no central recording of the relevant data, and partly because data concerning investment and locational decisions by firms are often unreliable. Even if positive advantages are secured by a particular locality, these are offset by the injury to competitors elsewhere and to taxpayers in the locality. In a national sense, the exemption is bound to be injurious.

Homestead and Veterans' Exemptions

Eleven states allow some exemption from the local property tax to owner-occupied homes or farms. Table 7-12 shows both the total dollar amount of this homestead exemption by states and the amount as a percentage of gross assessed value. Many states also grant some kind of property tax exemption to veterans. Only California, Iowa, Massachusetts, and New York exempted a substantial amount of veterans' property—$387 million, $128 million, $166 million, and

30. *Census of Governments, 1972,* vol. 2, pt. 1, p. 13.

Table 7-12. Homestead Exemptions, 1971

State	Assessed value removed by homestead exemptions, in millions of dollars	Percent of gross assessed value
California	1,955	3.3
Florida	6,971	13.5
Georgia	1,569	11.7
Hawaii	892	14.4
Louisiana	1,162	20.0
Mississippi	606ᵃ	23.5
Nebraska	73	1.3
Nevada	5	0.2
North Dakota	2	0.3
Oklahoma	522	12.2
Oregon	294ᵇ	1.4
Total	14,051	2.0

Source: *Census of Governments, 1972*, vol. 2, pt. 1, table G, p. 15, and table 1, p. 22.
a. Data are for 1970.
b. Includes exemptions for veterans and the elderly.

$906 million, respectively—in 1971; eight other states exempted a total of $382 million.[31]

Traditionally both the homestead exemption and veterans' exemption have been stated in flat dollar amounts. The homestead exemption provides tax relief on relatively inexpensive housing and the veterans' exemption is a way of expressing public esteem for a select group of individuals. The pattern of tax relief provided by the homestead exemption can be criticized for its failure to take into account the financial situation of the individual, and there can be little justification to a plan that distributes rewards to veterans according to their ownership of property. Programs to benefit veterans should rest on the need and merit of these individuals and be financed from the general revenues of the state. In general, property tax relief, whether for special groups or not, should take account of the individual's ability to pay. This has been the purpose of the circuit-breaker device.

Circuit Breakers

The ACIR describes circuit breakers as "tax relief programs designed to protect family income from property tax 'overload' the

31. Arizona, Florida, Maine, Nevada, New Mexico, Oklahoma, Rhode Island, Wyoming; Oregon also grants exemptions to veterans, but the amount is not separately available (ibid., table G, p. 15).

same way that an electrical circuit-breaker protects the family home from current overload."[32] That is, when the property tax burden on an individual exceeds a predetermined percentage of personal income, the circuit breaker goes into effect to relieve the excess financial pressure.

By 1974 twenty-four states and the District of Columbia had enacted circuit-breaker programs.[33] The ACIR has classified three types of circuit breakers—basic, expanded, and general—based on extent of coverage. Basic coverage provides relief to elderly homeowners and is used in six states. Expanded coverage offers relief to the elderly (either homeowners or renters) and is used in thirteen states. General circuit breakers are comprehensive in that the relief program applies to all overburdened taxpayers. That is, any family meeting the state income criteria may qualify for relief.[34]

One of the two methods used in designing the relief formula is the threshold approach. Under this scheme an acceptable level of taxation is defined as some fixed percentage of household income. The amount by which the actual property tax exceeds this level qualifies for relief. The other method is the sliding scale approach, under which a fixed percentage of property tax is rebated to taxpayers within each eligible income class; the percent of the property tax rebatable is lower the higher the income class.[35]

Generally the circuit breaker is built into the state income tax system. Either rebates are credited against the individual's state income tax liability or refund checks are sent. Although there are other techniques for administering the circuit breaker, the ACIR feels

32. ACIR, *Property Tax Circuit-Breakers: Current Status and Policy Issues* (Washington: ACIR, 1975), p. 2.

33. For a comprehensive listing of property tax relief policies for homeowners and renters, see ACIR, *Federal-State-Local Finances: Significant Features of Fiscal Federalism, 1973–74 Edition,* table 107, pp. 179–86.

34. ACIR, *Property Tax Circuit-Breakers,* p. 3.

35. Ibid., pp. 3–4. For a family with an income of $10,000 and a property tax burden of $600, the property tax relief would be $100 under a threshold approach that fixed the acceptable tax level at 5 percent ($600 burden minus $500 acceptable level). But under a sliding scale approach that allowed rebates of 15 percent for families with $7,000–$9,000 income, 12 percent for those with $9,000–$11,000, and 10 percent for those with $11,000–$13,000, the same family would be entitled to a $72 rebate (12 percent of $600). If the family's income were $12,000, the rebate would be $60.

"this method is not only efficient, its confidentiality preserves the dignity of the recipient."[36]

Since the circuit breaker is a relatively new device, detailed figures on the value of benefits provided are not readily available. An ACIR survey for the fiscal year 1974 reports about $450 million in total benefits were provided.[37]

The circuit breaker has two advantages over traditional homestead exemptions. First, in the distribution of benefits an attempt is made to take account of the individual's ability to pay. Second, the circuit breaker provides its relief without eroding local governments' property tax base.

The circuit-breaker idea, however, has not been free of criticism. The relief formulas built into circuit breakers are designed to offset a tax considered to be regressive. If, in fact, the tax is progressive, as some believe, the relief offered is perverse. Critics also point out that circuit breakers tend to subsidize those people with high ratios of property to current income and people with fluctuating incomes.[38]

An overall appraisal of the circuit-breaker device depends not only on whether the incidence of the property tax is thought to be regressive or progressive but also on how well it fits into the nation's system of income maintenance programs. There is no doubt that certain technical faults exist in circuit-breaker programs (for example, current income rather than permanent income is used to measure ability to pay). Nevertheless, circuit breakers provide cash payments to relatively poor people, and until a negative income tax or some other comprehensive income maintenance plan is established, the device has a place in the state tax structure.

The States' Responsibility

Most of the erosion of the local property tax base is a matter of state decision; state legislatures have thereby subsidized worthy purposes or groups at the indirect expense of local governments. This form of subsidy fails to provide equitable benefits since provision is denied to members of the group who do not own real property and quite often given to those who do, regardless of their need; it fails also in the equitable distribution of costs, since the amount of property

36. Ibid., p. 2.
37. Ibid., p. 5.
38. Aaron, *Who Pays the Property Tax?* pp. 71–91.

removed from the tax base of a locality is unrelated to its total financial situation. How, then, can one explain the use of property tax exemptions? State legislatures, responsive to organized pressure, use property tax exemption as a way to act without placing an expenditure in state (or local) budgets. But a slice is taken from the tax base of local governments. The indicated conclusion is that, if a state subsidy is to be offered, its weight should be on state rather than on local resources. An obvious step, when the subsidy takes the form of a property tax exemption, is reimbursement to local governments for the shrinkage in their tax base. The circuit breaker is a step in this direction.

State Assessment of Property

Some kinds of property are quite unsuitable for local assessment. Such an instance emerged a century ago with the railroads. Valuation of the operating property of a railway, piece by piece, made no sense; the valuation had to be of the whole system, or at least of the part lying within a state. As a result, most states decided to centrally assess railway property and most public utility property. Local governments, however, often are allowed to assess nonoperative property, that is, property with a local situs which, while owned by a utility, is not part of its business operations. In 1971, state-assessed property amounted to $53.5 billion out of a total of $694.6 billion of taxable property. The state-assessed property was classified as follows:[39]

Property	Billions of dollars
Railroads	5.1
Other public utilities	33.5
Other (mostly mining property)	14.9
Total	53.5

The shift to state assessment was not easily achieved; it had to overcome "both the hostile presumption against any state agency and the natural inertia supporting the local assessor."[40] And the shift did not

39. *Census of Governments, 1972*, vol. 2, pt. 1, table 3, pp. 26–27. Ten states and the District of Columbia have no state-assessed property; in fifteen states, under 10 percent of total local taxable assessed value is represented by state-assessed property; in fourteen, 10–20 percent; in four, 20–30 percent; in another four, 30–40 percent; in one, 40–50 percent; and in one, 50–60 percent; in Hawaii, 100 percent of the property is state-assessed (ibid.).

40. Jens P. Jensen, *Property Taxation in the United States* (University of Chicago Press, 1931), p. 420.

follow any simple pattern. Sometimes states not only valued but taxed the property for their own use; sometimes they apportioned the centrally assessed valuation for taxation by local units. The methods used to assess utility property were also very diverse.[41] The wisest step would be to abolish the congeries and replace them by some reasonable single substitute. But this seems unlikely to happen. Each state can and should, however, equate its taxation, intrastate, with the taxation of locally assessed property. The evidence seems to be that utility property is assessed in many states at values relatively higher than locally assessed property.

Interstate allocation of centrally assessed property is plagued by state over-reaching. The ACIR has commented that "a tendency exists for States to allocate to themselves fractions of value that add to more than 100 percent of total value."[42] Fair allocation formulas have been framed (notably by the Western States Association of Tax Administrators), but progress toward adoption has been very slight.

State Role in School Finance

In the United States the main responsibility for providing public schools has fallen to local government. This has brought with it much citizen involvement and control but has resulted in expenditure patterns favoring wealthier communities. The constitutionality of this expenditure pattern has been seriously questioned in the 1970s. A number of state courts ruled that wide disparities between school districts in expenditures per pupil are inconsistent with the equal protection clause of the Fourteenth Amendment to the Constitution.[43] In March 1973, however, the Supreme Court of the United States decided otherwise.[44] The Court did not condone expenditure patterns

41. *Census of Governments, 1962,* vol. 2, pp. 3–4, describes in detail the property tax bases used by the states for railway and other utilities. Often, policies differ toward different utilities. States differ among themselves in the scope of central assessment, and the extent of its application even to a given type of utility.

42. *The Role of the States in Strengthening the Property Tax,* vol. 1, p. 147.

43. These courts objected to systems where the quality of educaton received by a child appeared to be determined largely by the wealth of the school district and where state aid to equalize these disparities was insufficient. The most notable case was *Serrano* v. *Priest,* California Supreme Court, 938254, L.A. 29820 (1971). For detailed discussion of the problems involved in reforming school finance, see Robert D. Reischauer and Robert W. Hartman, *Reforming School Finance* (Brookings Institution, 1973); and ACIR, *Financing Schools and Property Tax Relief—A State Responsibility* (ACIR, 1973).

44. *San Antonio Independent School District* v. *Rodriguez,* 411 U.S. 1 (1973).

Table 7-13. Disparities in Cost of Equalizing Expenditures per Pupil, 1969–70

State rankings, by ability to equalize expenditures

Item	Poor shape	Pinched	Some- what pinched	Good shape	Mod- erately well off	Well off	Total
Number of states[a]	3	4	9	17	14	1	48[a]
Sample state	New York	Massa- chusetts	Pennsyl- vania	Michi- gan	Okla- homa	Nevada	All states
Expenditure ratio Highest district to lowest district	11.4	9.3	7.9	3.1	8.3	2.2	...
90th pupil percentile[b] to lowest district	1.9	2.1	2.1	2.2	2.1	1.2	...
Cost of leveling up to 80th pupil percentile, in millions of dollars	331.2	139.0	393.8	215.6	41.4	1.4	4,333.2
Untapped fiscal capacity,[c] in millions of dollars	190.4	315.1	1,652.5	1,543.2	654.4	187.2	27,328.9
Cost of leveling up, as a percentage of un- tapped capacity	174.0	44.1	23.8	14.0	6.3	0.8	15.9

Source: Advisory Commission on Intergovernmental Relations, *Financing Schools and Property Tax Relief—A State Responsibility* (Washington: ACIR, 1973), pp. 99–101, 108, and 119–21.
a. Hawaii and Alaska not included.
b. "The level at which 90 percent of the State's pupils are in districts with that level of per-pupil spending or less. Only 10 percent of the State's pupils are in districts with that level of per-pupil spending or more." Ibid., p. 101.
c. The difference between potential capacity and actual state and local tax collections. Potential capacity represents the sum of potential revenue-sharing funds to the state plus "the amount of potential revenue a State could raise if it made a tax effort midway between the highest tax effort State in the Nation and the highest tax effort State in its region." (ACIR also provides a more stringent and a less stringent measure of capacity.) Ibid., p. 113.

that favored the rich but indicated that reforming school finance was a legislative matter. It would now appear that the move toward greater intrastate equalization in school expenditures will proceed at a slower rate than anticipated before the Court's decision.

The extent of the existing disparities in school expenditures and the potential costs of equalization as calculated by the ACIR are summarized in table 7-13. The ratio of expenditures per pupil in the highest spending school district relative to the lowest spending district— 11.4 to 1 in New York, for example—overstates intrastate disparities since spending in the highest district reflects the specialized needs of certain students as well as the preferences and fiscal capacity of the area. A more realistic estimate is the comparison of per pupil expenditure at the 90th pupil percentile with that in the lowest district—a ratio that generally runs at about 2 to 1.

The ACIR has also calculated two other sets of figures: the costs to the state of providing sufficient funds to allow all school districts to spend in per pupil terms at a rate equal to the 80th pupil percentile, and the value of the state's untapped fiscal capacity. From these come the figures on the cost of leveling up as a percent of untapped fiscal capacity. The states' rankings by their ability to finance their own equalization program range from "well off" (one state—Nevada) to "poor shape" (three states—New York, Vermont, Wisconsin). The ACIR estimates that for the nation as a whole, the cost of leveling up as a percent of untapped fiscal capacity is 15.9 percent. Their conclusion is that although states should assume full responsibility for financing public schools, "a major Federal educational aid program . . . cannot be justified on the grounds that States confront insurmountable fiscal burdens."[45]

Conclusion

Unresolved problems remain in estimating the burden of distribution of the property tax among income groups. Whether the burden is regressive or progressive depends on whether it is assumed that the tax on capital improvements is shifted forward to consumers in the form of higher prices or the tax on property is felt primarily in the form of reduced income from capital. Whatever the incidence, however, the trend toward rehabilitation of the property tax should be strengthened and accelerated. This will require vigorous support from state governments. Is effective support likely to be forthcoming if it is not accompanied by restoration of the tax as a source of state revenue? State withdrawal from the use of the property tax in the past three decades has been widely approved—not, indeed, because of the inherent merit of "separation" of state and local revenues, or because of inequities in property taxation. Withdrawal by state governments is applauded because, thereby, local governments are provided with the only major tax from which they can safely secure a large and dependable revenue.

State supervision of local performance of many governmental

45. ACIR, *Financing Schools and Property Tax Relief*, p. 94.

functions—education, health, welfare—is extensive. It rests simply on a concept of state responsibility, unassociated with a concept of state financial gain. A state government is concerned with efficient performance of all duties by all its governmental units. State interest in establishing and maintaining reasonable standards of property tax administration should be as vital as its interest in public education. Moreover, efficient local use of the property tax will simplify for state governments the problems of financial transfers to localities.

There is a widespread belief in the United States that strong local governments are vital to successful democracy, and that their strength can be maintained only by possession of appreciable financial independence. These generalizations must, however, be given a reasonable interpretation. Strong local government does not mean anarchic autonomy; appreciable financial independence does not mean nonreceipt of state grants-in-aid. State governments should formulate a pattern of financial rules appropriate to the different types of local units; they should see that the rules are observed; they should supply needy units with grants that, when added to local revenues, will enable governmental services to be provided at an acceptable level. Local autonomy has meaning only within this framework.

Are state governments efficient enough to do their part in reforming the property tax? Do not many state governments themselves need reform which should, perhaps, precede reform of local taxation? Sometimes the answer should be affirmative. It would be retrograde if an inept and unrepresentative state legislature tried to reform administration of property tax in localities that, through professional assessors, had already secured uniformity in assessment of property. In most states, however, the glaring weakness of property taxation is displayed in governmental units that are too poor or too small. If attention is centered on them, state action can bring improvement nearly everywhere. Moreover, the framework advocated here for reforming the property tax does not, in any event, indicate state intrusion on local units that already perform well.

Some critics allege that rehabilitation of the property tax is inspired by a desire to restrain the growth of government. Talk of vigorous local governments financing important functions from their own revenues is subterfuge; the covert and real purpose is to hinder a shift of functions to a higher governmental level—state or federal—where paucity of financial resources would be a less serious obstacle to performance. The allegation is not without substance; some proponents of strong local government are concerned merely to secure less government. But such a manifestation of deceit should not obscure the merit of the traditional position. Strong local government has been the bulwark of democracy; strength and vitality in local government have been nourished by local decisions concerning the levy of taxes; the property tax is the only major tax that is suitable for local administration. And the admission should be made that even perfect rehabilitation would not provide many local governments with financial means adequate to their needs. It is the duty of each state government to see that the level of performance of governmental services is adequate everywhere within its boundaries, and this will require extensive use of intergovernmental transfers. Efficient use of the property tax will help rather than hinder this process. Besides supplying localities with a substantial portion of the revenue that they need, it will establish a fair base from which additional financial needs can be measured.

CHAPTER EIGHT

Nonproperty Taxes
and Nontax Revenue

After all the proper subjects of taxation have been exhausted, if the exigencies of the state still continue to require new taxes, they must be imposed upon improper ones.

The Wealth of Nations

THE DOMINANCE of the property tax as a source of tax revenue for local governments rests chiefly on the scarcity of alternatives. A local government has a limited and artificial territorial jurisdiction; movement of persons and of some types of property beyond its boundaries is easy, and this movement may be induced by differential local tax rates. But real estate—land and improvements—is immobile, and it can therefore be taxed by local governments with a less acute fear of consequences.

These simple generalizations are, however, less forceful and applicable for some types of local governments than others. A large city may, in some cases, have advantages as a center for distribution or manufacturing that are not greatly impaired by a city sales or income tax. A large city will, moreover, have administrative resources that may enable it to handle taxes quite beyond the capacity of a small city.

Local Nonproperty Taxes

It is not surprising that the first major employment of local nonproperty taxes was made by large cities. In 1934 New York City adopted a retail sales tax, and in 1938 New Orleans followed suit. Philadelphia in 1939 varied the pattern by adopting an earnings tax. The urgent and decisive force behind these experiments was the impact of severe depression. New York City was spending heavily for relief, and opposition to a sales tax was appeased by declaring the tax revenue to be "a contribution to relief." In Philadelphia similar financial pressures led, in 1938, to enactment of a sales tax; it was, however, repealed in less than a year because of the belief that trade was being diverted from the city. A flat-rate (1.5 percent) tax on income earned in Philadelphia by individuals and unincorporated businesses was accepted as a substitute. Dividends, interest, and corporate profits were not taxable.

These examples awakened the interest of city governments over the nation, an interest that was revivified in postwar years by the accumulation of a large backlog of desired public services. In two states, Ohio and California, "home rule" statutes allowed extensive tax powers to local governments; specific enabling legislation for such localities was not necessary. Accordingly, in 1945–46 five California cities enacted sales taxes, and other California cities soon followed. Before long these cities were imposing use taxes in attempts to protect the trade of their own merchants. Businesses that sold in many municipalities found it nearly impossible to comply with the numerous and dissimilar local requirements. The confusion was resolved in 1955 by converting local taxes to a 1 percent tax supplement to the state sales tax. In Ohio, a local income tax was adopted by Toledo in 1946 and other cities followed.

In 1947 the state government of Pennsylvania authorized local governments to utilize any tax not used by the state. The response was so exuberant that the state legislature was forced to draw up ground rules for the local use of taxing powers because many of the smallest jurisdictions levied income taxes. No adequate appraisal of the Pennsylvania experience is available, but it seems likely that the "tax anything" law was not one that should be copied in other states.

In the 1960s the growth continued; the steps taken in four states are important. In 1967 Texas authorized local governments to levy general sales taxes as supplements to the state tax. Maryland in 1967 authorized its counties to levy income taxes on residents at rates up to 50 percent of the state tax liability. And Michigan in 1964 enacted a "uniform city income tax" act with several unique features:[1] the content of the tax base was specified (this base was much broader than in other local income taxes, including dividends, interest, and capital gains); the rate was set at 1 percent for residents and 0.5 percent for nonresidents;[2] a per capita personal exemption of $600 was provided (which introduced some progressivity in effective rates). As of 1974 sixteen cities in Michigan had income taxes that were locally administered. In 1966 New York City added more variety by imposing an income tax that not only had a comprehensive income base and allowed exemptions and deductions, but also used graduated tax rates for residents (as of 1974 the rates ranged from 0.7 percent to 3.5 percent). Nonresidents are taxed at a lower rate than residents, and instead of deductions a vanishing exclusion related to the level of income is allowed.

Geographic Distribution

Local income taxes are levied in ten states, although in New York and Delaware only one city and in Missouri only two cities are involved. Table 8-1 shows the number of municipalities, by states, levying an income tax in 1973. Local income taxation is likely to yield $2.5 billion in 1975.

Local general sales taxes are now permitted in twenty-five states, and about 4,500 localities exercise the right. The largest number (over 1,200) is in Illinois, with Texas second. Table 8-2 shows the pattern.

Relative Importance of Various Taxes

The general sales tax was by far the most productive of local nonproperty taxes in 1973, yielding over 35 percent of total nonproperty

1. Detroit and Hamtramck adopted income taxes in 1962 under other state statutory authority; after passage of the 1964 act they reenacted their taxes. See A. L. Warren, "Detroit's Experience," in *Municipal Income Taxes, Proceedings of the Academy of Political Science, 1967,* vol. 28, no. 4 (1968), pp. 452–54.
2. The rate for residents of Detroit was raised to 2 percent in 1968.

Table 8-1. Local Income Taxing Units and Their Rates, by State, 1973

State	Units levying income tax	Rate
Alabama	5 cities	1–2 percent
Delaware	1 city	1.25 percent
Indiana	34 counties	0.5–1.0 percent
Kentucky	39 cities	0.25–2.50 percent
	3 counties	0.5–2.0 percent
Maryland	1 city	50 percent of state tax
	23 counties	20–50 percent of state tax
Michigan	16 cities	1.0–2.0 percent for residents,
		0.5 percent for nonresidents
Missouri	2 cities	1 percent
New York	1 city	0.7–3.5 percent
Ohio	20 cities	1–2 percent
	315 small cities	
	and villages	0.25–1.70 percent
Pennsylvania	15 cities and townships	0.5000–3.3125 percent
	3,750 other jurisdictions	0.25–1.00 percent

Source: Advisory Commission on Intergovernmental Relations, *Federal-State-Local Finances: Significant Features of Fiscal Federalism, 1973–74 Edition* (GPO, 1974), table 150. In all tables, years are fiscal unless otherwise noted.

tax revenue. As table 8-3 shows, selective sales taxes produced $1,725 million—19 percent of the total. The most important of these taxes was that on public utility gross receipts, levied in most states by local governments under their regulatory power. Income taxes, which accounted for 13 percent of nonproperty tax revenue in 1966, provided 27 percent of the total in 1973. This dramatic change is due mainly to the increased number of jurisdictions taxing income.

Because of the uneven distribution of nonproperty taxes, aggregate figures of collections for all local governments, or even for all cities, obscure their importance for some local governments. Table 8-4 lists twenty-three cities for which, in 1973, nonproperty taxes amounted to more than 40 percent of all their tax collections. For these cities, dependence on the property tax has weakened.

Development of new sources of revenue has, then, been mostly an urban phenomenon confined to a limited number of states. In these states—whether from a strong and positive home rule sentiment, or from a disinclination of legislatures to lift local problems to the state level—local governments have been allowed to experiment with taxes. But in most states this sort of experimentation has been unacceptable.

Table 8-2. Local General Sales Taxing Units and Their Rates, by State, 1973

State, and units levying sales tax	State tax rate, in percent	Number of units with local tax rate (in percent) of						
		0.50	0.75	1.00	1.25	1.50	2.00	3.00
Alabama	4.00							
206 municipalities		7	...	158	...	4	35	2[a]
25 counties		2	...	21	...	...	2	...
Alaska	...							
78 municipalities		...	...	10	...	4	33	31[b]
5 boroughs		...	...	1	...	1	2	1
Arizona	3.00							
36 municipalities		...	...	33	...	...	3	...
Arkansas	3.00							
1 municipality		...	...	1	...	...	...	...
California	4.75							
380 municipalities		...	...	380	...	...	...	...
58 counties		...	...	...	58	...	...	...
San Francisco Bay Area Rapid Transit District		1	...	...	...	...	...	...
Colorado	3.00							
89 municipalities		...	...	42	...	...	41	6
12 counties		1	...	8	...	...	3	...
Georgia	3.00							
2 counties		...	...	2	...	...	...	...
Illinois	4.00							
1,245 municipalities (approximately)		25	75	1,145	...	...	...	...
100 counties		...	4	96	...	...	...	...
Kansas	3.00							
3 municipalities		3	...	...	...	...	...	...
Louisiana	3.00							
93 municipalities		4	...	84	1	...	4	...
13 parishes		...	...	10	...	2	1	...
49 school districts		4	1	44	...	...	...	...
Minnesota	4.00							
1 municipality		...	...	1	...	...	...	...
Missouri	3.00							
83 municipalities		2	...	81	...	...	...	...

Nebraska	2.50						
2 municipalities					2		
Nevada	3.00						
10 counties		10					
New Mexico	4.00						
3 counties		3[c]					
New York	4.00						
21 municipalities				11	2	5	
44 counties					2	11	
North Carolina	3.00						
88 counties					88		
Ohio	4.00						
28 counties		28					
Oklahoma	2.00						
300 municipalities					270	30	
South Dakota	4.00				1	11	1
13 municipalities							
Tennessee	3.50						
24 municipalities		15		40	9		2[d]
85 counties					43		
Texas	4.00						
757 municipalities					757		
Utah	4.00						
150 municipalities (approximately)		150					
26 counties		26					
Virginia	3.00						
38 cities					38		
96 counties					96		
Washington	4.50						
260 municipalities		260					
37 counties		36	1[e]				

Source: ACIR, *Significant Features, 1973–74 Edition*, table 136.
a. One municipality at 2.50 percent.
b. Eight municipalities at 4.00 percent, and two at 5.00 percent.
c. Two counties at 0.25 percent.
d. Two counties at 1.75 percent.
e. One county at 0.8 percent.

Table 8-3. Local Nonproperty Tax Revenue, by Type of Tax, 1973

Type of tax	Amount, in millions of dollars	Percentage of total
General sales	3,199	35.3
Selective sales	1,725	19.0
Motor fuel	65	0.7
Alcoholic beverages	78	0.9
Tobacco products	174	1.9
Public utilities	1,005	11.1
Other	403	4.4
Income	2,406	26.6
Licenses and all other	1,731	19.1
Total	9,061	100.0

Source: U.S. Census Bureau, *Governmental Finances in 1972–73*, p. 20.

Table 8-4. Local Nonproperty Taxes as a Percentage of Total Local Tax Collections, Selected Cities, 1973

City	Percentage of local tax collections	City	Percentage of local tax collections
Columbus	84	Cleveland	56
Toledo	83	Seattle	54
Kansas City	76	Oklahoma City	53
Philadelphia	71	Norfolk	50
St. Louis	71	San Jose	50
Washington	71	Los Angeles	49
Tulsa	69	San Diego	46
Phoenix	67	Detroit	45
Cincinnati	64	New York	43
Louisville	64	Omaha	41
New Orleans	63	Pittsburgh	41
Denver	59		

Source: Dervied from Census Bureau, *City Government Finances in 1972–73*, table 7.

Defects of the Taxes

The defects of these local nonproperty taxes are plain. Because of the limited geographic jurisdiction of the governmental units, the distribution of employment and of purchasing is distorted. Decisions of workers, firms, and consumers are altered, impairing efficiency. Compliance costs are high, especially for firms that do business in many taxing jurisdictions. The injurious effects of the taxes may not be confined to the local areas that levy them; they may affect the economic development of the state, and, more obviously, state governments may find their future freedom to use taxes hindered by the prior occupancy by their local units. The types of nonproperty taxes in common use do not, moreover, rate highly on grounds of equity even when levied by a geographically large jurisdiction. Local levy aggravates and adds to the inequities, since incidence depends on residence inside or outside the boundaries of a city. Proponents of the local nonproperty taxes have, nonetheless, one effective retort to complaints; admitting all of the defects, what of the faults of alternative local taxes? Are they greater or smaller?

State Intervention and Administration

State governments, if fearful of excesses of local autonomy, may intervene with restraint or with vigor. A state government might, for example, provide local governments with information, training facilities, and technical advice. State legislation might, furthermore, enable localities to act in concert in framing and administering a revenue measure. Or the state might take more vigorous action by authorizing localities to levy a supplement to a state tax, or by permitting a tax credit. Both of these devices require the prior adoption of a tax by the state government, and both may be suspect or unwelcome to localities because they bring state control.

The tax supplement means that local governments are allowed to add a local tax rate to the state rate. Each local government has the responsibility of imposing the tax and of specifying its rate (within limits). The state administers the total tax, sharing an appropriate amount of collections with the local governments. As of 1972, local sales taxes were state administered in twenty states. In thirteen of these states, state collection was mandatory; in the other seven it was optional.[3] The tax supplement could not be employed where segments of the base of a tax are not plainly definable as within a local jurisdiction. Local supplements to a state income tax, for example, would raise questions concerning the location of income that could be solved only by arbitrary decision.

The tax credit allows taxpayers to offset (credit) an amount paid as a specified local tax against their tax liability for a similar state

3. For the details of local sales and local income tax administration, see John F. Due and John L. Mikesell, "Local Sales and Income Taxes," in J. Richard Aronson and Eli Schwartz, eds., *Management Policies in Local Government Finance* (Washington: International City Management Association, 1975), pp. 124 and 131.

tax. Although complete state collection and administration of the local tax is not a necessary feature of crediting (or even identical state and local definitions of tax base), such steps seem likely to be the rule. At present, however, local credits have little application.

Tax sharing has long been used extensively between state and local governments. As indicated in chapter 4, when state governments sliced off types of property from the base of the general property tax, they usually agreed to share with localities the proceeds of the state taxes levied as substitutes. Centralization at the state level, for the sake of efficient collection, led to sharing the proceeds with local units on some agreed basis. Frequently the basis was changed when the formula—based on origin of collections—provided too much revenue for rich localities and too little for poor ones. The shared taxes, in such cases, have lost their distinctive feature; they resemble grants-in-aid except that, unlike grants, their annual amount depends on annual yield.

The theoretical similarity between the tax supplement, the tax credit, and tax sharing between state and local governments is obvious. The different names reflect a different historical origin rather than a difference in substance. All the devices bring centralization; all reflect the ineluctable fact that local governments are narrowly circumscribed in their capacity to tax.[4]

Nontax Revenue

State governments first ventured extensively into commercial enterprises in the 1820s. By this time population had moved westward, and streams of internal commerce had begun to take shape. Internal improvements would swell this commerce; they would, moreover, enhance the economic growth of states served by them. But the improvements were too risky and required too much capital for private enterprise to handle.[5] Why might not large-scale improvements be federal? Because the Constitution had made no provision for federal

4. Data and details of the various programs of state aid to local government can be found in Advisory Commission on Intergovernmental Relations, *Federal-State-Local Finances: Significant Features of Fiscal Federalism, 1973–74 Edition* (GPO, 1974), tables 52–59.

5. At this time no industrial enterprise in the nation had a capital of as much as a million dollars.

expenditure of this sort. To use the welfare clause as justification for federal action might endanger the Union because it would obliterate the functional boundaries between federal and state responsibility.

Since federal intervention was debarred, use of direct state enterprise or state guarantees seemed indicated. It happened that, at this very time, state governments could borrow with unprecedented ease. The nation was prosperous, and foreign capital (especially British capital) was flowing into the United States. The safest use of this capital was in federal securities, but in the 1820s they were being retired out of federal surpluses at a remarkable rate. What was more natural than that foreign investors, unacquainted with the intricacies of federalism, should regard state securities as a close substitute for federal? Accordingly, the issuance of state debt for internal improvements found a ready market.

Almost all of the state enterprises proved unprofitable. And when, after 1837, the nation suffered first a severe economic crisis and then a prolonged depression, states that had borrowed for internal improvements suffered acute financial difficulties. Some defaulted, and in all of them a revulsion of opinion led citizens to amend state constitutions to prohibit the use of state credit for business undertakings.

Public Service Enterprises

When interest in public ownership revived, local rather than state governments were to be the instruments. A keen debate developed late in the nineteenth century over public versus private ownership of public service industries—the supply of water, gas, electricity, transportation, and so on. These enterprises were "natural" monopolies. Competition in the supply of such services was not sensible. The choice was either to make the activity a public function, or to assign it to a private company subject to public regulation. More than a century and a quarter ago, John Stuart Mill stated the alternatives clearly:

When, therefore, a business of real public importance can only be carried on advantageously upon so large a scale as to render the liberty of competition almost illusory, it is an unthrifty dispensation of the public resources that several costly sets of arrangements should be kept up for the purpose of rendering to the community this one service. It is much better to treat it at once as a public function; and if it be not such as the government itself could beneficially undertake, it should be made over entire to the company or association which will perform it on the best terms for the public.[6]

On what grounds might a choice be made between public ownership and operation, and private ownership and operation with public regulation? Here a split in opinion developed which continued into the twentieth century. Delos F. Wilcox, long a leading advocate of municipal ownership, believed that "the complexity and difficulty of public control, either by franchise contract or by police regulation," were so great that public ownership and operation were indicated.[7] The public service corporations required a franchise in order to get under way; they had to secure government permission to use the streets, or to acquire land by the right of eminent domain. Government, and especially local government, had to grant special privileges to public service enterprises. On grounds of efficiency alone, Wilcox favored public ownership and operation.

F. W. Taussig, while much less certain, still believed that "the experiment of public ownership and operation should be tried, and every effort made to bring it to a successful issue. The most promising field would seem to be the municipality of moderate size."[8]

It was important, however, to select for the experiment those ventures that might, on economic grounds, be most likely to be successful as government enterprises, and here a number of general tests were offered: Did the business have a small capital account? Were its operations routine in nature? Was the flow of revenue certain and steady?[9] A small capital account was desirable because government, at least at the local level, often seemed unable to establish and maintain an accurate system of accounting for depreciation. The Census Bureau has regularly complained that such statistics of municipal public service enterprises are defective. When, in 1951–52, Robert M. Haig and Carl S. Shoup examined the financial problems of New York City, they found that "the best data available on the financial sig-

6. *Principles of Political Economy,* W. J. Ashley, ed. (London: Longmans, Green, 1920), pp. 143–44.

7. *Municipal Franchises,* vol. 2: *Transportation Franchises; Taxation and Control of Public Utilities* (New York: Engineering News Publishing Co., 1911), p. 803.

8. *Principles of Economics* (Macmillan, 1921), vol. 2, p. 433.

9. Adam Smith explained the success of the post office as a government enterprise as follows: "The capital to be advanced is not very considerable. There is no mystery in the business. The returns are not only certain, but immediate." *The Wealth of Nations,* bk. 5, chap. 2, pt. 1.

nificance of the various public enterprises to the city are those published by the Census Bureau."[10] The desirability of routine operations arose because government enterprises seemed not to be energetic in introducing technological changes. If, moreover, the operations were subject to easy scrutiny by users of the services, performance could be kept up to the mark. The advantage of a certain and steady flow of income was that the government enterprise could operate on a semicash basis, avoiding the accumulation of debts and reserves.

For the first four decades of this century, municipal ownership and operation of public service companies progressed, and great expectations were entertained by proponents. But in the last three decades municipal ownership has lost its appeal, as public regulation has become more effective, and the actual results of municipal ownership and operation have proved disappointing.

WATER SUPPLY. Most localities operate publicly owned water systems, making this the most extensive example of municipal utility enterprise. Here the welfare consideration of public health has been decisive. Private enterprise cannot be expected to give adequate weight to the health benefits accruing to the whole community through a supply of pure water. Similar considerations arise out of the need for adequate fire protection. Moreover, municipalities— especially the large ones—have to reach out to distant areas in order to secure a water supply, and this often requires the use of extraordinary powers not readily delegated to a private concern.

During the twenty-year period 1953–73, local utilities showed an increase in the ratio of operating expenditures to revenues. Table 8-5 shows that operating expenses plus interest on debt as a percent of revenues for water supply systems increased from 67.2 percent in 1953 to 76.5 percent in 1973. A continuing upward trend in this ratio would be a signal of future financial difficulties for these systems. It should also be noted that the companies pay no taxes, that they borrow at a low rate because they issue tax-exempt bonds,[11] and that adequate amortization charges are not included as costs. But no attempt can be made to adjust the figures.

OTHER PUBLIC SYSTEMS. Public ownership of electric power is

10. *The Financial Problem of the City of New York: A Report to the Mayor's Committee on Management Survey* (Finance Project of the Mayor's Committee, 1952), p. 319.

11. See chapter 9 for a discussion of this aspect of local debt.

Table 8-5. Operating Revenue and Expenditure, Local Water Supply Systems, 1953, 1966, and 1973

Year	Revenue, in millions of dollars	Expenditure, in millions of dollars[a]	Expenditure as a percentage of revenue
1953	939	631	67.2
1966	2,115	1,505	71.2
1973	3,463	2,650	76.5

Sources: Table A-17; and *Governmental Finances in 1965–66*, p. 26.
a. Includes interest on utility debt.

much less usual, and, at the local level, is usually confined to distribution systems. Some aggregate figures of revenue and expenditure appear in appendix table A-17. Public systems of gas supply appear to be financially self-supporting (table A-17). Public transit systems, however, do not manage to cover operating expenses and the deficits continue to mount at an accelerated pace (table A-17). No simple explanation of transit deficits is plausible, and no simple remedy can be offered. An increase in fare would cause some riders to use their private automobiles instead, leaving some transit capacity unutilized and adding to the congestion of city streets. In metropolitan areas, attempts to change from a flat charge to differential fares based on distance or the time at which a ride is taken have met with strong and effective resistance. The New York subway system, for example, has had a flat rate for decades. The fare was increased from 5 to 10 cents in 1948, from 10 to 15 cents in 1953, and from 35 to 50 cents in 1975. The system pays no taxes, either federal, state, or local; costs of construction, new equipment, and debt service are borne by the city.

SELF-SUPPORT OR DEFICIT. It is commonly held that public service enterprises should be self-supporting. As must now be apparent, the generalization hides ambiguities. Sometimes it means merely that the enterprises should cover operating costs, or operating costs plus depreciation and interest. But since the enterprises do not pay taxes, a sum equivalent to the taxes that would be paid by a private concern should also be included as a cost. Unless this is done, consumers of the services are subsidized in kind, the amount of the subsidy depending on the amount of their consumption. And even if a decision is made to include as costs all expenses that would be borne by a similar private enterprise, debate will arise concerning equivalents. What are the appropriate amounts to include in lieu of taxes? What amount of subsidy is provided by the right to issue bonds with provisions exempting the income from federal income tax? Answers to these questions are hard to come by, and yet without standard municipal accounting no factual basis exists for determining or evaluating pricing policies.[12]

A local government may make a deliberate decision to operate a public enterprise at a deficit. Such a plan may be thought desirable if it promotes some collective goal, or if it brings about a redistribution of income from richer to poorer persons. Thus a deficit in a water supply enterprise may be thought desirable on the ground that some portion of the benefits from water consumption accrues to citizens collectively rather than to them as individuals. Similarly a deficit in a public transit system may be accepted on the ground that consumption is largely by low-income users, and that the amount of consumption varies inversely with income.

The situation where benefits from the enterprise accrue, in some degree, to nonconsumers of its services is difficult to make precise. Spillovers occur from actions by private enterprise. A firm, by its location and existence in an area, may bring increases in property values; it may bring other collective benefits of which no account can be taken in its pricing policy. One might argue, therefore, that unless the external benefits resulting from a public enterprise are both widespread and of obvious significance, pricing below cost requires some other justification—perhaps a welfare one.

The question relevant to this case is: Who are the recipients of the subsidy when the price is less than cost? Obviously the users, and they receive a subsidy in kind rather than in money. If all users have low incomes, or indeed if the percent of consumption to income falls as income rises, the subsidy would seem to be properly directed. Actual measurement of use in relation to income status is difficult. But the common situation is that some users of the services of a transit system

---

12. There is also the problem of whether prices should be based on marginal cost or average cost; whether or not two-part tariffs should be used; and the conditions under which peak-load pricing systems are appropriate. See Harold Hotelling, "The General Welfare in Relation to Problems of Taxation and of Railway and Utility Rates," *Econometrica*, n.s. vol. 6 (July 1938); W. Arthur Lewis, "The Two-Part Tariff," *Economica*, n.s. vol. 8 (August 1941); and Marcel Boiteux, "The Green Tariff of the Electricite de France," trans. Eli W. Clemens and Lucienne C. Clemens, *Land Economics*, vol. 40 (May 1964), pp. 185–97.

have low incomes, and some do not; some low-income users are large users, some are small, and some are nonusers. Subsidization in kind (through a deficit) has the built-in defect that it is specific rather than general. A low-income person who is a nonuser gains no subsidy. Therefore government, when subsidizing for welfare reasons, should be wary of subsidization through pricing of commercial services below unit cost.

Still another awkward question arises when the incidence of the deficit is examined. The annual deficit of, for example, a transit system has to be met by taxes. The taxes may offset—wipe out—the subsidy. If the incidence of these taxes is regressive, their burden, as a percentage of income, falls more heavily on low- than on high-income persons. The likelihood—almost the certainty—is, however, that individual low-income persons who are steady users of the transit system will retain a substantial subsidy. Local tax systems, while regressive, do collect much larger absolute amounts from persons as their income rises. Thus, a sales tax with an effective rate of 4 percent for a person with an income of $2,000, and 2 percent for a person with an income of $10,000, collects $80 and $200 from each, respectively. A flat subsidy via a low transit fare of $100 yearly per steady user would, therefore, be cut into but not wiped out for a low-income user by a regressive tax; it would be negative for a high-income user.

In view of the imperfections of subsidization through public enterprises, one may wonder why it is so extensive. Part of the explanation seems to be inflexibility in the face of changing circumstances, and part the familiar intrusion of "political" decisions. Rising money costs, coupled with a rising price level, have prevailed for three decades; increases of prices of the products of public enterprises have lagged. The visibility of unit increases in transit fares is great; the effectiveness of protest in checking action has been demonstrated; the certainty that repeated deficits will not bring a decrease in supply of the service—all these factors encourage irrational pricing by municipal enterprises despite the desperate need of local governments for additional revenue.[13]

13. J. A. Stockfisch estimated that in 1957 Los Angeles could have raised $35.0–$37.6 million if a more rational method of pricing had been followed by its enterprises (the Harbor Department, the Airport Department, and the Department of Water and Power). This revenue could have been used either for tax relief or for

Highways

Except for streets and toll roads, the highway system is financed mainly through user taxes, especially on motor fuel. This is a form of indirect pricing. Almost all of the revenue of governments from taxation of motor fuel and motor vehicles is earmarked for highway purposes. It is, therefore, plausible to describe the highway system as a sort of public utility, operated by government. The analogy is, however, imperfect since the linkage between individual payment and benefit is imprecise. In particular, most highway users in thinly settled areas secure benefits in the form of good roads for which they do not make equivalent payments in the form of highway user taxes; the reverse is true for highway users in urban areas.

Streets are financed mainly from general taxes; in addition, a limited mileage is financed by tolls—direct pricing—which link cost with benefit to the user. A major factor in the decision to utilize one or the other method is cost of administration. Toll highways have limited entry and egress points, and this feature implies and requires a heavy traffic density in order to meet administrative costs.

Toll roads in the modern sense are a phenomenon of the 1930s and the postwar years. Interest in them was stimulated because too much of the revenues from users of motor vehicles had gone to lightly traveled roads, and too little to roads with heavy traffic. When people became convinced that more resources should be devoted to the latter, several obstacles stood in the way. Formulas for allocation of revenues from user charges were often firmly embedded in state legislation, and proposals for alteration raised objections. Increase of user charges was unpalatable, and, besides, would not meet the problem unless a new allocation of expenditure could be secured. Toll roads did seem to be a feasible solution. In areas of heavy traffic they could be financed on the benefit principle so that users would pay tolls covering the costs of construction and maintenance. The toll method of finance, moreover, allowed borrowing for construction through revenue bonds, thus avoiding constitutional or statutory restrictions applicable to regular borrowing.

For a number of years toll road mileage grew very rapidly, and

---

financing additional activities. "Fees and Service Charges as a Source of City Revenues: A Case Study of Los Angeles," *National Tax Journal,* vol. 13 (June 1960), pp. 111–21.

Table 8-6. Highway Expenditure, by Level of Government, 1973

Millions of dollars

	Highway expenditure		
Level of government	Direct	Intergovernmental	Total
All levels	19,173	...	19,173ª
Federal	558	5,276	5,834
State	12,072	2,953	15,025
Local	6,543	56	6,599

Source: *Governmental Finances in 1972–73*, p. 22.
a. Duplicative transactions between levels of government excluded.

continued growth seemed likely in areas of heavy traffic. But the Federal-Aid Highway Act of 1956 put an effective damper on new toll road construction. The act provided (among other things) for construction of a national system of interstate and defense highways of 41,000 miles. Ninety percent of the cost is paid for by federal grants from a Highway Trust Fund into which revenue from federal excises on gasoline, tires, and so forth, is deposited. Although the roads have limited access (and the existing toll roads are incorporated into the system), federal money cannot be used to construct toll roads. Since much of the mileage suitable for toll roads is now part of the interstate system, future toll road construction seems likely to be modest. Nonetheless, for many years ahead, a modest highway mileage will be financed by the levy of tolls on users—a direct pricing system. Expenditure for operation and construction of the toll road system in 1973 was $734.2 million, while revenue was $890.8 million.

On all other highways, some $19,173 million was spent by all levels of government in 1973 (see table 8-6). Most federal expenditure—90 percent—was intergovernmental, in the form of grants; 20 percent of state expenditure was intergovernmental.

Revenue from highway users in 1973 was $17,136 million. Table 8-7 shows, by level of government, the sources from which this was obtained.

User Charges for Noncommercial Activities

Besides the commercial enterprises outlined above, state and local governments carry on noncommercial activities for which they collect user charges. While all of these activities yield collective benefits,

Table 8-7. Revenue Collected from Highway Users, by Level of Government, 1973

Millions of dollars

	Source of revenue			
Level of government	*Motor fuel*	*Motor vehicles*	*Current charges*	*Total revenue*
All levels	12,525	3,636	975	17,136
Federal	4,402	...	n.a.	4,402
State	8,058	3,386	975	12,419
Local	65	249	n.a.	314

Sources: *Governmental Finances in 1972–73*, p. 20; and Census Bureau, *State Government Finances in 1973*, p. 23. Figures are rounded.
n.a. = not available.

they also yield to individuals some direct and measurable benefits that justify a user charge. At one end of the spectrum are charges that are barely distinguishable from those made for business-type services— for example, housing. At the other end are charges, usually called fees or license charges, that are primarily for regulatory purposes— court fees, licenses for restaurants, and so on.

The basis on which the level of charges for a particular service is set will often be some rough estimate of the value of a particular benefit or of the cost of rendering the service. But the charge will usually fall short of the benefit value or unit cost, and this shortfall may be justified either for reasons of equity—that is, for welfare or redistributional reasons—or as spillovers of benefits or costs. For example, the provision of elementary and secondary education yields benefits to people generally that spill over to such an extent that taxes, rather than fees, are used as the means of finance. Moreover, the amount of education provided becomes a public decision and parents are compelled to send their school-aged children to school.

Considerations of equity may be advanced even when the benefits from a governmental service are direct and divisible, and when spillovers are unimportant. When some of the recipients are indigent, the fact of direct benefit is irrelevant since, by definition, such persons cannot pay the charge. When some of the recipients are low income, equity may indicate that the user charge be reduced for them if a progressively graduated charge is feasible to take account of the varied income status of users.

Should local governments give weight to equity considerations in determining user charges? A negative answer can be, and has been, offered. Equity, when interpreted to mean redistribution of income, can only be handled fairly and efficiently at the national level. Action at the local level is bound to be uncoordinated and discordant. When particular governmental services are furnished free, or at less than cost, the incidence of redistribution to individual users is likely to be unequitable. Benefits accrue to users in proportion to their consumption of these services. Ideally, redistributional benefits should be in money form (generalized purchasing power), and not in the form of particular services. Otherwise, those recipients who have high preferences for the particular services benefit, while other low-income persons with low preferences do not benefit. Again, redistribution that applies only to persons in a small geographic area will either be so trivial that it has a small effect, or so strong that it endangers the economic position of an area.

The abstract cogency of these arguments is undeniable, and yet they are often irrelevant to actual situations. For example, besides absorbing the hospital charges of indigent persons, most local governments levy user charges on low-income persons that are less than cost. Any other course of action would be politically unattractive and repugnant to humanitarian sentiment.

For many services, however, the justification of uniform user charges that fail to cover cost is not apparent. If water is unmetered and is supplied at low charges, its use is often wasteful and frivolous; if on-street parking is free, or if, when metered, the charge is low and enforcement is lax, downtown shopping areas are injured and driving is impeded. Individuals and groups whose activities require special governmental regulation (for example, elevators, boilers, ownership of animals, operation of restaurants, and sale of milk) should be charged adequate fees. Numerous instances exist where user charges, based on cost, would serve as a crude rationing or control device to limit expansion of consumption of services for which, when the charge is low, the demand is elastic. This elasticity is enhanced when individual consumption is gradual and represents a small part of total consumption. Administrative problems are, however, sometimes an impediment to collection of any charge.

RECENT TRENDS. In postwar years, state and local collection of user charges has grown relatively as well as absolutely. Table 8-8 shows that the ratio of user charges to general revenues at both the state and local levels was much higher in 1973 than in 1953. For the

Table 8-8. Ratio of Local and State Government User Charges to General Revenue from Own Sources, 1953, 1963, 1966, 1969, and 1973
Percent

Year	Local ratio	State ratio
1953	12.8	6.8
1963	16.3	9.6
1966	16.3	10.4
1969	17.1	11.0
1973	17.4	10.7

Sources: Tables A-18 and A-19; and *Governmental Finances in 1965–66*, p. 20, and *in 1968–69*, p. 20.

decade 1963–73, however, the relative contribution of current charges to general revenues remained constant. Charges provided 16.3 percent of general revenues collected by local governments in 1963 and 17.4 percent in 1973. For state governments the corresponding figures were 9.6 percent and 10.7 percent. Whether or not user charges can be expected to grow in relative importance as a source of state and local revenue cannot be predicted. Charles Goetz, analyzing data similar to those presented in table 8-8, finds no support for the hypothesis that there is a trend toward increasing reliance on charges. He concludes: "Unless technological developments or changes in social attitudes are postulated, it is not clear why state and local governments would be expected to place an increased emphasis on user charges. In most cases, moreover, federal tax deductibility suggests advantages for the more traditional forms of taxation."[14] Nevertheless, state and local governments do provide many services —higher education, recreation and parking facilities, and so on— that yield direct and measurable benefits to individuals for which collection of user charges based on cost would seem justified. The charges would bring a desirable linkage between individual payment and benefit; they would not result in significant shrinkage of collective benefits; and they would provide needed revenue.

LOCAL SERVICE REVENUES. Table 8-9 shows the principal services for which local governments levied user charges in 1973 and table 8-10 shows the ratios of charges to expenditure on these services in 1953 and 1973. The most noticeable changes have taken place in

14. Charles J. Goetz, "The Revenue Potential of User-Related Charges in State and Local Governments," in Richard A. Musgrave, ed., *Broad-Based Taxes: New Options and Sources* (Johns Hopkins University Press, 1973), p. 114.

Table 8-9. Local and State User Charges for Governmental Services, 1973

	User charge, in millions of dollars		Percentage of total charges	
Governmental service	Local	State	Local	State
Nonhighway transportation	956	178	7.8	2.1
Natural resources, parks, and recreation	443	275	3.6	3.2
Hospitals	3,405	1,306	27.7	15.2
Housing	689	19	5.6	0.2
Sewerage and other sanitation	1,951	...	15.9	...
Education	2,714	4,891	22.1	56.8
Highways	a	975	a	11.3
Other	2,128	965	17.3	11.2
Total	12,285	8,609	100.0	100.0

Source: Tables A-18 and A-19.
a. Included in "other."

hospital finance and sanitation where the ratios have risen and in the housing category where the ratio has dropped. For education and highways the ratios are low. Education is viewed as a collective function and the chief user charges are for school lunch sales ($1.5 billion of the $2.7 billion collected in 1973); highways, at the local level, are also viewed as collective, and collection of charges (except for parking) raises severe administrative difficulties.

STATE SERVICE REVENUES. The purposes for which state governments collect user charges are more concentrated (table 8-9). Education is the largest item; user charges amount to more than half of total state user charges. They furnish, however, only one-quarter of state expenditures on education (exclusive of local school costs). Eight-tenths of this state expenditure (again exclusive of local school costs) is for state institutions of higher education. A controversy of long standing over the financing of these institutions has, in recent years, become much more acute. This controversy relates to the low level of charges (fees) of state, compared to private, institutions. Private institutions complain of unfair competition, and certainly the subsidy here has a peculiar bias, since it goes to some institutions in a state and not to others that nonetheless are providing similar or identical services.

Of the other types of state user charges, the steady rise of highway charges stems from toll facilities, and state user charges from hospi-

Table 8-10. Ratio of Local and State User Charges to Expenditures
for Governmental Services, 1953 and 1973
Percent

	Local		State	
Governmental service	*1953*	*1973*	*1953*	*1973*
Nonhighway transportation	55.7	59.5	47.8	43.2
Natural resources, parks, and recreation	16.6	13.8	15.3	10.5
Hospitals	27.1	59.3	10.9	24.3
Housing	35.8	23.8	...	7.2
Sewerage and other sanitation	17.0	36.7	...	...
Education	4.6	5.3	27.6	27.5
Highways	4.3	a	3.7	8.1
Total[b]	8.7	10.8	8.7	12.8

Source: Tables A-18 and A-19, and sources listed in table A-19.
a. Included in "other," which is not listed here but is included in total.
b. Includes "other," which is not listed here.

tals come largely from mental institutions. The two classes of state user charges that approach the category of commercial charges are housing and nonhighway transportation (including air transport, and water transport and terminals). Subsidization of these two classes of charges raises again familiar questions.

LOTTERIES. The fiscal pressures of the 1960s brought renewed interest in the public lottery as a source of revenue for state and local governments. In 1964, state lotteries were introduced in New Hampshire and in 1967 in New York. The results were disappointing because in both cases actual revenues were far less than anticipated revenues.[15] New Jersey's experience was somewhat different. Its lottery, established in 1971, offered more prizes more frequently and charged a lower price for its tickets than the others. The New Jersey experiment led to modifications in both the New Hampshire and New York games. Since 1971 ten other states have adopted lotteries based more or less on the New Jersey model.[16]

15. See Tax Foundation, *Nontax Revenues* (New York: Tax Foundation, 1968), p. 41; J. Richard Aronson, Andrew Weintraub, and Cornelius Walsh, "Revenue Potential of State and Local Public Lotteries," *Growth and Change,* vol. 3 (April 1972), pp. 2–8; Sam Rosen, "New England's State Operated Lotteries," *New England Journal of Business and Economics,* vol. 1 (Spring 1975), pp. 1–10.

16. Connecticut, Massachusetts, Pennsylvania, Michigan, Maryland, Rhode Island, Maine, Delaware, Illinois, and Ohio.

The revenue potential of lotteries is not great. In general none of the lotteries provides a very good buy for the gambling consumer. Prizes as a percent of gross receipts are much lower for state-run lotteries than for casino gambling or the illegal numbers game.[17] Moreover, the lottery is continuously attacked as being regressive and immoral. Funds provided by these games have amounted to only a small fraction of total revenues. In Massachusetts, for example, net receipts in 1972–73 were $32.1 million, or only 0.7 percent of total state-local general revenues from own sources; in New Jersey, net receipts for 1972–73 were $56.7 million, or just 1 percent of total state-local revenues from own sources.

Summary

The notable result of the search of local governments for nonproperty taxes has been that local sales and income taxes have become important sources of revenue to some large cities. In smaller localities freedom to levy miscellaneous taxes has been of questionable value. Indeed, it may be that the use of sales and income taxes by local governments is fiscal perversion. State intervention, sooner or later, seems likely to come.

Development of nontax revenues seems to have promise. In the past, considerations of equity and of redistribution have led public enterprises to price their services far below cost, and have persuaded local governments to levy user charges for noncommercial activities that do not reflect particular benefits. The probability is that, in these respects, the pursuit of equity has been misdirected; the inefficiencies of applying an equity test at the state and local level have been forgotten. Subsidization in kind has, moreover, serious built-in defects, and these are exaggerated when action is confined to a small geographic area. It would seem, therefore, that if public service enterprises followed a more rational system of pricing, they could provide local governments with additional revenue.

17. Rosen, "New England's State Operated Lotteries," p. 7.

CHAPTER NINE

State and Local Debt

So foul a sky clears not without a storm.

King John

HISTORICALLY, the volume of state and local borrowing has proceeded in waves, usually being heaviest when the volume of federal borrowing is lightest. The first wave of state borrowing developed in the 1820s and 1830s when many states engaged in "internal improvements"—canals, highways, railways, and so on. This effort was feasible not only because the nation was prosperous and had begun to accumulate savings, but also because the federal debt was being retired with great celerity. Holders of this debt, forced to seek new outlets for their capital, were attracted to state issues. Unfortunately, many of the internal improvements turned out to be unprofitable; the debt issued for them proved to be deadweight. When, in 1837, severe depression struck and continued for several years, the burden of this deadweight debt was aggravated. Nine states and one territory defaulted.[1] All state credit was impaired, and borrowing by state governments came to an abrupt halt. Most of the states resumed interest payments before 1850, although four states repudiated some debt.[2]

1. Default is a broad term, meaning that a government, for whatever reasons, is failing to pay interest, or installments of principal, when due. The default may be temporary or long-continued. No satisfactory method of weighting the seriousness of a default is available.

2. B. U. Ratchford, *American State Debts* (Duke University Press, 1941), pp. 98–99 and 105–14.

In a spirit of reaction against the mistakes that had been made, many state constitutions were framed to restrict future state borrowing.

The Civil War brought a new wave of state borrowing. Defense had not, at this time, become wholly a federal function, and the state governments borrowed to finance military operations. But at the close of the war the debts of the northern states were retired, usually through federal financial assistance. In the Reconstruction period, after 1865, carpetbag governments in the southern states issued considerable amounts of bonds, the proceeds of which were often wasted. After ejection of the carpetbaggers, nine southern states made extensive adjustments. Most of the debt was repudiated; the remainder was scaled down and, in the process, a few states reduced pre-Civil War debts.[3]

In the last two decades of the nineteenth century, borrowing by state governments declined sharply. State debt, less sinking funds, was $9.15 per capita in 1870 and only $3.10 in 1900. Bitter experience, coupled with a conservative philosophy, had led voters in most states to endorse severe constitutional or statutory limitations on state borrowing.[4]

It turned out, however, that some local governments in the 1870s had become creditworthy; they stepped into the vacuum and began to borrow extensively to finance internal improvements, notably railways. Their experience paralleled the earlier experience of the states. Borrowing was overdone; much of the capital was wasted; the annual carrying charges were beyond what local governments were prepared to finance. During the depression of 1873, defaults were widespread —perhaps 20 percent of the total.[5] State governments nearly everywhere imposed limitations on local borrowing, usually in the form of a debt-to-property ratio.

For two decades these limitations were restrictive, but in the twentieth century they proved to be elastic. Local governments, especially

3. Ibid., pp. 191–96.
4. A. James Heins, *Constitutional Restrictions Against State Debt* (University of Wisconsin Press, 1963), pp. 7–9, gives a brief history of state action.
5. A. M. Hillhouse, *Municipal Bonds: A Century of Experience* (Prentice-Hall, 1936), p. 17. Defaults amounted to about $100 million to $150 million during the 1870s out of outstanding bonds that ranged from $516 million in 1870 to $821 million in 1880 (ibid., pp. 36 and 39).

Table 9-1. State and Local Debt Outstanding, Selected Years, 1902–73

Millions of dollars

Year	Local debt	State debt	Total
1902	1,877	230	2,107
1913	4,035	379	4,414
1927	12,910	1,971	14,881
1932	16,373	2,832	19,205
1938	16,093	3,343	19,436
1946	13,564	2,353	15,917
1948	14,980	3,676	18,656
1960	51,412	18,543	69,955
1964	67,181	25,041	92,222
1966	77,487	29,564	107,051
1970	101,563	42,008	143,570
1973	129,110	59,375	188,485

Sources: U.S. Census Bureau, *Historical Statistics of the United States: Colonial Times to 1957* (GPO, 1960), pp. 728 and 730; and Census Bureau, *Governmental Finances*, annual issues. In all tables and figures, years are fiscal unless otherwise noted. Figures are rounded.

large cities, borrowed at an accelerating pace for the construction of schools and streets. In 1902, as table 9-1 shows, local debt was eight times larger than state debt.

The onset of depression in the 1930s did not at first slacken state and local borrowing. But as the depression continued and deepened, the reaction was very severe; after 1932, net borrowing was extremely low and during a few years repayments actually exceeded new borrowing. The rate of interest paid by state and local governments rose sharply, despite a marked drop in flotations (in 1932, 52.5 percent of the issues bore a rate of 5 percent or more, and many offerings could not be marketed at all); interest remained high, compared with the rate on federal debt. Table 9-2 shows state and local interest payments per $1,000 of personal income for selected years from 1902 to 1973. As income fell after 1929, the rise in these figures was startling.

Equally startling was the rise in defaults. By the mid-1930s, perhaps 10 percent of municipal bonds—$1.5 billion out of more than $15.0 billion—were in default. Some rough indication of the impact of the depression is provided by the growth in the number of defaults. For the five years prior to March 1932, about 226 defaults took place—an average of 45 yearly. On November 1, 1932, 678 local

Table 9-2. Interest Expenditure of State and Local Governments per $1,000 of Personal Income, Selected Years, 1902–73

	Interest	
Year	*In millions of dollars*	*In dollars per $1,000 of personal income*[a]
1902	68	3.37
1913	147	4.36
1927	584	7.34
1932	741	14.79
1934	739	13.79
1948	399	1.89
1957	1,106	3.18
1960	1,670	4.17
1962	2,008	4.57
1964	2,826	6.12
1966	3,268	6.14
1970	5,123	6.88
1973	7,828	8.37

Sources: Derived from *Historical Statistics*, pp. 139, 728, and 730; and *Governmental Finances*, annual issues.

a. Personal income data are for calendar years, and beginning in 1964 the data are for the preceding calendar year.

units were listed as in default; two years later the figure was 2,654, and on November 1, 1935, it was 3,251.[6] Default was not confined to bonds of inferior quality, since 90 percent were, in 1929, rated as Aa or higher.[7]

What lay behind the traumatic record? State and local debt had doubled in the 1920s, while the gross national product had risen by only 40 percent. Much more significant in impact was the fall in the price level, incomes, and employment, each of which added to the burden of debt. Despite increases in rates, local tax revenues declined by 17 percent in the years from 1930 to 1934. Tax delinquency in 1934 was more than 23 percent in 150 cities with populations over 50,000.

6. Ibid., pp. 17–21. One-quarter of the defaulting governmental units were reclamation, irrigation, and special assessment districts. Only one state, Arkansas, defaulted on its debt. During the 1920s Arkansas borrowed heavily for highways and Confederate pensions. Spending of the borrowed money was both wasteful and corrupt. Default came in 1932–33, followed by a bitter struggle over refunding. See Ratchford, *American State Debts,* chap. 15.

7. The quality ratings range from Aaa (the best rating) down to Caa.

Table 9-3. Relative Growth of State and Local Debt, Selected Years, 1938–73

Base year 1938 = 100.0

Year	Local debt	State debt	Total
1938	100.0	100.0	100.0
1948	93.1	110.0	96.0
1960	319.5	554.7	360.0
1962	367.1	657.2	417.0
1964	417.5	749.1	474.5
1966	481.5	884.4	550.8
1970	631.1	1,256.6	738.7
1973	802.3	1,776.1	969.8

Sources: Table 9-1; and *Governmental Finances in 1962*, p. 26.

During World War II state and local net borrowing remained low. Public construction for civilian purposes was at a standstill, and, as revenues picked up with full employment, state and local governments had large surpluses which they used to retire debt. At the end of 1946 their gross debt was 18 percent less than in 1938. And this was not the only favorable financial circumstance. Yields on state and local bonds were low beyond all precedent, with the result that new borrowing cost less and old debt could be refunded on a favorable basis.

The contrast between the market reception of state and local bonds in 1946 and the middle 1930s was marked. In 1937 the average yield of high-grade long-term state and local bonds was 3.10 percent, compared to a yield of 3.26 percent for Aaa corporation bonds—the differential as a percentage of the corporate yield was 5 percent. In 1946 this differential was 36 percent (yields of 1.64 percent on state and local bonds and 2.53 percent on corporation bonds). The main force behind this surprising performance was the exemption of interest on state and local bonds from federal income tax. The value of this exemption had risen because of the marked wartime increase in the level and progression of federal income tax rates, coupled with the decrease in the volume of exempt bonds and pessimistic market expectations concerning future increase in their volume.

This overview of state and local debt should call attention to differences between the growth of state debt and local debt in recent decades. Beginning in the 1930s, state debt grew at a faster rate than did local debt (table 9-3). The severity of the depression forced states

Table 9-4. Change in Per Capita Total Debt of State Governments and 48 Large Cities, 1966–73

Change in debt per capita (dollars)	Number of state governments	Number of large city governments
Decrease, all magnitudes	4[a]	4[b]
Increase		
0– 49	16	8
50– 99	8	4
100–149	8	7
150–199	2	8
200–249	3	6
250–299	4	4
300–349	0	1
350 and over	5	6

Sources: Census Bureau, *State Government Finances in 1966*, p. 15, and *in 1973*, p. 15; and Census Bureau, *City Government Finances in 1965–66*, tables 5 and 6, and *in 1972–73*, table 7.
a. Colorado, $14; Kansas, $23; Utah, $28; Arkansas, $0.65.
b. Honolulu, $66; Jacksonville, $175; Memphis, $204; San Jose, $73.

to assume governmental tasks that, in ordinary circumstances, were local. But it also led them to assume new governmental responsibilities, a factor that has, since World War II, grown in importance. Nonetheless, the actual amount of local debt in 1973 was still more than twice as large as state debt (see table 9-1).

Table 9-3 shows the remarkable overall increase in state and local debt during the postwar period. The increase, however, has not been uniform among governmental units. For example, for the time period 1966–73, state outstanding debt per capita increased by $130 from $152 to $282. But table 9-4 shows that in three states a sizable decrease occurred; in one state there was virtually no change; and sixteen states experienced an increase of less than $50 per capita. Table 9-4 also shows the uneven increase in per capita debt among large cities over the period 1966 to 1973. In eleven of the largest forty-eight cities, per capita debt increased by $250 or more. At the same time, however, per capita debt in four cities actually fell.

In postwar years the default record in municipal bonds has been quite good. Only two have created alarm and evoked memories of the 1930s: the West Virginia Turnpike Commission ($133 million of revenue bonds) in 1958 and the Calumet Skyway Toll Bridge ($101 million of revenue bonds) in 1963. Yet the dramatic increase in the quantity of debt, both short- and long-term, raises questions concerning its quality.

George H. Hempel, in his study of the period 1948–68, concluded that the quality of state and local debt had weakened.⁸ Debt service charges generally increased faster than state and local general revenues. Moreover, the revenue structure of state and local governments had undergone a relative shift in the direction of relatively elastic sales and income taxes and away from the property tax. As a result, these governmental units have become more vulnerable to slowdowns in economic activity. Hempel also concluded, however, that state and local governments experience extreme difficulty in managing their debt only during the latter stages of depressions and that widespread defaulting on municipal debt is more a result than a cause of depression.

In a more recent study the ACIR has focused attention on the ability of cities to meet their debt obligations.⁹ An attempt is made to pinpoint warning signs of financial trouble. The following are considered important:

- an operating fund . . . imbalance in which current expenditures significantly [exceed] current revenues in one fiscal period;
- a consistent pattern of current expenditures exceeding current revenues by small amounts for several years;
- an excess of current operating liabilities over current assets (a fund deficit);
- short-term operating loans outstanding at the conclusion of a fiscal year (or in some instances the borrowing of cash from restricted funds or an increase in unpaid bills in lieu of short-term operating loans);
- a high and rising rate of property tax delinquency;
- a sudden substantial decrease in assessed values for unexpected reasons.¹⁰

The study concludes that "in general, the present fiscal problems facing cities need not cause a financial emergency in the technical sense, provided local financial management is reasonably good and provided there is no major national economic depression."¹¹

In general, it would appear that during the period 1966–73 the debt burden of state and local governments in relation to their ability

8. *The Postwar Quality of State and Local Debt* (Columbia University Press for National Bureau of Economic Research, 1971), chap. 5.
9. Advisory Commission on Intergovernmental Relations, *City Financial Emergencies: The Intergovernmental Dimension* (GPO, 1973).
10. Ibid., p. 4.
11. Ibid.

Table 9-5. Debt Service Estimates of State and Local Governments, 1966, 1969, and 1973

Item	1966	1969	1973
Debt, in billions of dollars			
Long-term, outstanding	101.0	123.5	172.6
Long-term, retired	5.6	6.5	9.0
Short-term, outstanding	6.1	10.1	15.9
Interest	3.3	4.4	7.8
Revenue,[a] in billions of dollars	75.0	101.3	159.5
Debt service[b] *as percentage of revenue*	*20.0*	*20.7*	*20.5*
Personal income,[c] in billions of dollars	532.1	683.7	935.4
Debt outstanding,[d] *as percentage of personal income*	*20.1*	*19.5*	*20.2*
Debt per capita, in dollars	547	661	898

Source: *Governmental Finances in 1965–66, in 1968–69,* and *in 1972–73,* pp. 18, 28, and 52 in each.
a. General revenue of state and local governments from own sources plus utility revenue.
b. Long-term debt retired, short-term debt outstanding, and interest on debt.
c. U.S. total, for calendar years 1965, 1968, and 1972, respectively.
d. Long- and short-term debt outstanding.

to pay has remained constant. Table 9-5 shows that although per capita debt of state and local governments increased from $547 in 1966 to $898 in 1973, debt service payment in relation to general revenue has remained at about the 20 percent level. An alternative measure of debt burden—the ratio of total debt outstanding to total personal income—has also remained about 20 percent during this period.[12]

Forms of Debt

Most of the debt of state and local governments is secured by the full faith and credit of the issuing unit. Approximately 40 percent, however, is nonguaranteed. State and local debt nowadays is almost always in serial form. When the debt is incurred, a percentage of the issue comes due every year. The annual service charge for a twenty-

12. Fiscal pressure has become serious in a number of large cities, however. In late 1975, to avert New York City's default on its debt, the state created the Municipal Assistance Corp. (Big Mac) to buy up and manage the city's debt obligations, and the federal government authorized the Treasury to lend the city up to $2.3 billion to finance seasonal short-term borrowing. Rough estimates of debt service payment as a percentage of general revenue, following the formula in table 9-5, show an increase from 35 percent in 1966 to 44 percent in 1973 for New York City. For a comprehensive analysis, see Attiat Ott and Jang H. Yoo, *New York City's Financial Crisis: Can the Trend Be Reversed?* (Washington: American Enterprise Institute for Public Policy Research, 1975).

Table 9-6. Functional Distribution of State Long-Term Debt, 1941 and 1973

Function	Amount, in millions of dollars		Percentage of total		
	1941	*1973*	*1941*	*1973*	*Change*
Highways	1,373	16,088[a]	45.8	29.0	−16.8
Education	123	14,304	4.1	25.8	+21.7
Hospitals	50	1,200	1.7	2.2	+0.5
Water transportation and terminals	151	563	5.0	1.0	−4.0
Public welfare	449	n.a.	15.0	n.a.	...
Other[b]	855	23,242	28.5	42.0	+13.5
Total	3,001	55,397	100.0	100.0	...

Sources: Census Bureau, *Financial Statistics of States, 1941*, vol. 3, *Statistical Compendium* (1943), p. 66; and *State Government Finances in 1973*, pp. 40–41.
n.a. = not available.
a. Includes $6.9 billion for toll facilities.
b. Includes general control, natural resources, public welfare, parks and recreation, veterans' aid, and housing and community development.

year issue includes the repayment of, say, one-twentieth of the principal, as well as the required interest. This method is superior to the older device of sinking funds which required the accumulation of large sums for the final redemption of the whole issue at maturity. The temptation to raid such funds, or to alter the terms, was often irresistible to hard-pressed state and local governments.[13]

Most state and local borrowing is for capital expenditure such as roads, buildings, and public service enterprises. Table 9-6 shows the purposes for which state long-term debt had been incurred in 1941 and 1973. Besides an eighteenfold increase in the total amount, there were significant shifts in particular items. While highway debt was dominant in both years, borrowing for toll roads—negligible in 1941—was 43 percent of the highway debt in 1973. Debt for educational purposes rose from 4 percent in 1941 to 26 percent in 1973, while debt for public welfare—important in 1941—was negligible in 1973.

13. The old-fashioned sinking fund, however, did provide a financial advantage for state and local governments. Sinking fund assets could be invested in U.S. government securities which, because they are not tax exempt, generally carry a higher yield to maturity than do municipals of the same maturity. See Roland I. Robinson, "Debt Management," in J. Richard Aronson and Eli Schwartz, eds., *Management Policies in Local Government Finance* (Washington: International City Management Association, 1975), p. 233.

Table 9-7. Functional Distribution of Long-Term Debt of 43 Largest Cities,
1941 and 1973

	Amount, in millions of dollars		Percentage of total	
Function	1941	1973	1941	1973
General debt[a]	3,210	16,853	50.6	71.5
Education	589	1,865	9.3	7.9
Highways	653	1,684	10.3	7.1
Sewerage	373	1,928	5.9	8.2
Housing and urban renewal	n.a.	2,780	n.a.	11.8
Other and unallocable	1,595	8,596	25.1	36.5
Utility debt	3,136	6,723	49.4	28.5
Water supply systems	1,148	2,892	18.1	12.3
Other utilities	1,988	3,831	31.3	16.2
Total debt	6,346	23,576	100.0	100.0

Sources: Census Bureau, *Financial Statistics of Cities Having Populations over 100,000, 1941*, vol. 3, *Statistical Compendium* (1943), pp. 101–05; and Census Bureau, *City Government Finances in 1972–73*, table 7. To make the 1973 estimates comparable with those of 1941, the debts of the five smallest of the 48 cities in the 1973 list (Birmingham, Norfolk, St. Paul, El Paso, and Newark) were subtracted from the total.
n.a. = not available.
a. The Census Bureau cautions that the scope of municipal government operations differs. In particular, public schools may be operated by the municipal corporation or by an independent school district. Such differences mean that the debt figures do not include all debt of the cities as geographic units.

Table 9-7 shows the purposes of the long-term debt of the forty-three largest cities in 1941 and 1973 (figures for all local debt are not available). General debt had risen, relative to utility debt, from 50.6 percent to 71.5 percent of the total. One new function, housing and urban renewal, had emerged and, in 1973, accounted for 11.8 percent of total debt.

The life of most state and local debt is geared to the expected life of the asset provided by the debt, or to an estimate of the revenue to be derived from the asset—but the gearing is loose. The life of water and sewer issues is usually thirty years, a maturity that readily assures receipts covering interest and annual maturities.[14]

Borrowing by state and local governments is generally contracyclical. The peak rate of bond sales during the years from 1952 to 1970 was reached in recession troughs. Not all types of projects are affected. Schools, water, and sewer projects are carried forward without regard to the condition of the money market, but other types of state

14. Roland I. Robinson, *Postwar Market for State and Local Government Securities* (Princeton University Press for National Bureau of Economic Research, 1960), pp. 46–47.

and local capital projects "have shown a very pronounced contra-cyclical movement."[15] This is so even though officials responsible for the technical details of issuance may commit themselves not when interest rates are lowest, but when the market will provide a rate within the ceiling specified by the legislative body in authorizing the issue, and even though voters, as well as state and local officials, are more disposed to endorse borrowing for capital purposes in good years, that is, in years when interest rates are high.

From a Federal Reserve survey of interest rates, borrowing, and capital spending in 1966 it appears that the larger state and local governments had greater flexibility than small governments in reacting to the rapid escalation of interest rates.[16] McGouldrick and Petersen show that although the high interest rates of 1966 had a great effect on the borrowing plans of the large governments, the effect on capital spending was marginal. Small governmental units, however, were likely to completely abandon rather than temporarily delay their bond offerings. The difference in behavior was apparently due to the larger cash cushion of the larger governments. Examining the relationships between monetary policy and real and financial flows in the economy, the authors suggest that withdrawal from capital markets in the face of rising interest rates may very well demonstrate financial strength rather than weakness and that continued borrowing under increasing interest rates may be a signal of weakness.

In 1973, 92 percent of state and local debt was long term (table 9-8). This is in distinct contrast to federal practice, since 47 percent of federal marketable interest-bearing debt matures within one year. The federal Treasury also issues a variety of intermediate-term debt that has no parallel in state and local practice. State and local governments use short-term debt mostly in anticipation of tax receipts; they seldom use it to finance the start of capital projects. State and local officials are less close to, and less versed in the behavior of, money markets; they are unwilling to issue short-term debt in the expectation that a more favorable long-term market will develop. They have, in

15. Frank E. Morris, "Impact of Monetary Policy on State and Local Governments: An Empirical Study," *Journal of Finance,* vol. 15 (May 1960), p. 234.

16. Paul F. McGouldrick and John E. Petersen, "Monetary Restraint and Borrowing and Capital Spending by Large State and Local Governments in 1966," and "Monetary Restraint, Borrowing, and Capital Spending by Small Local Governments and State Colleges in 1966," *Federal Reserve Bulletin,* vol. 54 (July and December 1968), pp. 552–81 and 953–71.

Table 9-8. Outstanding Long-Term and Short-Term State and Local Debt, 1966 and 1973[a]

	Debt, in billions of dollars			Percentage of total debt		
Period of debt	State	Local	Total	State	Local	Total
1966 total	29.6	77.5	107.1	100.0	100.0	100.0
Long-term	28.5	72.5	101.0	96.3	93.5	94.3
Short-term	1.1	5.0	6.1	3.7	6.5	5.7
1973 total	59.4	129.1	188.5	100.0	100.0	100.0
Long-term	55.7	116.9	172.6	93.8	90.5	91.6
Short-term	3.7	12.2	15.9	6.2	9.5	8.4

Sources: *Governmental Finances in 1965–66* and *in 1972–73*, table 14, p. 28, in each.
a. Debt at end of fiscal year. Short-term debt is repayable within one year.

any case, less flexibility and discretion, since refunding of short-term credit is subject to constitutional or statutory limitations and is, moreover, frowned upon by local banks. Nevertheless, as table 9-8 shows, short-term debt has risen in recent years from 5.7 percent to 8.4 percent of the total of all state and local debt. The short-term component of local debt alone was approximately 10 percent of the total in 1973.

Tax Exemption

The most important and distinctive characteristic of state and local issues is their freedom from federal taxation.[17] The federal government does not tax the interest on state and local securities through income tax, and state and local governments cannot tax federal securities. The federal government does tax the interest on its own securities. State and local governments may tax their own securities, although most do not exercise this right; they may, and generally do, tax each other's securities.

The failure of the federal government to tax income from state and local securities rests on the specific statutory exclusion of such income by Congress. When the Sixteenth Amendment to the Constitution was in process, assurance was given to some state governors that the amendment merely was to remove the constitutional requirement that a federal income tax, as a direct tax, be apportioned among the

17. Interest on arbitrage bonds and large industrial aid bonds is taxable. Realized capital gains on municipal bond transactions are also taxable. However, the implicit interest embodied in a bond originally issued at discount is not taxable.

states according to population. And when Congress passed the individual income tax of 1913, it implicitly accepted this position by providing that interest on state and local securities be excluded from income. This statutory exclusion has been retained.

The Supreme Court has never decided the question of the constitutional right of Congress to delete the exclusion and to tax interest on state and local securities as income. For some years after 1913, the inference of many decisions seemed to be that the amendment had not altered the taxable status of state and local securities. But in the late 1930s several decisions that curtailed the immunity of governmental instrumentalities raised doubts anew.

These decisions seemed to depend on the theory that nondiscriminatory taxation, federal or state, was permissible and tolerable. The epigram of Chief Justice Marshall in *McCulloch* v. *Maryland,* that "the power to tax involves the power to destroy," had been capped by the epigram of Justice Holmes that "the power to tax is not the power to destroy while this Court sits." The courts, as the referees of a federal system with a dual sovereignty, would protect the states even if, as Justice Butler believed, the doctrine of reciprocal immunity was "presently marked for destruction."[18]

So far this has not happened, but if it should happen and if, by statutory provision, the state and local governments were given the right to tax federal securities and the federal government the right to tax state and local securities, the position of the state and local governments would legally be much more insecure. A statutory right of the states to tax the income on federal bonds could be repealed by any subsequent Congress. The federal right to tax state and local securities would, presumably, be a constitutional right; it would continue even if the state right were repealed. One can argue, of course, that a future Congress would not take the unjust action of taxing state and local securities without permitting state and local taxation of federal securities. State and local interests are adequately represented in the Congress, and this is protection against mistreatment. But the states and localities have been unwilling to trust this assurance. They maintain that their present position should be altered only by constitutional amendment. If Congress itself simply removed the exclusion,

18. *McCulloch* v. *Maryland,* 4 Wheat. 316, 431 (1819); Holmes, dissenting, in *Panhandle Oil Co.* v. *Mississippi,* 277 U.S. 218, 223 (1928); and Butler, dissenting, in *Graves* v. *New York ex rel. O'Keefe,* 306 U.S. 466, 493 (1939).

this would indicate congressional opinion that the exclusion was undesirable. The Supreme Court then, in the event of a state-local appeal against the exclusion, would be forced to make a decision that should rest with the people of the nation.

For more than fifty years the federal Treasury has made intermittent efforts to abolish the exemption, at first only for future issues, but in 1942 for outstanding issues as well. All efforts have failed, in the face of sharp resistance by state and local governments and the unwillingness of Congress to impair the financial powers of these governments at a time when their financial responsibilities were large and expanding. One proposal, a municipal bond subsidy program, has, however, had some support in Congress. Under this plan state and local governments would have the option of issuing either taxable or tax-exempt securities. If the local government chose to issue taxable securities, the federal government would subsidize some portion of the interest cost. Such a plan should raise the before-tax yield on municipals and thereby make these instruments more attractive than at present to individuals and institutions (for example, pension funds) in low tax brackets. At the same time, the taxing of municipal bond interest would remove much of the tax advantage now enjoyed by those in the higher tax brackets.[19]

Yield Differentials

Tax-exempt bonds have always sold at a lower yield than taxable bonds of similar quality and maturity. The yield differential depends chiefly on the relative expected supply of the two kinds of bonds and on the anticipated amount of tax that can be avoided. The holder of tax-exempt bonds does not pay income tax on the interest. If all other income were taxed proportionally, and all bondholders were subject to the tax, then the provision for tax-free interest on certain bonds would bring about an increase in their price equal to the value of the exemption to every buyer. The public sector would not be the loser since the lower yield of the tax-exempt municipal bonds would be

19. The "taxable bond option" plan first appeared in the House version of the Tax Reform Act of 1969. For further discussion, see Harvey Galper and John Petersen, "An Analysis of Subsidy Plans to Support State and Local Borrowing," and Harvey Galper and George E. Peterson, "The Equity Effects of a Taxable Municipal Bond Subsidy," *National Tax Journal*, vol. 24 (June 1971), pp. 205–34, and vol. 26 (December 1973), pp. 611–24.

equivalent to the taxes the federal government agreed to forgo. But when income is taxed progressively, the value of the exemption becomes worth more to buyers as the size of their taxable income increases, and this graduated value will not be fully reflected in the price of an issue.

For example, a taxpayer in the top (70 percent) bracket who buys a taxable bond yielding $60 annually can keep only $18. To him, the exemption from income tax is worth forty-two–sixtieths (70 percent) of the yield. He would be as well off to purchase at par a tax-exempt bond yielding 1.8 percent as a taxable one yielding 6 percent. A taxpayer in the 20 percent bracket keeps $48 out of $60, and to him exemption is worth only twelve-sixtieths of the yield. An exempted yield of 4.8 percent is equivalent to 6 percent from a taxable bond.

If it is assumed that the actual supply of tax-exempt bonds is relatively small, then perhaps all could profitably be bought by persons in the top bracket, and the market yield would be 1.8 percent. But if the supply is so large that buyers in the lower brackets must be tapped, the yield for those in the 20 percent bracket would have to rise to 4.8 percent. These are the marginal buyers, whose income after taxes is the same whether they buy tax-exempt or taxable securities. Since the market is undifferentiated, all buyers get the same yield as the marginal buyers and the high-income buyers secure a sort of surplus of tax saving.

Over the decades the differential between the yield of taxable and tax-exempt securities has widened or narrowed in response to pressure from various forces. In the 1920s, when the rates and progression of the federal individual income tax were sharply decreased and these trends were widely expected to continue, the differential was narrow (see table 9-9). Thus, the advantage to high-income persons from holding tax-exempt bonds was modest, and so was the loss to the federal Treasury from its inability to tax the income from exempted bonds. During World War II the differential widened; by 1946 the yield of high-quality tax-exempt bonds was about 63 percent that of similar taxable bonds. Behind this lay the marked increase in the level and progression of federal income taxes, as well as the decrease in the volume of exempted bonds. In postwar years the differential narrowed, partly because of a modest decrease in federal income tax rates but mostly because of the great rise in the volume of exempted bonds. The gross proceeds from issues of state and local

Table 9-9. Comparative Yields on High-Grade Long-Term Municipal and
Corporate Bonds, Selected Years, 1928–73

Percent

| | Yield | | | Differential as |
| | Municipal | Corporate | | a percentage of |
Year	bonds[a]	bonds	Differential	corporate yield
1928	4.02	4.55	0.53	12
1938	3.01	3.19	0.18	6
1946	1.60	2.53	0.93	37
1963	3.16	4.26	1.10	26
1966	3.88	5.13	1.25	24
1973	5.29	7.44	2.15	29

Sources: *The Bond Buyer's Municipal Finance Statistics, 1974*, vol. 13 (June 1975), p. 19; Board of Governors of the Federal Reserve System, *Banking and Monetary Statistics* (The Board, 1943), p. 468; and *Economic Report of the President, February 1975*, p. 317.

a. Average of high and low yields for the year; the data are for twenty municipal bonds.

securities, which in 1946 amounted to 6.2 percent of all new issues, rose in the mid 1960s to about 28 percent and by the early seventies was averaging about 23 percent. As a result, the advantage to state and local governments from the exemption privilege has diminished; the advantage to high-income buyers has increased. This trend, however, may be in the process of reversing. The school-aged population is expected to fall and new highway construction will probably not continue at historic rates. All this should act to reduce the pressure on state and local governments to increase the amount of debt outstanding. The result of such a trend would be an increased yield differential between taxable and tax-exempt securities. This potential change would be to the advantage of issuing governments and at the expense of high-income buyers.

Holders of Tax-Exempt Securities

As table 9-10 indicates, only a small portion of state and local interest-bearing securities is held in investment funds of state and local governments themselves (2.1 percent in 1973).[20] The three groups that hold the bulk of these securities are commercial banks, high-income individuals, and insurance companies—each of these groups is, of course, exposed to high federal income tax rates. One significant change in the distribution of ownership appears to have

20. Since state and local governments are not taxed by the federal government, it makes little sense for them to hold tax-exempt bonds yielding less than taxable U.S. government securities.

Table 9-10. Estimated Holdings of State and Local Securities by Various Types of Owners, 1966 and 1973

Type of owner	Value, in billions of dollars		Percentage of total	
	1966	*1973*	*1966*	*1973*
Households	40.0	50.5	37.8	26.6
Commercial banks	41.2	95.7	38.9	50.4
Insurance companies	15.7	33.8	14.8	17.8
State and local governments[a]	4.6	3.9	4.3	2.1
Other	4.4	6.0	4.2	3.2
Total	105.9	190.0	100.0	100.0

Source: *The Bond Buyer's Municipal Finance Statistics, 1974,* p. 17. Estimated on Dec. 31. Figures are rounded.

a. General fund and retirement fund holdings.

taken place between 1966 and 1973. In 1966, commercial banks and households were about tied in the portion owned, 39 percent and 38 percent each. By 1973, commercial banks had increased their share to 50.4 percent; the proportionate holdings of households had decreased to 26.6 percent. A possible explanation for this shift is the reduction in tax rates on individual income relative to the rate on corporate income that has taken place since 1964.

The volume of tax-exempt securities held by high-income persons has always been less than an inspection of the tax advantages might suggest. Many of these persons prefer to be active rather than passive investors; they prefer an investment that may bring either appreciable capital gains, or, as with ownership of equities, that involves participation in the operation of a business. To them the tax advantages of exempted issues are not decisive. They are erratic buyers, shifting into and out of exempts inversely to the attractiveness of other investments. Holdings of tax-exempt bonds by commercial banks are also quite variable. When the demand for loans by business is large and growing, the banks will not buy, and may sell, exempts; when business demand declines, they buy exempts. For casualty insurance companies, whose earnings vary because of unpredictable losses from year to year, exempts provide fair liquidity, as well as a secure and tax-free income.

As a consequence of the variability in the holdings of these important groups, fluctuations in interest rates of tax-exempt securities are greater than those of other comparable long-term holdings.[21]

21. Robinson, *Postwar Market,* pp. 89–93.

Proposals for Abolition

Most proposals for abolishing tax-exempt issues have assumed that mere reciprocal abolition—permitting state and local governments to tax income from federal securities, and the federal government to tax the income from state and local securities—would not be attractive to state and local governments. Such a move would, it seems, bring a net financial gain to the federal Treasury which could tax this addition to the income tax base at high and progressive rates. But state and local governments would suffer a net financial loss, since the interest rates payable on their bonds would rise, while the additional revenue that they might secure from taxation of interest on federal debt would be modest. Some extra inducement, such as the municipal bond subsidy program described above, would therefore be needed to secure state and local consent.

The benefits derived by state and local governments from the issuance of tax-exempt bonds accrue more to governmental units in high-income areas than in low simply because the former units issue more debt. High-income states have a high state-local debt per capita, low-income states a low debt (see table A-20). Regarded as a subsidy, therefore, exemption is inefficient. And even though the exemption may not be more valuable to governmental units with high credit ratings than it is to those with low, the exemption is not distributed according to need.[22]

In January 1962 the Brookings Institution sponsored a conference of experts on taxation of state and local securities.[23] Discussion appeared to indicate that even if a satisfactory financial compensation could be devised for state and local governments' loss of exemption benefits, some state and local governments would remain fearful on political grounds. An arrangement would rest on legislation by Congress which, conceivably, future congresses could alter. Even if at some future time Congress did not alter the money value of the compensation, it might assert federal control over how the money was

22. See Carolyn V. Kent, "The Subsidy to State and Local Governments Implicit in the Exemption of Municipal Bond Interest from Federal Tax" (doctoral dissertation, Lehigh University, 1975).

23. See David J. Ott and Allan H. Meltzer, *Federal Tax Treatment of State and Local Securities* (Brookings Institution, 1963), for an exploration of the economic issues involved and a summary of the conference.

used. A key problem to removal of the exemption is, therefore, devising a plan to allay this fear.

Debt Limitations

Most states impose limitations on the authority of the state legislature to borrow. The limitations reflect impulsive reactions to misdirected overborrowing; their objective is to protect taxpayers, and the credit of the governments, against recurrences of past mistakes. There are different types of restrictions. In some states a constitutional amendment is required for authorization of debt. Or the restrictions may be in the form of referendum requirements or monetary limits placed on debt authorizations. There are also legal provisions for exceeding limits.[24]

Attempts have been made to classify states by the severity of these restrictions. B. U. Ratchford, a pioneer in the study of state debt, divided the states into three groups; and the differences between the groups in the amount of state debt per capita appeared to support the hypothesis that restrictions were effective in limiting the amount of debt.[25] A. J. Heins, however, has warned that care must be taken in reaching this conclusion. The groupings are somewhat arbitrary, a few very large and unusual debt issues are included in the data, and the importance of local debt in the state-local total is neglected.[26] Heins, from data similar to Ratchford's, concludes that "constitutional provisions have been less effective—if effective at all—in limiting state debt than most people would have supposed."[27]

Besides limiting their own borrowing power, states also impose constitutional or statutory limitations on the borrowing power of their local governments. A common limitation is to set a ceiling on debt as a percentage of the property tax base of the local govern-

24. For a convenient listing of these restrictions see ACIR, *Federal-State-Local Finances: Significant Features of Fiscal Federalism, 1973–74 Edition* (GPO, 1974), table 95, pp. 155–58.

25. In one group the constitution prohibits state borrowing except as authorized by a constitutional amendment; in a second, borrowing proposals must be enacted by the legislature and then approved by a popular referendum; and in a third, legislatures make the borrowing decisions ("State and Local Debt Limitations," in National Tax Association, *Proceedings of the Fifty-first Annual Conference on Taxation* [1959], p. 226).

26. Heins, *Constitutional Restrictions Against State Debt*, chap. 3.

27. Ibid., p. 35.

ment.[28] Another device, mandated by constitution or statute in all but eight states, is a requirement that the issuance of debt be approved by referendum.[29]

State limitations on local government borrowing are designed to protect the solvency of local governments (as well as that of the state), and to protect bondholders. The ACIR has rephrased the purposes as follows: "To empower local governments to make use of borrowing, prudently and in a responsible and locally responsive manner, as one means for financing their requirements."[30]

The limitation that sets a ceiling on local borrowing in terms of the property tax base has often been criticized. Some critics declare that it is technically deficient. It focuses on the property tax base of the individual local government, even though that same base may be shared by several overlapping local governments. Summation of the ratios of debt to assessed value of property for all the governmental units in a geographic area might produce an aggregate ratio that would seem alarming to voters. If consolidation of the units in order to achieve a simpler and more efficient governmental structure were under consideration, some officials would oppose this step simply because of their fear that, in the process, the aggregate borrowing power of the area would be curtailed.

Conversely, the creation of new governmental units has been induced and stimulated by a desire to gain new borrowing power. Fragmentation of governmental functions through proliferation of special districts and authorities destroys the unity of governmental budgets and deprives citizens of understandable information concerning government finances. A basic premise of responsible state and local government is thereby impaired.

Limitations tied to the property tax base are less relevant now than in the past. Thirty or forty years ago the property tax supplied 95 percent of the tax revenue of local governments; in 1973 it supplied 83 percent. The debt-carrying capacity of local governments is, therefore, not measured by their property tax base alone. This is the more so because state-imposed limits usually relate to assessed value,

28. For a summary of these restrictions, see ACIR, *Significant Features, 1973–74 Edition,* table 93, pp. 143–52.

29. No referendum is required in Connecticut, Hawaii, Indiana, Massachusetts, New Jersey, New York, Tennessee, and Washington. See ACIR, *Significant Features, 1973–74 Edition,* table 94, pp. 153–54.

30. ACIR, *State Constitutional and Statutory Restrictions on Local Government Debt* (ACIR, 1961), p. 39.

which, in most cases, is less than full value. The result is that the impact of debt limitations depends mostly on local assessment practices. In an area where assessed value is less than full value, assessors can lift the debt ceiling by lifting the assessed value, or lower it by dropping the assessed value. The ACIR feels that this situation exposes assessors to undesirable pressures wholly unrelated to their duties. Decisions to borrow should be made by elective bodies; they should not be subject to the irrelevant decisions of assessors. Moreover, the impact of a debt-to-property limitation within a state will not be uniform among localities unless assessment is uniform. In most states uniformity of assessment by local governments has not been achieved.

Another and major defect of this debt limitation is that usually it applies only to full faith and credit debt, secured by the general revenues of the government, and not to nonguaranteed debt, secured only by the revenues of the enterprise or activity for which this debt is contracted. The volume of the latter type of debt has been growing much more rapidly than that of the former.

The Nonguaranteed Bond

The most important device used to avoid debt limitations has been the revenue bond, a form of nonguaranteed debt. Strictly defined, revenue bonds are those for which interest and principal are payable exclusively from the earnings of a specific enterprise. In such case they are not serviced from the general revenues of a local or state government; they are not, therefore, subject to the constitutional or statutory limitations imposed on the issuance of full faith and credit bonds.

In their original use, revenue bonds were mostly issued to finance revenue-producing enterprises—public utilities, toll facilities, and so on. This use of nonguaranteed debt was greatly enlarged during the 1930s when the Public Works Administration was attempting to stimulate state and local construction of public works. State and local limitations on borrowing stood in the way. The legal division of the PWA decided that nonguaranteed bonds were a device that would circumvent the limitations, and it offered to help state and local governments in drafting bills authorizing the issuance of such bonds. The help was widely accepted. In 1931 only fifteen states permitted local governments to use nonguaranteed bonds; by 1936 the number had risen to forty; and now nonguaranteed bonds are used in every state.

Table 9-11. Long-Term Debt of State and Local Governments, 1949, 1963, 1968, and 1973[a]

Year	Debt, in billions of dollars			Full faith and credit debt as percentage of total	Non-guaranteed debt as percentage of total
	Total long-term	Full faith and credit	Non-guaranteed		
State and local					
1949	20.2	17.7	2.5	87.6	12.4
1963	83.2	50.7	32.4	60.9	38.9
1968	112.7	65.1	47.7	57.8	42.3
1973	172.6	102.9	69.7	59.6	40.4
State					
1949	4.0	3.4	0.6	85.0	15.0
1963	22.8	10.7	12.1	46.9	53.1
1968	33.6	14.7	18.9	43.8	56.3
1973	55.7	28.4	27.3	51.0	49.0
Local					
1949	16.2	14.3	1.9	88.3	11.7
1963	60.4	40.0	20.4	66.2	33.8
1968	79.1	50.4	28.7	63.7	36.3
1973	116.9	74.5	42.4	63.7	36.3

Source: Table A-21. Data are for end of fiscal year. Figures are rounded.

Even more surprising than the growth in the volume of such bonds was the expansion in the types of projects financed by them. In addition to the usual public utilities, local governments constructed swimming pools, golf courses, college dormitories, and so on.

Since World War II the nonguaranteed bond has been widely utilized by both state and local governments. As table 9-11 and figure 9-1 show, in 1949 full faith and credit debt accounted for 87.6 percent of all state and local long-term debt, while in 1973 it had fallen to 59.6 percent. While the relative use of full faith and credit debt diminished at both the state and local levels, the decline was greater at the state level where, in 1973, full faith and credit debt was only 51.0 percent of the total. Similarly, the figures show that the postwar growth of nonguaranteed debt was greater at the state level.[31]

The annual publication *State Government Finances* supplies debt figures for individual states. In 1941 more than half of the net long-

31. Heins, *Constitutional Restrictions Against State Debt*, pp. 22–24, gives information concerning the purposes for which outstanding state nonguaranteed debt in 1958 had been issued. Of the total, 70 percent was for bridges and roads, 13 percent for education, and 9 percent for power and water.

Figure 9-1. Percentage of State and Local Debt in Full Faith and Credit and Nonguaranteed Form, 1949 and 1973

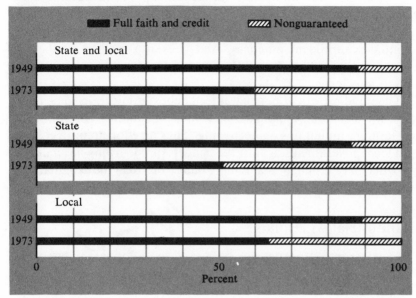

Source: Table A-21.

term debt of thirty-four states was in the form of full faith and credit bonds; in 1973 the number was twenty-two (see table A-22). Eight states in 1941, and sixteen in 1973, had less than half of their long-term debt in full faith and credit form. Again, in 1941, six states had no long-term debt in full faith and credit form; in 1973 the number was twelve. Five of the six states in 1941, and the twelve in 1973, were not free of long-term debt; except for Florida in 1941, all of them had some nonguaranteed debt (see table A-23).

Among the disadvantages of nonguaranteed bonds is the long time period for which they are issued, usually in order to provide "a safe margin for coverage of costs and debt charges."[32] Extension of maturity tends to increase the rate of interest that must be paid. Another of their faults is their tendency to bias the use of government resources toward purposes for which the device is readily applicable.

The most serious present danger of nonguaranteed bonds arises from their extensive use for purposes that are not self-financing and that therefore burden the budgets of state and local governments. If

32. ACIR, *State Constitutional and Statutory Restrictions,* p. 55.

these purposes are public, and if they should be financed by borrowing, issuance of full faith and credit debt is superior in all respects to the issuance of revenue bonds. By concealing or obscuring what state and local governments are doing, the use of nonguaranteed bonds stimulates imprudent practices. And if even a modest number of these bonds should default, all state and local credit would be adversely affected.

The rapid growth of nonguaranteed debt is ironical. In some measure, the technique of nonguarantee aims at avoiding constitutional or statutory limitations on borrowing. Thus an effort to protect state and local governments against the dangers of borrowing has induced growth of a type of debt that is more dangerous than the debt that was restricted.

Industrial Aid Bonds

Nonguaranteed bonds have been used to aid private industry. In over forty states, local governmental units have been authorized to issue revenue bonds in order to acquire land, buildings, and equipment that are leased to private firms. The firms pay a rental to cover servicing of the debt.

This practice, which has been discouraged by 1968 tax legislation, is objectionable for several reasons: it exploits the interest exemption of state and local bonds from federal income taxation for purposes that are proprietary and private rather than public; it enables recipient firms to derive a cost advantage over other private firms; it induces firms to move from one state to another when market forces by themselves are not favorable.

Often, such nonguaranteed bonds are not the obligations of local government. A governmental unit issuing revenue bonds to finance an industrial aid project incurs no legal obligation to pay interest or redeem the debt out of its own resources. The bonds are secured through the earnings of the firm occupying the facility, and the market judges the bond issue on the basis of the credit quality of the firm. Since investors, in effect, lend their credit to the private firm, the governmental unit merely serves as the organ through which the firm borrows. Under nonguaranteed industrial aid bond financing, therefore, the debt of private companies is effectively converted into tax-exempt obligations.

Table 9-12. Industrial Aid Bonds in Relation to Total State and Municipal Bonds Sold, Selected Years, 1966–74

	Bonds, in millions of dollars		Industrial aid as percentage of total
Year	Industrial aid	Total, long-term	
1966	504.5	11,088.9	4.5
1968	1,585.3	16,374.3	9.7
1970	47.6	17,761.6	0.3
1972	470.7	22,940.8	2.1
1974	340.0	22,824.0	1.5

Source: *The Bond Buyer's Municipal Finance Statistics, 1974,* pp. 7 and 8.

During the 1960s an upsurge occurred in the number of local units issuing industrial aid revenue bonds and in the amount of debt issued. This form of debt reached the height of its popularity in 1968, according to table 9-12, when $1.6 billion in industrial aid bonds were issued; they represented 9.7 percent of the total state and municipal bonds sold that year. Federal legislation enacted in 1968 removed the tax-exempt status of industrial aid bonds issued to finance projects with costs of more than $5 million.[33] The effect of this legislation has been a dramatic reduction in the use of industrial aid financing. In 1970 these bonds represented only 0.3 percent of total state and municipal bonds sold. The increase in use from the 1970 low is due to growing popularity of the pollution control bond which is a special class of industrial development bond, whose tax-exempt status is not restricted by the congressional legislation of 1968.

Reform of Borrowing Limitations

The ACIR in 1961 recommended a complete revision of "the present maze of constitutional and statutory restrictions upon local government borrowing." Authority to issue bonds "should be legally vested in the governing bodies of local governments, subject to a permissive referendum only, on petition, and with participation in any such referendum available to all eligible local voters and the results determined—except under unusual circumstances—by a sim-

33. See *Renegotiation Amendments Act of 1968, Etc.,* H. Rept. 1951, 90:2 (GPO, 1968), pp. 7–9. The legislation as enacted applies to bonds issued after Jan. 1, 1969. The $5 million limitation does not apply in the case of bonds held by a firm occupying a facility constructed out of proceeds of the bond issue.

ple majority vote on the question." Limitations that tie local debt or debt service to the local base for property taxation should be replaced. The commission implied that the states might find a substitute control "by reference to the net interest cost of prospective bond issues in relation to the currently prevailing interest rate on high quality municipal securities." In any case, state provisions concerning local indebtedness should "take cognizance of all forms of local borrowing and debt."[34]

In 1941 Professor Ratchford took a cautious attitude toward change. The legislatures of some states for many decades had borrowed "with discretion," despite the absence of limitations.[35] The legislatures of some other states were, in his view, less to be trusted. At present a bolder position seems indicated. Limitations on the state legislative power to borrow have probably had little effect in restraining borrowing and they have had a bad effect on the form of debt. Borrowing by nonguaranteed debt has been stimulated, and, except for limited purposes, this is an imprudent instrumentality. State constitutions should be overhauled to limit the use of nonguaranteed debt to specified self-financing purposes, and to repeal constitutional and statutory limitations on legislative borrowing power.

34. *State Constitutional and Statutory Restrictions*, pp. 4 and 5.
35. Connecticut, Delaware, Massachusetts, and Vermont are mentioned; *American State Debts*, p. 592. The first three had low per capita state debts in 1941, but by 1973 they all had high debts.

CHAPTER TEN

Earmarked Revenues, Retirement Systems, and Capital Budgets

If to do were as easy as to know what were good to do, chapels had been churches, and poor men's cottages princes' palaces.

The Merchant of Venice

IN MAKING fiscal decisions, executive officers and legislative bodies of state and local governments are concerned with satisfying the public desires that fall within their jurisdiction. The task of spending, taxing, and borrowing to meet these demands is one of efficient allocation of resources, and a budgetary process has evolved that is designed to provide the necessary funds and to establish priorities of need.

This state-local job differs from the federal budgetary process in two major respects: it is concerned only minimally with problems of economic stabilization, and with alterations in the distribution of income and wealth. Stabilization is a national objective for which responsibility must rest chiefly with Congress and the federal executive. While state-local budgeting may perhaps be arranged to assist federal action, such efforts are supplementary. That alterations in the distribution of income are a federal responsibility may be less obvious

215

and, in practice, has not been accepted by state governments. Nonetheless, the possibility of interstate movement of people and resources limits the force of state initiative in this area.

Behind the state-local budgetary process lie policy decisions. These are rooted in the past; year-by-year alterations can only affect details. Provision of most state and local services must continue, subject to modest enlargement and contraction. But new social objectives do emerge that may, in time, be translated into governmental policies, and then into governmental provision.

Most of the problems of governmental decisionmaking lie in the field of political science. Three issues that are now topics for sharp debate and that are important to the budgetary process—earmarking, retirement systems, and capital budgets—are discussed here.

The Budgetary Process

State and local budgeting aims at an accurate determination of governmental needs and an efficient appraisal of how these needs can be met. Competing needs must be weighed, and revenues must be raised and allotted to them. After formulation and enactment, budget programs must be executed according to plan.

The time period of a budget depends on the timing of legislative sessions. In about a third of the states, sessions are biennial and therefore budgets must be planned for a two-year period. Local budgets are for a one-year period. A fiscal year may, but usually does not, coincide with the calendar year. The most common opening and closing dates are July 1 and June 30, respectively. However, since the federal government has moved to an October 1–September 30 fiscal year, a similar change can be expected at the state-local level.

A standard textbook rule is that a budget should be comprehensive —all expenditures and receipts should be reported in it. Only in this way can proper allocations be made. In practice comprehensiveness is seldom achieved, and for understandable reasons. Some types of spending seem to require different and special treatment. For example, government enterprises are excluded from the budgetary process in an effort to secure nonpolitical and efficient business-type operation. What of capital expenditures, which are irregular and often provided by borrowing? And what of special funds, with earmarked tax revenues? Have they features that justify their exclusion from the budgetary process?

The first step in governmental budgeting is preparation of the budget. This should be the job of the executive and, in almost all states and a growing number of cities, this is the case. An executive budget is constructed and presented. But the force of executive recommendations may be strong or weak. It is weak when important agencies, or departments, or activities are exempt from executive control. In some states, departments headed by elective officers are exempt on the ground that they receive a direct mandate from the electorate. Activities financed by earmarked revenues, and those of business-type enterprises, are usually free from executive control since they depend on assigned or earned revenues and do not compete in the budgetary process with other programs. Budgets of the judiciary and the legislature are exempt in conformity with the theory of separation of governmental powers. Similarly, the budgets of institutions of higher learning—the "fourth branch" of government—are frequently quite free from executive control.

Most—perhaps all—states require the state government, and local governments as well, to present a balanced budget. This does not mean that current expenditures and revenues must equate, but merely that any excess of expenditures is covered by borrowing. Authorized receipts from loans serve to balance the budget. The balance is often tricky. Estimates of revenue are frequently higher, and those of expenditure lower, than a candid appraisal would provide. At the local level, fudging of this sort may be curbed by requiring that local estimates be reviewed by a state authority; it is less easy to curb at the state level.

The form in which the budget should be presented to the legislature has been much debated. A line-item budget shows estimates of the sums needed to provide specific objects—salaries for so many clerks, sums for purchase of office supplies, and so on. It leans heavily on prior expenditures, and it does not indicate what the clerks are to do or what the supplies will be used for. When a government is small, this method is useful both to the executive and to the legislature. But when the government is large, a line-item budget becomes bulky and incomprehensible; it conceals any view of functions or programs. Executives, legislatures, and citizens should be concerned with what government is trying to do, and with reckoning the cost of a program in comparison with what it provides. Budgets should therefore be framed on a functional basis, with subdivisions that indicate what functions will be performed.

After the budget has been framed, the next step is its transmittal to the legislative body. The primary job of the legislative branch is to examine, modify, and approve the budget. In a state where the budgetary powers of the executive are large, agencies are expected to support the budget as presented. But sometimes this is not the situation. Instead, elected officials make requests to the legislature that do not coincide with what the budget offers.

The most common legislative organization at the state level for review of the budget provides for an appropriations and revenue committee in each house. As at the federal level, the drawback to this procedure is that separate consideration of expenditure and revenue results, and that repetitive presentation, appraisal, and recommendation occur. Modifications exist in some states—one appropriations committee and one revenue committee, or a combined appropriations and revenue committee. The efficiency of legislative examination depends heavily on proper staffing, since members of the legislature cannot themselves find time to analyze budgetary programs in detail. In a few states the power of the legislature to alter the budget—especially the power to add items—is restricted. In New York, for example, the legislature may eliminate or reduce items; it may add items only if they are "stated separately and distinctly from the original items of the bill and refer each to a single object or purpose."[1] Moreover, legislative alteration of a budget has been curbed by giving governors the right of item veto; the curb is even more effective when the governor has the power not only to veto, but also to reduce, items.

Execution of the budget is the step in the budgetary process that follows legislative approval. Expenditure must not only go to the proper purposes, it must also be properly timed. Usually a schedule is set up by which a flow of money will be made available to be spent. This ensures a pattern of spending that fits appropriations, and the executive may be empowered to modify the pattern in the light of changed conditions. The legislature in providing appropriations recognizes that some flexibility must be allowed in execution of the

1. New York Constitution, art. 7, sec. 4.

budget, usually by permitting the transfer of items within broad categories. Flexibility at different phases of the business cycle has received little explicit recognition in state budgets. New York, however, has enacted a simple and logical scheme. Two tax reserves were set up in 1946, one for local assistance and the other for the remainder of the state budget. An operating surplus is transferred to, or a deficit is withdrawn from, these reserves. By this device state spending in recession can be maintained or expanded, and, at the same time, the budget kept in balance as the law requires.

In postwar years, as governmental activities have grown, application of new managerial techniques to the budgetary process has been a dramatic development. Program and performance budgets, accrual accounting, integrated purchasing—these and others have been applied by some state and local governments. The old objective of checking irregularities, which inspired the early advocates of formal budgeting, has been supplemented by the objective of making the budget a positive tool in the appraisal of competing uses for government money. Before performance budgeting was brought to public attention by the Hoover Commission, some state and local governments had utilized functional or program budgeting which separated the budget items into program areas. A legislative body, limited in the time it can give to details, should economize on the attention it devotes to separate items and focus on programs. "There now are procedures for costing out work and activities, projecting future spendings, and presenting program comparisons."[2]

In the early 1960s the Department of Defense experimented with planning techniques, and these efforts led President Johnson in 1965 to direct most federal departments to apply planning-programming-budgeting systems (PPB) to their programs. Interest among state and local officials heightened, and an intergovernmental, pilot demonstration of planning-programming-budgeting systems was undertaken in five cities, five counties, and five states.[3]

The distinctive characteristics of PPB are: identification of governmental objectives; explicit consideration of future implications;

2. Allen Schick, *Budget Innovation in the States* (Brookings Institution, 1971), p. 192.
3. State-Local Finances Project of the George Washington University, directed by Selma J. Mushkin. See Harry P. Hatry and John F. Cotton, *Program Planning for State, County, City* (State-Local Finances Project of the George Washington University, 1967).

consideration of all pertinent costs; and systematic analysis of alternatives. The process of program analysis is, of course, complicated by difficulties in obtaining quantitative measures for many economic and social aspects of programs, especially when those programs serve various objectives. At present, program analysis usually lacks rigor; it consists of a question and answer review that provides decision-makers with a rational ordering of alternatives, rather than cost-benefit analysis.

After attracting much attention for several years, planning-programming-budgeting lost ground. Allen Schick reported in 1971 that "in spite of the fact that most state budget officials profess an interest in PPB, there are few success stories to emulate, few examples of what works, and no solid evidence of the benefits to be derived from PPB. The traditions established in earlier years continue to dominate the budget process, while PPB stands on the outside, a fashionable but peripheral feature of state administration."[4]

Earmarked Revenues

Earmarking may be defined as a restriction imposed on the use to which a governmental revenue may be put. The legislative body is required by statute or by constitutional provision to channel certain revenues to specified purposes. Quite commonly earmarking is accomplished by providing special funds, which are not included in the budget. But sometimes revenue that flows into the general fund may have its use restricted.

Earmarking is much more extensively used at the state level than at the federal or local level of government. Local budgets earmark the revenue from special assessments and use it to pay the cost of improvements, such as construction of a boulevard; revenue from fees collected for hunting and fishing licenses is earmarked and used to support related governmental activities; revenue or contributions collected for employee retirement funds are earmarked for benefit payments. More important, and more questionable on logical grounds, is the financing of local education almost everywhere by earmarked revenues, especially property tax collections. Although there are but a few purposes for which revenues are earmarked at the federal level, the dollar amount is large. Table 10-1 shows that in

4. *Budget Innovation in the States,* p. 103.

Table 10-1. Governmental Insurance Trust Revenue by Purpose and by Level of Government, 1973

Billions of dollars

Purpose	Federal	State	Local	Total
Unemployment compensation	0.1	4.9	*	5.1
Employee retirement	2.1	8.3	1.8	12.2
Old-age, survivors, disability, and health insurance benefits	56.1	...	...⎫	57.3
Railroad retirement	1.2	...	...⎭	
Other	0.7	1.5	...	2.1
Total	60.2	14.7	1.8	76.7

Source: U.S. Census Bureau, *Governmental Finances in 1972–73*, p. 27. Years are fiscal in all tables unless otherwise noted. Figures are rounded.

* Less than 0.05.

1973, federal insurance trust revenue was $60.2 billion. Earmarking for these purposes is sound practice. But earmarking by state governments goes far beyond these purposes; indeed, it is remarkable for its diversity.

Rationale

Many writers in the field of public finance have been critical of earmarking, and certainly the actual practice offers scope for legitimate criticism. But a rationale can be offered, resting on a linkage of benefits received by particular users of a governmental service and the taxes collected from them. A level of government will spend appropriately for some purpose such as provision of highways, and this expenditure will render particular and measurable benefits to highway users. Taxes may reasonably be imposed, and limited to highway users, in an amount that will roughly equate benefits and payments for each user. This is an example of indirect pricing. The government should not collect less in annual revenues than the cost of these services because, in such case, it would have to meet the deficiency by general taxes, levied according to ability or sacrifice. The government should not collect and use more because this would finance collective benefits through taxes raised from particular groups of taxpayers.[5] On

5. The argument is sometimes made, erroneously, that persons who are forced to pay particular levies should receive particular governmental services in return— that, for example, there should be a linkage between the collections of liquor and tobacco taxes and expenditure of the collections for the benefit of consumers of liquor and tobacco. This inverts the relationship. Government does not try to discover what benefits are received by users of liquor and tobacco. Its decision to

what ground could collection of more be justified? If this seemed to be a better method than any other by which to finance expenditures that yielded collective benefits. On what ground could collection of less be justified? If a legislature estimated that the collective benefits from the excess expenditure justified the levy of general taxes equal to the deficiency.

The abstract concepts of this rationale are, to be sure, not always readily applicable to clear-cut government functions or to administratively feasible taxes. Moreover, many types of state and local expenditure may seem to yield some benefits that are particular rather than collective. The loose statement has been made, for instance, that local expenditure for police, fire protection, streets, and so forth, benefits property and that therefore the property tax is a benefit levy. This is an unacceptable description. Property tax is assessed on the value of property as a general tax, without consideration of the value of the benefits accruing from local government expenditures. Most of these benefits accrue collectively to all residents of the community, regardless of how much or how little property they own or use.

Sometimes, however, the concepts are applied accurately, but to trivial situations. In Montana the constitution requires that the proceeds of a property tax on livestock be used to pay bounties for destruction of predatory animals. While this linkage between cost and benefit may be accurate, petty earmarking of this sort impairs efficient budgeting. The same fault is to be found with the earmarking of many regulatory fees and license charges.

Quite frequently, pragmatic—if illogical—reasons lie behind the earmarking. Pressure groups have sought to ensure that a type of government expenditure will be provided by revenues outside of the appropriation process. They wish to avoid the annual legislative scrutiny, evaluation, and vote of money. Assignment of all, or some part, of the revenue from a well-established tax fulfills their aim. The more socially significant the expenditure, or the more powerful the pressure group, the more persuasive will be the appeal to the legislature. The incidence of the allocated tax on individuals may be wholly unrelated to the benefits that individuals receive. Indeed, a tax

---

tax them grows chiefly out of the sumptuary purpose of limiting and controlling consumption. Taxation raises the price of the taxed product. In itself, this may not be an effective curb on consumption. But it is the only power of a sumptuary tax, and if government is not satisfied, other steps are available.

based on ability or sacrifice has no linkage with any particular governmental expenditure. The amount paid by an individual as income, sales, or property tax is unrelated to the benefits he receives either from aggregate or from particular government expenditures.

Another pragmatic reason for earmarking has been the association of a needed and widely approved expenditure with new and unpalatable methods of finance. When the city of New York, in 1934, introduced its retail sales tax, the proceeds were earmarked for welfare expenditures; when New Hampshire, in 1963, introduced a state lottery, it earmarked the expected receipts for education. After the new revenue measure has been enacted, inertia—and the obstacles in the way of statutory or constitutional alteration—leads to the continuance of artificial earmarking.

Defects

Even when earmarking meets the test of direct linkage of cost and benefit, it has the fault that it removes certain governmental revenues and expenditures from regular and periodic legislative control. For activities that are similar to those provided by government enterprise, this has recognized advantages. Government enterprises will ordinarily be run more efficiently if they are somewhat outside the budgetary process and if the legislature, when it wishes to act with respect to them, must do so by altering existing legislation. A parallel infringement of the budgetary process may be sensible when pricing for the service is indirect. But earmarking does impair the unity of the governmental budget. The total impact of government finance can be judged only when the spending and receipts of all special funds (or at least the algebraic sum of their surpluses and deficits) are added to those of the legislative budget.

Another practical and related defect is that numerous earmarking formulas, some quite intricate, complicate administration. Although this may seem to be a legislative aberration, subject to legislative remedy, it often arises because of attempts to make precise and exclusive tie-ins between particular services and tax collections.

When earmarking does not meet the test of direct linkage of cost and benefit—when finance of a general or collective function of government is segregated from other functions—its faults are more serious. In such case the legislature is abdicating an essential duty. It should, through the budgetary process, determine the appropriate

Table 10-2. Distribution of States by Percentage of Tax Collections Earmarked, 1954 and 1963

	Number of states	
Percentage	*1954*[a]	*1963*
90–100	0	0
80–90	4	2
70–80	6	2
60–70	6	7
50–60	8	9
40–50	14	7
30–40	4	13
20–30	2	3
10–20	1	1
Up to 10	2	5
None	1[b]	1[c]

Source: Tax Foundation, *Earmarked State Taxes* (New York: Tax Foundation, 1965), p. 12 and appendix tables.

a. Alaska and Hawaii not included.
b. Delaware.
c. Georgia; but gasoline taxes, which are paid into the general fund, are used to set the subsequent year's appropriations.

expenditure for each collective function, and also indicate how the annual revenues are to be provided. Except when particular expenditures and revenues are naturally linked, failure to make such decisions will allow the levels of particular expenditures and revenues to become too large or too small in relation to current needs. For example, the annual revenue from a state meals tax, earmarked for payment of old-age assistance, may be larger or smaller than is needed to meet established standards. Earmarking delays recognition of the situation and, even more, it delays rectification. Excessive segmentation—multiplication of special funds—builds rigidities into the aggregate revenue system. In the early sixties the state government of Michigan, which constitutionally earmarked nearly 60 percent of its tax revenues, faced chronic fiscal crises chiefly because of the inflexibility of its revenue system. Deficits in the general fund could not be met by special fund revenues.

Status

Earmarking is provided for either constitutionally or by statute. Current material showing the status of earmarking can be gleaned only by laborious scrutiny of state budget reports, diverse in accounting practices and tax classifications. The Tax Foundation's compilations for 1954 and 1963, summarized in table 10-2, show that in

Table 10-3. Distribution of States by Percentage of Constitutionally Earmarked Tax Revenue, 1960

Percentage	Number of states
60–70	1
50–60	2
40–50	3
30–40	11
20–30	6
10–20	2
Up to 10	6
None	15
Not available	4[a]

Source: Citizens Research Council of Michigan, *Constitutional Earmarking of State Tax Revenues*, research paper 7 (Detroit: The Council, 1962), pp. 7–8.

a. Alabama, Oregon, Mississippi, and Georgia.

1954 twenty-four states earmarked over half of their tax collections, but by 1963 the number had dropped to twenty. The average had declined from 51.3 percent to 41.1 percent because of removal of some earmarking provisions and growth of tax revenues that were not earmarked. In 1960 thirty-five states had some constitutional earmarking. For thirty-one of these states the percentages of tax revenues so earmarked are shown in table 10-3. Fifteen states had no constitutional earmarking, although some of them earmarked by statute. Unfortunately, no current data are available to determine whether or not there are any trends in the use of this financing technique.

HIGHWAY USER TAXES. For many years federal policy encouraged the states to earmark all motor fuel tax revenue for highway purposes. Diversion to other purposes was frowned upon. When the depression of the 1930s pushed a number of states into using some of this revenue for relief and education, Congress responded in 1934 by passing the Hayden-Cartwright Act which penalized such diversion by cutting federal grants for highway construction. A federal motor fuel tax was first imposed in 1931. Not until twenty-five years later, with the Highway Revenue Act of 1956, was revenue from it earmarked. Thereafter, a large slice of the revenue from the motor fuel tax and from the manufacturers' excises on automobiles, trucks, parts, tires, and so on—over $3 billion a year—was assigned to the Highway Trust Fund.

Earmarking of a large portion of highway user revenues for the purposes of highway construction and maintenance is now given widespread approval. These taxes provide indirect pricing of the benefits of highway use. To be sure, some collective benefits accrue (although how much is still a matter of controversy) and therefore some part of the cost of highways may be placed on revenues from other sources. Moreover, it is clear that, over time, assignment of revenues by type of highway has been inaccurate, notably by favoring nonurban roads. Part of the explanation is that allocation formulas get out of date, and yet are inflexible against alteration. And until recently rural areas were overrepresented in state legislatures and in Congress. At any rate, the amount of motor fuel tax and of other user charges paid by an individual can only be a rough measure of the benefits received by this individual. These are important flaws in the application of indirect pricing, and they admit of no sure remedy.

At present the old controversy concerning diversion is being re-kindled. State governments may spend more for highways than they collect from highway users, and when this is so, diversion makes no sense. But an excess of highway user revenue may be an appropriate way to finance nonhighway expenditures. The motor fuel tax, in such cases, is as a good a source of general revenue as many other taxes currently in use.

DEBT SERVICE. State governments have very often assigned spe-cific taxes, or some segments of them, to service specific security issues. This practice complicates the debt structure and builds up a confusing system of prior and subordinate liens on state revenues for different issues. The correct technique is to declare by statute (or even constitutional provision) that debt obligations are to be secured by a preferred and equal claim on the general fund. The state credit would thereby be enhanced and the cost of borrowing reduced. Bor-rowing would have an immediate and direct impact on general fund revenues; it might, therefore, encourage responsible borrowing de-cisions.

MISCELLANEOUS EARMARKED REVENUES. The justification of ear-marking for such purposes as retirement funds, unemployment insur-ance, and workmen's compensation is rooted in their origins. At the outset all of these schemes leaned heavily on the analogy of private insurance. Contributors made payments that earned them the right to benefits; they were thus insured against the danger of legislative cuts in their subsequent receipts. General taxpayers were assured that benefits, being linked to contributions, would not be liberal-ized for political reasons. With the growth and acceptance of these systems the social aspects of social insurance have become more important, especially in the federal systems. But the linkage of contributions and benefits does seem to have induced responsible legislative behavior, and therefore earmarking remains justifiable.

EDUCATION. State governments have been very eclectic in their choice of taxes earmarked for education, since no major type is unutilized. Indeed, in many states part of the revenue from several taxes is pledged. The broad-based and productive taxes on retail sales and income are most utilized. In all of this there is no linkage of cost and benefit. The benefits that flow from governmental expenditure for primary and secondary education are mainly collective, and the costs should, therefore, be provided through general taxes. In this sense the practice of many states is correct. But earmarking all or part of these revenues is questionable since there is no provision for recurrent legislative appraisal of what the state government spends in aid to education. Another drawback is the variation in annual amounts available from earmarked taxes as economic conditions change.

PUBLIC WELFARE. Earmarking revenues for public welfare was a phenomenon of the 1930s. Many states, in order to finance the great expansion of welfare payments, introduced sales taxes and pledged all or part of the receipts. The same period witnessed the repeal of prohibition and, as states secured new revenues from taxation or sale of alcoholic beverages, some chose to assign them to welfare expenditure. However, in recent years, as other demands on state budgets have grown in relative importance, state reliance on earmarked taxes to finance welfare has lessened.

LOCAL GENERAL PURPOSES. The practice of earmarking revenues for local general purposes developed over many decades as state governments removed some types of property from the local property tax base. A revenue-equivalent was usually promised. A number of state-collected locally shared taxes emerged, and in many states the practice continues. It is, however, of declining importance. Moreover, since in many states the local governments are allowed to spend their allocations as they choose, no specific earmarking occurs.

Conclusion

The popularity of earmarking is a major illustration of the distrust shown by voters in the wisdom and integrity of state legislatures. A group of citizens, deeply interested in state performance of a particular activity, will try to free that activity from legislative control by having earmarked funds provided for it. Legislatures often acquiesce, debarring themselves from periodic exercise of judgment concerning segments of the state budget. This practice also hampers the chief executive of a state who should frame a budget with full knowledge of how all state governmental resources are utilized and with freedom to recommend changes. Earmarking limits the powers of the executive. When the limitation has a logical rationale—a linkage of benefits and costs—the advantages outweigh the disadvantages. Some students of public finance would, however, limit the autonomy even of legitimate earmarking by requiring legislative appropriation of the maximum amount to be used in a budgetary period, and reversion of surpluses to the general fund. These two restrictions seem misdirected; they would interfere with the efficient operation of government activities.

What is required is effective compromise between independent operation and periodic legislative scrutiny. Just as governmental enterprises need to be free from legislative heckling, so do those activities for which earmarking is legitimate. And yet some periodic legislative scrutiny is necessary in order to weigh performance of the governmental activities.

State and Local Retirement Systems

The retirement system of a state or local government is a complex financial arrangement.[6] A package of benefits must be agreed upon and a financing scheme must be adopted. Eligibility rules for membership must be established. A variety of matters must be carefully weighed: whether employees should be accepted into the plan immediately or should serve a probationary period; what kind of benefits should be provided (should disability, death, and survivor benefits be included, or should the plan be limited to providing pensions to retirees?); whether benefits should be set as a fraction of the employee's average salary or be determined by the future value of the periodic contributions made by the employee and his government employer;

6. This section is adapted from David J. Ott, Attiat F. Ott, James A. Maxwell, and J. Richard Aronson, *State-Local Finances in the Last Half of the 1970s* (Washington: American Enterprise Institute for Public Policy Research, 1975), chaps. 3 and 4.

how rights to the government's contribution become vested in the employee before retirement; what the retirement age will be, and whether early retirement should be permitted.

Retirement systems contain so many features that it is not surprising to find wide variations in the plans adopted by state and local governments. Yet it is possible to describe a typical plan.[7] The most common benefit formula bases the employee's annual pension on the number of years he has worked multiplied by 1.67 percent of his average salary in the five highest-paid of his last ten years of service. Thus an individual who has worked for thirty years retires with a pension equal to 50 percent of his final average salary. A cost-of-living adjustment guarantees that pension benefits will increase with the consumer price index up to a maximum of 3 percent a year.

Retirement is compulsory at age seventy. For an employee with at least ten years of service, the normal retirement age is sixty and the early retirement age, at a reduced pension, is fifty-five. The same is true for an employee who leaves after ten years of service and does not withdraw his contributions; this means that the government's contributions become vested in the employee after ten years of service.[8]

A disability pension is provided for those who have at least ten years of service. The benefit is guaranteed to be not less than 25 percent of final average salary unless that amount exceeds what the employee would receive under normal retirement at age sixty. The service requirement is waived if the disability was the result of a job-connected accident.

The typical plan includes a variety of death benefits. If an employee dies after at least one year of employment, his beneficiary is entitled to a half year's salary. If he has been employed for ten years, the benefit is usually a full year's salary. If the employee dies at a time he is eligible to retire, his widow is entitled to an annuity equal to what she would have received if he had retired just before his death.

Some 160 of the largest systems, representing about 80 percent of

7. See Robert Tilove, *Public Employee Pension Funds* (Columbia University Press, 1976), chap. 2.

8. For a discussion of vesting provisions in retirement plans, see Joseph J. Melone and Everett T. Allen, *Pension Planning: Pensions, Profit Sharing, and Other Deferred Compensation Plans* (Irwin, 1966), p. 53; and *Bulletin of the Commission on Insurance Terminology of the American Risk and Insurance Association,* vol. 1, no. 4.

the total membership in retirement plans, use actuarially determined contribution rates with the objective of becoming fully funded.[9]

Methods of Funding and Intergeneration Equity

The alternative schemes for financing a pension system range between pay-as-you-go financing and a fully funded approach. From a narrow point of view, the cost of a pension plan to the community as a whole is the same no matter what financing scheme is adopted. Assume that a governmental unit enters into a pension arrangement with some of the employees, that it agrees to pay the full costs of the plan, and that its expected payments to pensioners will be zero in the first three years of the plan, $100 in the fourth and fifth years, and zero thereafter.[10] If the plan is financed on a pay-as-you-go basis, the $100 payments in the fourth and fifth years will, with a 5 percent rate of discount, cost the government (in present value terms) $160.70.

The government might, however, consider funding the pension plan with a single lump-sum contribution at the time the plan is initiated. The amount needed to cover all of the obligations of the plan is, of course, $160.70. Assuming a 5 percent rate of interest, $160.70 will grow to $195.33 by the end of the fourth year. At that time $100 must be paid to pensioners. The $95.33 left in the trust fund will grow to $100 by the end of the fifth year, providing exactly the amount needed for pensioners.

The amount needed to finance the benefits could also be accumulated by equal annual contributions of $45.32 over four years. Assuming a 5 percent rate of interest, these contributions will grow to $195.33 in four years. The cost to the government of this plan is the same as the cost of the other two plans. The present value of four payments of $45.32 at a 5 percent rate of discount is $160.70.

The fact that the present value of the future obligations of a pension plan is not affected by the method of finance does not mean, however, that the schemes are equally satisfactory. A pay-as-you-go system has some undesirable features. For example, for the pension plans of private firms, pure pay-as-you-go financing offers no security to the claims of pensioners. If the fortunes of the firm were to take a bad turn, there would be pressure on the firm to renege on its promise and reduce the level of pension benefits. If the firm were to go bank-

9. See Tax Foundation, *State and Local Employee Pension Systems* (New York: Tax Foundation, 1969), pp. 28–29.
10. This example is drawn from Ott and others, *State-Local Finances*, pp. 66.

rupt, the claims of pensioners would be worthless. Under a trust fund (the fully funded approach) the assets of the retirement system would be segregated from the other assets of the firm and as a result the claims of the pensioners would be protected.[11]

The chance of a state or city ceasing operations is slight. Moreover, the rights of public employees to their pensions are protected by law. Thus, the reasons for using the fully funded approach in public employee retirement systems must be something more than the protection of the claims of retired and active workers. The trust fund (fully funded) approach is preferable to a pay-as-you-go approach because some degree of intergeneration equity between present and future taxpayers is assured and because the governmental unit is protected from potential fiscal strain.

The problem of intergeneration equity is seen most clearly in the government's financial obligations to the plan. Under pay-as-you-go provisions, the pension benefits due in each year are financed by general taxation in that year. Tax rates to finance pension benefits need not rise over time as long as the tax base (income and wealth of the community) rises at a higher rate than that at which pension benefits rise. Continuous growth in the wealth of states and cities, however, is not to be expected. The population and the tax base of some states and cities will decrease, and the number of public employees and membership in retirement plans are likely to fall also. Nevertheless, the level of pension benefits will not decrease for a considerable period of time. If it is assumed that any existing employee contribution rate is held constant and that there is no trust fund, then the burden of the pension plan would be felt in the form of higher tax rates. A pay-as-you-go system will present a problem of intergeneration equity, since, to support the plan, future residents of the community will face higher tax rates than current residents. Moreover, the necessary increase in tax rates, at a time when the tax base is shrinking, will aggravate the fiscal problems of the community and for smaller governmental units may even lead to further reductions in the tax base.[12]

11. Of course, it is impossible to provide perfect protection for the claims of pensioners. Trust fund assets can be mismanaged and private insurance companies can fail.

12. For an analysis of how changes in tax rates can induce changes in the tax base of a community, see J. Richard Aronson and Eli Schwartz, "Financing Public Goods and the Distribution of Population in a System of Local Governments," *National Tax Journal*, vol. 26 (June 1973), pp. 137–60.

The fully funded approach avoids these problems. Since the employee and the government (taxpayers) contribute to the fund when pension liabilities accrue rather than when payments are made, intergeneration equity is preserved.[13] Moreover, higher future tax rates to finance benefits are not inevitable when the tax base of the governmental unit declines. The trust fund and its interest earnings, along with a constant government contribution rate based on covered payroll, provide the funds to meet benefit payments. As long as the community tax base does not decrease at a faster rate than covered payroll, tax rates need not rise.

Trends and Future Outlook

In recent years, membership in state and local government retirement systems has expanded more rapidly than has the number of state and local employees. In 1972, 98 percent of full-time employees were members of the state and local systems—a figure that must be close to the practical ceiling. Future growth in membership is likely to do no more than keep pace with growth in employment, and the likelihood is that employment will not rise at the pace of the last decade. No less than 2,304 different state and local retirement systems were in operation in 1972. Although they do have a common form and pattern, the variation among them in size and composition of membership, amount of assets, and financial structure of payments and benefits is great. In 1972 the 157 largest systems contained 93 percent of total membership. Nonetheless, small systems persist: 1,437 of the systems had fewer than 100 members in 1972.

The diversity of the systems means that it is impossible to make generalizations about their finances. Systems that are new and expanding in membership have few current beneficiaries and a considerable excess of annual receipts over annual payments. Older systems have a relatively large number of beneficiaries and a rising annual ratio of payments to receipts. The diversity is compounded because some systems, even when new, pursue a full-funding policy, while others operate on a pay-as-you-go basis, and still others in between.

13. At the time when the plan is initiated or when benefit provisions are liberalized, current employees are given past service credits even though no contributions have been made in their behalf. This financial obligation is usually referred to as a supplemental unfunded balance and generally amortized over a rather lengthy period. These credits interfere with intergeneration equity because their costs must be spread over future generations.

Table 10-4. Number of Beneficiaries and Ratio of Beneficiaries to Membership in State and Local Retirement Systems, 1957, 1962, 1967, and 1972[a]

Item	1957	1962	1967	1972
	Thousands of beneficiaries			
Benefit base				
Normal retirement	424.2	600.2	844.5	1,241.0
Disability	43.4	60.7	77.2	92.3
Survivors	54.8	78.1	108.2	130.1
Total	522.4	739.1	1,029.8	1,463.4
	Percentage of total membership			
Beneficiaries in system				
All systems	13.0	13.8	14.6	16.1
State administered	9.3	10.5	11.7	13.9
Locally administered	24.2	26.3	27.5	26.7

Sources: Census Bureau, *Census of Governments, 1967*, vol. 6, no. 2, *Employee-Retirement Systems of State and Local Governments* (1968), p. 10; and *1972*, vol. 6, no. 1, *Employee Retirement Systems of State and Local Governments* (1973), p. 10. Figures are rounded.
a. Last month of fiscal year.

This diversity means that, over time, trends are obscured. They are further obscured because of the time lag in the impact of most changes in a system. Lowering the retirement age, for example, affects immediately only the annual trickle of members who retire. Higher benefit payments affect existing retirees, and they are only a fraction of membership. In short, financial liberalization (or retrenchment) of a retirement system has a lagged rather than an immediate affect.

Among significant overall changes in retirement systems is the rise in the ratio of beneficiaries to membership between 1957 and 1972 from 13.0 percent to 16.1 percent (see table 10-4). In 1972, the ratio of beneficiaries to membership in locally administered systems in eighteen states was 30.0 percent or more, while this ratio was reached in only one state under state-administered plans. Receipts of all systems grew remarkably, and the growth was attributable, aside from the growth in membership, to growth in the rate of earnings on investments from 2.78 percent in 1957 to 5.05 percent in 1972 (see table 10-5). This growth was marked by a shift in the composition of assets. In 1957 two-thirds, and in 1972 only 9 percent, of assets were in the form of government securities. As table 10-6 shows, the systems had turned sharply to nongovernmental securities, including corporate stocks. Although the shift was not yet complete in 1972, growth in the rate of earnings on investments could not reasonably be expected to continue to rise. The responsibility of providing future payments

Table 10-5. Assets and Earnings of State and Local Retirement Systems, 1957, 1967, and 1972

Year	Book value of assets	Earnings on investments	Average rate of return on investments
	Millions of dollars		*Percent*
1957	12,834	357	2.78
1967	39,265	1,565	3.99
1972	68,760	3,471	5.05
	Relative value (1957 = 100)		
1957	100	100	100
1967	306	438	144
1972	536	972	182

Source: *Census of Governments, 1967*, vol. 6, no. 2, p. 11; and *1972*, vol. 6, no. 1, p. 10.

Table 10-6. Assets of State and Local Retirement Systems, 1957, 1962, 1967, and 1972

Type of asset	1957	1962	1967	1972
	Billions of dollars			
Governmental securities	8.4	10.2	9.1	6.1
Nongovernmental securities	4.2	12.8	29.7	61.8
Corporate bonds	3.4	9.5	20.3	37.9
Corporate stocks	0.2	0.7	2.4	12.6
Mortgages	0.5	2.1	4.8	7.0
Other	0.2	0.6	2.2	4.3
Cash	0.2	0.3	0.4	0.8
Total	12.8	23.3	39.3	68.8
	Percentage distribution			
Governmental securities	65.7	43.6	23.1	8.9
Nongovernmental securities	32.7	55.2	75.7	89.9
Corporate bonds	26.3	40.9	51.6	55.1
Corporate stocks	1.4	3.0	6.1	18.3
Mortgages	3.5	8.8	12.3	10.2
Other	1.4	2.5	5.7	6.2
Cash	1.7	1.2	1.1	1.1
Total	100.0	100.0	100.0	100.0

Source: Same as table 10-5. Figures are rounded.

to beneficiaries will thus fall more heavily on employee and government contributions, mostly on the latter. The governmental contribution has already risen substantially—it was $1.2 billion in 1957,
$3 billion in 1967, and $5.7 billion in 1972. Governmental contribution has accelerated and seems likely to accelerate further in the
years ahead as the systems mature and as benefit provisions are lib-

Table 10-7. Receipts and Payments of State and Local Retirement Systems, 1957, 1962, 1967, and 1972

Retirement system	1957	1962	1967	1972
All systems				
Receipts, in millions of dollars	2,455	3,997	6,580	12,620
Payments, in millions of dollars	958	1,589	2,684	4,920
Payments as a percentage of receipts	39.0	39.8	40.8	39.0
State administered				
Receipts, in millions of dollars	1,504	2,695	4,656	9,285
Payments, in millions of dollars	522	948	1,654	3,279
Payments as a percentage of receipts	34.7	35.2	35.5	35.3
Locally administered				
Receipts, in millions of dollars	951	1,302	1,924	3,336
Payments, in millions of dollars	437	641	1,030	1,641
Payments as a percentage of receipts	46.0	49.2	53.5	49.2

Sources: *Census of Governments, 1962*, vol. 6, no. 1, *Employee-Retirement Systems of State and Local Governments* (1963), p. 13; *1967*, vol. 6, no. 2, p. 11; and *1972*, vol. 6, no. 1, p. 10.

eralized, especially in response to inflation. No other elastic source for larger receipts will be available.

These generalizations are not wholly dependable because of the diversity of the various funds. Some of the funds recently have strengthened their finances, and as indicated in table 10-7 the ratio of payments to receipts of funds in the aggregate fell from 40.8 in 1967 to 39.0 in 1972. But the ratio in twenty-three states and the District of Columbia in 1972 exceeded 50.0 and in nine states exceeded 70.0. Perhaps the most vulnerable systems will be those of large cities with a declining population.

Projecting the financial position of state and local retirement systems through examination of the past record has a serious fault. Most of the current disbursements of a retirement system are the result of costs that accrued a generation earlier; they do not reflect costs that will accrue in the future. Prospective disbursements arising out of wage and salary adjustments or benefit improvements in the form of earlier retirement or larger payments need to be reckoned with. The best way to project costs is to apply actuarial methods that estimate the accrual of future costs and translate these costs into present values. This device implies a fully funded system.

Most of the 2,304 state and local retirement systems are partially funded. To ascertain the degree of funding of all of them is an undertaking of impressive magnitude because the individual differences in the systems are many and actuarial reports exist for very few. The

American Enterprise Institute has, however, developed an elementary present-value model of pension fund financing that can be used to project the potential future fiscal impact of retirement systems on state and local governments. The projections indicate that contributions to state-local trust funds will have to increase significantly over current levels if these systems are to approach a fully funded position in a reasonable period of time.[14]

Capital Budgets

At the state-local levels some kinds of expenditures raise special difficulties, notably those that are large and irregularly timed. Most commonly, these finance construction of new facilities yielding services over a considerable span of years. On the other hand, state and local governments have to make, year after year and with modest variation, expenditures for current services.

Simply as a matter of procedure, it makes sense to separate out in the budget those items that create special difficulties in planning and execution. School buildings, streets, sewage facilities, and so on, demand long-range planning, and their annual provision must be regularized in order to minimize the problems of financial support. Priorities have to be arranged in advance. In short, state and local governments find it sensible to bundle together certain items into a capital budget in order to facilitate financial planning and decisions. Nonetheless, the capital budget is properly a section of the total comprehensive budget. The total budget is a device for handling one-year segments of longer range operating and capital programs; comprehensiveness is a vital feature.

A capital budget[15] in this sense should be distinguished from the budgets of government enterprises. A government enterprise spends annually for capital and for current items, but none of its expendi-

14. Ott and others, *State-Local Finances*, chap. 4; it includes details of the pension fund projection model.

15. A descriptive account of state organizations for central capital budgeting—including the preparation, legislative review, and execution of capital budgets—is provided in A. M. Hillhouse and S. K. Howard, *State Capital Budgeting* (Council of State Governments, 1963). For an analysis of capital budgeting techniques, see J. Richard Aronson and Eli Schwartz, "Capital Budgeting," in Aronson and Schwartz, eds., *Management Policies in Local Government Finance* (Washington: International City Management Association, 1975).

tures is appropriated by a vote of the legislature. All of its budget should, ordinarily, be removed from the budgetary process (although the general budget should show any subsidy granted or revenue received from an enterprise). Similarly, trust funds as a whole are outside the budgetary process.

Pay As You Go versus Pay As You Use

What is the character of the items to be placed in a capital budget? Their distinctive feature is a yield of returns that stretches into the future. Such budget items, it is argued, should be financed by borrowing. Ordinary items that are consumed currently should be financed by annual taxes, on a pay-as-you-go basis, but items that are used over a considerable time period should be financed on a pay-as-you-use basis. The term of the borrowing should coincide with the life of the capital item, and the current budget should merely carry charges equal to interest and depreciation, paying off the principal of the debt as the benefits from the initial outlay are secured. Only through financing public durable goods by loans will intergenerational equity be provided. A project that yields services over many years should be paid for by people according to their use, so that an aged person pays less of the cost of a new project that a younger one. This principle, so Professor Musgrave states, is particularly important in municipal finance "where the composition of the resident group is subject to more or less frequent change."[16] An elderly person who became resident in a locality that, soon thereafter, made large expenditures on durable items that were financed on a pay-as-you-go basis would be treated inequitably. And so would a young person who became a resident in this locality just after a spate of capital expenditures had ended. In order to secure intergenerational equity, debt should be used to finance all public durable goods, the loan running for the life of a good and being paid off according to use by annual taxes. Equity requires that benefits received and payments made should coincide.

Another justification of loan finance relates to items of expenditure that are irregular in time and large in amount. Assume a small district is in need of a new school. If the whole cost were provided by raising

16. Richard A. Musgrave, *The Theory of Public Finance: A Study in Public Economy* (McGraw-Hill, 1959), p. 563.

tax rates for one or two years, the effects would be unnecessarily disturbing. One alternative would be to establish reserves that could be drawn on to meet such episodic expenditures; and still another would be to borrow to construct the school, raising annual taxes only enough to cover interest and depreciation. The irregularity argument for loan finance, however, can be overemphasized. The expenditure of a large, or even a moderate-sized, unit on each particular type of public works will be irregular, but the yearly aggregate expenditure is, or can be made, approximately constant.

Table 10-8 illustrates the effects of a shift from pay-as-you-go to pay-as-you use financing.[17] Assume that a government has a stream of capital projects yearly amounting to $1 million, and that its other expenditures are $4 million. If they were financed on a pay-as-you-go basis, and if the budget were balanced, the tax levy would be $5 million. But suppose the government shifts to a two-budget system, providing $1 million yearly by borrowing at 4½ percent with amortization on a ten-year basis. Table 10-8 and figure 10-1 indicate the financial effects of the shift. Tax collections—always assuming a balanced budget—would go down by $1 million in the first year minus annual amortization and interest. Thereafter, expenditures would gradually rise as interest and amortization rose. In the eighth year, the total collected in taxes to balance the current budget would be $5,034,000, that is, it would exceed the amount of yearly collections ($5 million) under the pay-as-you-go plan. In the tenth year, tax collections would be $5,247,500 and at that figure they would remain.

What would be the financial gain and loss by adoption of the capital budget? In the first year, tax collections would decrease by $855,000 ($1 million minus amortization of $100,000 and interest of $45,000). Thereafter, the tax levy would rise steadily until the tenth year in which it would stabilize. However, neither the decreases in tax collections of the first seven years nor the increases afterwards should be regarded as financial gains or losses to the community. The net present value (at 4½ percent) of the tax savings minus the tax

17. For a more detailed analysis of the differences between pay-as-you-go and pay-as-you-use financing, see James A. Maxwell and J. Richard Aronson, "The State and Local Capital Budget in Theory and Practice," *National Tax Journal*, vol. 20 (June 1967), p. 165–70; Earl R. Rolph, " 'Pay-As-You-Use Finance'; A Comment," and Maxwell and Aronson, "Reply," ibid., vol. 21 (June 1968), pp. 210–12 and 213–14.

Table 10-8. Illustrative Effect of Capital Budgeting on Total Annual Spending and Taxing
Dollars

| | Expenditures | | | | Tax collections | | | |
| | | Capital projects | | | Budgeting method | | | |
Year	Current	Interest	Amortization	Total	Pay as you go	Pay as you use	Decrease	Increase
1	4,000,000	45,000	100,000	4,145,000	5,000,000	4,145,000	855,000	...
2	4,000,000	85,500	200,000	4,285,500	5,000,000	4,285,500	714,500	...
3	4,000,000	121,500	300,000	4,421,500	5,000,000	4,421,500	578,500	...
4	4,000,000	153,000	400,000	4,553,000	5,000,000	4,553,000	447,000	...
5	4,000,000	180,000	500,000	4,680,000	5,000,000	4,680,000	320,000	...
6	4,000,000	202,500	600,000	4,802,500	5,000,000	4,802,500	197,500	...
7	4,000,000	220,500	700,000	4,920,500	5,000,000	4,920,500	79,500	...
8	4,000,000	234,000	800,000	5,034,000	5,000,000	5,034,000	...	34,000
9	4,000,000	243,000	900,000	5,143,000	5,000,000	5,143,000	...	143,000
10	4,000,000	247,500	1,000,000	5,247,500	5,000,000	5,247,500	...	247,500
11	4,000,000	247,500	1,000,000	5,247,500	5,000,000	5,247,500	...	247,500
12	a	a	a	a	a	a	a	a

a. No change.

Figure 10-1. Illustrative Effect of Capital Budgeting on Total Annual Spending and Taxing

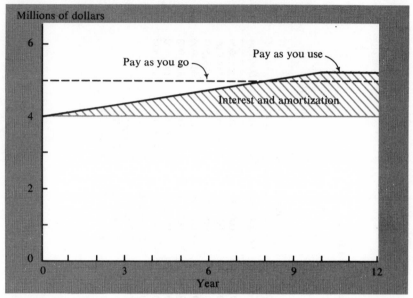

Source: Table 10-8.

increase is zero.[18] Therefore the choice between a pay-as-you-go and a pay-as-you-use system cannot be based on purely monetary considerations.[19]

Practical Difficulties

There are some practical difficulties involved in capital budgeting. Accurate depreciation of public durable consumer goods is hard to calculate, and borrowing has often been abused. Expenditure must be assumed to represent the value of an asset; estimates must be made of the time period of benefits from an outlay. In short, the apparatus of asset accounting should be applied. Depreciation rates for public consumer durables must be either quite subjective or quite routine. In Massachusetts the state law specifies the purposes for which local

18. The interest and debt repayment changes do, however, bring transfer costs and distributive effects that may be considered unfortunate.

19. Because of the tax exemption privilege on municipal bond interest, citizens of any one given community are better off borrowing through their government rather than individually. Thus there exists a tax-induced advantage to pay-as-you-use over pay-as-you-go financing.

governments may borrow, and the duration of the loans. The categories of purposes are broad: "stone, block, brick . . . or other permanent pavement of similar lasting character," "extension of water mains and for water departmental equipment," "remodeling [or] reconstructing . . . private buildings owned by the city or town," and so on. The investment value and the period of depreciation of each project in such categories should not be uniform; yet to determine an appropriate period for each would be difficult. For commercial outlays, public or private, such calculations rest on market factors that are moderately objective; for noncommercial public outlays, they rest on social appraisals, the nature of which defies analysis. The difficulty does not lie chiefly or wholly in the character of the goods. Individual consumer durables are quite frequently financed by formalized borrowing. In this way individuals try to synchronize individual benefit and cost over time. For public consumer durables a parallel process must assume a social judgment, so that a city council or state legislature balances social benefits against social costs for the city or state.

Should a capital budget be formulated to include only tangible assets? The argument has been made that this procedure rests on the business concept of net worth which is inappropriate for social accounting. Educational training, for instance, brings future benefits; it adds to the productivity of the economy over a period of years. But if such expenditure is accepted as an investment, what should be the time period of borrowing? What should be the depreciation rates?

The purport of these questions is that many unsolved operational issues prevent logical development of full-fledged capital budgets. The merit of capital budgets as a procedural device has been perceived by many state and local governments. But controversy over pay-as-you-go versus pay-as-you-use financing remains unresolved. As a practical compromise, a considerable slice of public consumer durables has been loan-financed without formal depreciation through the techniques of asset accounting. But state and local governments have utilized a rough and ready financial equivalent in the form of serial bonds, which mature in installments throughout the life of the issue. They have, moreover, sometimes indicated an intuitive awareness that social appraisals, unless restrained, are likely to lead to overborrowing with unfortunate long-run results. The financing of some capital items through the ordinary budget has, therefore, been customary. And state and local governments have failed to place "investment in human resources" in capital budgets, not so much because of a "prejudice in favor of expenditures on hardware"[20] as because of a complete inability to measure the effects of such investment on that part of the economy they can reach by taxes.

Adoption of full-fledged capital budgets, financed on a pay-as-you-use basis, would tend to amplify swings of the business cycle. Countercyclical financing calls for debt creation in recession and debt reduction in boom. A complete capital budget would infringe this rule by coupling debt creation with certain types of government spending, regardless of cyclical conditions. But if the device of capital budgets persuaded state and local governments to plan stable annual expenditures on a long-run basis, it could readily be adapted to serve countercyclical needs. This would require that, in a normal year, capital items be financed partly by pay-as-you-go methods and partly by borrowing. The former portion would be diminished in years of recession and enlarged in years of boom.

20. Musgrave, *The Theory of Public Finance,* p. 562.

CHAPTER ELEVEN

Whither State and Local Finance?

Read not to contradict and confute, nor yet to believe and take for granted, nor to find talk and discourse, but to weigh and consider.

Francis Bacon

THE FUTURE of state and local finance can be predicted by extrapolating past financial trends and modifying them according to expectations of change.[1] This, however, is neither an objective nor a certain technique, and it should, therefore, be regarded with a sturdy skepticism. Prior chapters have, moreover, occasionally recalled past predictions. Their frailty, even when made by experienced observers, should heighten skepticism. The course of history has often confounded the prophets.

Reallocation of Functions

As the preceding chapters have indicated, the performance of most civil functions is now the responsibility of state and local governments. The federal government plays a minor role. Forty years ago,

1. The title, as well as certain ideas in this chapter, are borrowed from an article by L. L. Ecker-Racz in *Journal of Finance*, vol. 19 (May 1964), pp. 370–81. See also the discussion of the article by Jesse Burkhead, ibid., pp. 385–89.

a semirevolution in the allocation of governmental functions erupted —the first in the history of the federation. But its force petered out with World War II, and in the postwar years a new intergovernmental equilibrium seems to have been established. Despite a marked expansion in the overall expenditure on major civil functions, the state-local share has been dominant and constant. This generalization hides some ambiguity. Through grants, the federal government participates in the financing of more civil services than ever before. But performance of the services has been left in state and local hands, subject to a modicum of federal conditions. Only occasionally, as in the case of the 1972 supplemental security amendment to the Social Security Act, which "nationalized" federal aid to the needy aged, blind, and disabled, have grants been a prelude to centralization.

This practice of cooperative federalism does not correspond to the theory of separation of functions that was in the minds of the Fathers of the Constitution. But the theory was infringed by practice from the beginning, so that nowadays, in the words of Morton Grodzins, "as colors are mixed in the marble cake, so functions are mixed in the American federal system. . . . From abattoirs and accounting through zoning and zoo administration, any governmental activity is almost certain to involve the influence, if not the formal administration, of all three planes of the federal system."[2] Even when the function receives no aid, intergovernmental collaboration is common. But grants have proliferated, and they enable Congress to recognize growth of a national interest in new functions, while leaving administration in state and local hands. State and local governments, responsive to the diversity of civilian needs and demands, secure financial assistance that enables them to achieve a level of performance acceptable to Congress. No reallocation of functions from the state to the federal level is required. And by passage of the State and Local Fiscal Assistance Act of 1972, Congress has enlarged its responsibility to provide financial aid with few or no strings.

Expenditure Trends: 1948–73

In the twenty-five years from 1948 to 1973, state and local expenditure for general government (less federal grants) rose by $123.5

2. "The Federal System," in *Goals for Americans,* Report of the President's Commission on National Goals (Prentice-Hall, 1960), pp. 265 and 266–67.

Table 11-1. State-Local General Expenditure, Excluding Federal Grants, by Function, 1948 and 1973

	Expenditure, in billions of dollars			*Percentage of total increase*
Function	*1948*	*1973*	*Increase*	
Education	5.0	60.9	55.9	45.3
Highways	2.7	13.3	10.6	8.6
Public welfare	1.4	11.5	10.1	8.2
Health and hospitals	1.2	12.1	10.9	8.8
Other	5.6	41.6	36.0	29.1
Total	15.9	139.4	123.5	100.0

Source: Table A-5. In all tables and figures, years are fiscal unless otherwise noted.

billion (from $15.9 billion to $139.4 billion). Some part of the rise was illusory, being attributable to a rise in the prices of what state and local governments bought. The relevant price rise during this period was approximately 196 percent, and deflation of state and local expenditures would reduce the figure for 1973 from $139.4 billion to $47.1 billion. In addition, population had grown by 42.9 percent and allowance for this increase would reduce the figure to $33.0 billion. If, therefore, the effects of both price and population changes are removed, the increase is not from $15.9 billion to $139.4 billion but from $15.9 billion to $33.0 billion, that is, by 108 percent. This figure indicates roughly the quantitative and qualitative growth from 1948 to 1973 in provision of goods and services by state and local governments.

What kinds of state and local expenditures grew most rapidly after deduction of expenditure financed by federal grants? What functions account for the aggregate increase of $123.5 billion? As would be expected, education is the leader, and nearly one-half ($55.9 billion of the $123.5 billion) went to it. Table 11-1 and figure 11-1 show that highways, public welfare, and health and hospitals account for another quarter of the increase. These four major functions together were responsible for nearly seven-tenths of the increase.

Very probably the aggregate price rise of 196 percent in state and local goods was reflected in the prices of goods for each of the major functions; certainly, unusual changes in school population, in the number of the aged, and in the number of motor vehicles help explain the particular functional increases in expenditure. Public school population rose much faster than did total population from 1948 to

Figure 11-1. Increase in State-Local General Expenditure, Excluding Federal Grants, for Civil Functions, 1948–73

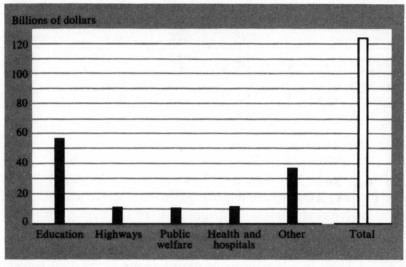

Source: Table 11-1.

1973 (95 percent compared to 43 percent), and so did enrollment in state and local institutions of higher education; the number of persons aged sixty-five and over increased by 85 percent; motor vehicle registration rose by more than 200 percent. The old and the young are heavy consumers of state and local expenditure on education, public welfare, and health and hospitals. Nonetheless, some real increase took place—qualitative and quantitative—per relevant unit for all of the functions.

Revenue Trends: 1948–73

The record of state and local governments in raising revenue during the years 1948–73 was remarkably good (see table 11-2 and figure 11-2). Nobody in the immediate postwar years predicted the yields that were, in fact, achieved. Total revenue from own sources grew almost tenfold. The largest absolute contributor to the increase was the property tax. Its receipts responded with unexpected elasticity to new construction, higher property values, and higher tax rates. The next largest amount was provided by taxes on sales and gross receipts—the retail sales tax and selective excises. Seventeen states enacted a retail sales tax during the years 1948–73; many states raised their rates and a few broadened their bases. All of these moves rein-

Table 11-2. State-Local General Revenue Collected from Own Sources, 1948 and 1973

	Revenue, in billions of dollars			Percentage of total increase
Source	1948	1973	Increase	
Taxes	13.3	121.1	107.8	79.6
Property	6.1	45.3	39.2	28.9
Sales and gross receipts	4.4	42.0	37.6	27.7
Individual income	0.5	18.0	17.5	12.9
Corporation income	0.6	5.4	4.8	3.5
Other	1.6	10.4	8.8	6.5
Charges and miscellaneous	2.0	29.8	27.8	20.5
Total	15.4	150.9	135.5	100.0

Sources: U.S. Census Bureau, *Historical Statistics of the United States: Colonial Times to 1957* (GPO, 1960); and Census Bureau, *Governmental Finances in 1972–73*, p. 20. Intergovernmental revenues grew by $41.5 billion (from $1.6 billion to $43.1 billion) from 1948 to 1973 (see table 3-1). Figures are rounded.

Figure 11-2. Increase in State-Local General Revenue Collected from Own Sources, 1948–73

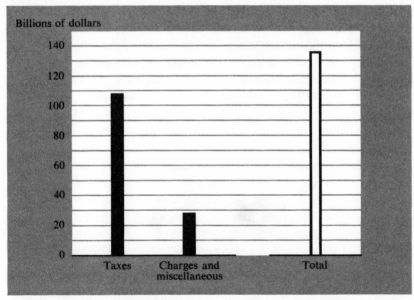

Source: Table 11-2.

forced the revenue productivity of the rapid rise in consumption. Eleven states enacted a broad-based tax on individual income during the period 1948–73. The important forces behind the remarkable growth in receipts were the rising base, improved administration (especially by withholding), and small increases in the level of rates.

The revenue elasticity of the income tax is high. "Charges and miscellaneous" added more than one-fifth of the total increase in revenue from own sources.

Federal Intergovernmental Transfers

The revenues of state and local governments have, for many decades, been supplemented by federal grants. The upsurge in grants in the 1960s was, however, paralleled only by the emergency (and temporary) grants of the 1930s. While state and local revenue from own sources rose almost tenfold from 1948 to 1973, that from federal grants grew almost twenty-sevenfold (from $1.6 billion to $43.1 billion). In 1948, grants to local governments were small, but by 1973 they amounted to $11.1 billion—one-quarter of the total of $43.1 billion. The tumultuous growth of federal grants in the 1960s raised or aggravated many problems. State governments, and local governments even more, could not keep track of the services for which grants were available; they could not cope with the great variety of formulas, application forms, reporting requirements, and so on, that arose. Those recipient governments with the personnel and the wit to keep abreast of what was offered usually did well. But they were seldom the governments most in need of federal assistance. Gamesmanship was rewarded; financial need was not. Many of the principles on which grants were justified were obscured by a cloud of bureaucratic red tape.

A backlash developed that demanded consolidation of specific-purpose grants into bundles or blocks, with allocation of the grants by formula rather than by application to federal authorities. Moreover, a strong agitation for federal general-purpose grants arose and, as a response, Congress passed the State and Local Fiscal Assistance Act of 1972 which, over a period of five years, authorized grants of $30.2 billion, one-third to go to the state governments and two-thirds to local governments.

The federal government has therefore embarked on distribution of large and growing annual amounts of money to aid state and local governments in financing many services that have, or are thought to have, a national significance. The distribution is disorderly in many features—definition of eligibility, allocation formulas, administrative rules, reporting requirements. But it does represent a response to a perceived fiscal imbalance in American federalism. State and local governments have suffered from an excess of responsibility for provision of services in relation to the financial resources within their reach.[3] Federal grants are an important instrument by which the imbalance can be alleviated.

State-Local Intergovernmental Finances

In this book financial comparisons have usually been made, state by state, of aggregates of state plus local expenditure or revenue. The reason is that the division of responsibility for provision of services or the raising of revenue between a state government and the local governments that are its creatures varies widely among the fifty states. Some state governments themselves provide services that others leave in local hands and assist by grants. No simple explanation of these diversities can be offered; it is not possible to declare that, in principle, the one arrangement is clearly better than the other.

Overall, however, most state governments leave critical and unfulfilled responsibilities to their local units. Property tax is the one natural and normal source of major tax receipts for these units. But effective utilization of the tax requires state help, and the nexus of that help is the framing and enforcement of rules of behavior. Perverse use—competitive undervaluation and inaccuracies of assessment of individual properties—must be controlled, if not eliminated. Recently, local units in some states have levied nonproperty taxes, and in several large cities these have been fiscally productive. Nonetheless, the spread prompts forebodings that the distribution of employment and purchasing power may be distorted, that compliance and administrative costs will prove excessive, and that the structure of federalism will be damaged. Alternatives both fiscal and nonfiscal are available. The fiscal program should include reform of the property tax, extension of local user charges, and expansion of state grants. The nonfiscal program should rationalize the structure of local governments. State grants to localities have expanded greatly in the postwar years: in 1948 they were 29 percent, and in 1973, 35 percent of local general revenue. The evidence seems to be that

3. James A. Maxwell and J. Richard Aronson, "Federal Grants and Fiscal Balance: The Instrument and the Goal," *Public Policy*, vol. 20 (Fall 1972), pp. 577–93.

the states should be more alert to couple aid with local governmental reorganization. And sometimes, as an alternative to aid, state takeover of performance of a service will be indicated, especially in states that are compact in size and homogeneous in economic structure.

The states also display a diverse pattern of revenue preferences, and much of this diversity is natural and desirable. Perverse use of taxes by state governments is, however, objectionable. It is a perversion when state governments reach outside their boundaries to enlarge their tax base, as, for example, when the value of sales in the state of destination is given heavy weight in allocating the net income base of a corporation; when the income earned in a state by individuals who reside in a different state is included in the tax base of both states; or when buyers who make out-of-state purchases are charged a use tax by the home state and a sales tax by the other state. When different tax definitions are used by the states, the fact that each definition would be acceptable, if generalized, is not enough. The actual operation of the rules of taxation, like rules of the road, should be uniform. If the states cannot, by themselves, achieve this goal, multiplication of inequities will, in time, justify and bring about federal intervention.

State-Local Debt

In the years since World War II, borrowing by state and local governments has grown even more rapidly than ordinary spending and taxing. This increase has been almost entirely for capital purposes because state and local governments are narrowly limited in their legal powers to borrow to finance deficits on current operations. The market for state and local bonds has remained receptive, yet several aspects of the state-local debt structure are worrisome. One weighty but unattractive reason for the relatively low yield is the exemption of interest from federal income taxes. This privilege or subsidy is firmly rooted against change, even though change is needed. By offering a legal method of tax avoidance, the exemption impairs the logic of a progressive tax on income and reduces federal revenues. A subsidy geared to the volume of borrowing by a governmental unit is objectionably stimulative of borrowing.[4]

4. Most projections of state and local finances indicate a potential slackening in the need for additional public capital facilities. If there is a relative drop in the

Combined with self-imposed constitutional and statutory limitations on debt, the subsidy has tempted state and local governments into dangerous forms of debt, especially by the issuance of nonguaranteed bonds. Almost nonexistent at the state level before the war, these now make up 37 percent of the total outstanding debt (short term plus long term) of state and local governments. Through industrial aid bonds, some state and local governments are exploiting the interest exemption for projects that are private rather than public. And the enormous use of nonguaranteed bonds for purposes that are not self-financing is utterly imprudent.

Projections

Many investigators have estimated the rate of expansion of state-local expenditures and revenues for the last decade. Some expect the pressures of recent years to diminish so that, in the last half of the 1970s, state and local governments should have surpluses.[5] These projections rely heavily on demographic predictions that the relative growth in the number of school-aged children and those of college age will slacken. Other anticipated changes working in the same direction are a substantial slowdown in real state and local construction outlays, and a growth of federal grants for pollution control and mass transit at a more rapid pace than other grants because of higher federal matching rates.

The optimistic forecasts are, of course, subject to many hazards. Some investigators suspect that these reckonings may "underemphasize current deficiencies in State-local services," as well as "the

---

supply of municipal debt such that people in the lower income tax brackets need not be induced to buy these securities, then the yield spread between taxable and tax-exempt securities should widen.

5. Advisory Commission on Intergovernmental Relations, *Fiscal Balance in the American Federal System* (GPO, 1967), vol. 1, pp. 60–66, examines projections made by the State-Local Finances Project at George Washington University (summarized in Selma J. Mushkin and Gabrielle C. Lupo, "Project '70: Projecting the State-Local Sector," *Review of Economics and Statistics,* vol. 49 [May 1967], pp. 237–45); by the Tax Foundation in *Fiscal Outlook for State and Local Government to 1975* (Tax Foundation, 1966); and by the Committee for Economic Development in *A Fiscal Program for a Balanced Federalism* (CED, 1967). See also David J. Ott, Attiat F. Ott, James A. Maxwell, and J. Richard Aronson, *State-Local Finances in the Last Half of the 1970s* (American Enterprise Institute for Public Policy Research, 1975).

demand for increased *quality* of these services."[6] In an affluent society, governmental willingness to increase spending for domestic services is great. The low level of state-local expenditure in many states is partly attributable to low urbanization; more urbanization will mean higher expenditure. And new social needs may burgeon. An aggregative process that lumps together the state and local governments on which financial pressures will be great with those on which these pressures will be light seems to underestimate the force of financial distress.

Another uncertainty is the prospective behavior of state and local retirement plans. For many years these have run substantial surpluses. Most of the plans are funded, at least to a considerable degree, on an actuarial basis. They accumulate reserves by setting contribution rates at such a level that receipts exceed payments. When a plan is fully funded, a sufficient reserve is accumulated to meet all obligations for all benefits accrued under the plan from its beginning to its end.

While generalizations about the 2,300 systems now in operation must be precarious, the likelihood is that financing of many of them will be a serious problem for many state and local governments in the next decade. Especially in the big cities, pension benefits have been liberalized without a careful reckoning of the long-run effects. The liberalization brings no immediate increase in current costs, and it is a politically tempting move because it places the future impact on a different mayor and a different city council.[7]

Conclusion

A federalist in the 1970s is plagued with anxiety concerning the problems of American federalism. History will inform him that the course of federalism has seldom run smooth, and that, periodically, for almost one hundred and ninety years similar worries have been endemic. This information will, perhaps, be a consolation, but it is unlikely to be a sedative. Are not the flaws now displayed by Ameri-

6. Walter W. Heller and Joseph A. Pechman, "Questions and Answers on Revenue Sharing," in *Revenue Sharing and Its Alternatives: What Future for Fiscal Federalism?* Hearings before the Subcommittee on Fiscal Policy of the Joint Economic Committee, 90:1 (GPO, 1967), p. 116.

7. Harry H. Wellington and Ralph K. Winter, Jr., *The Unions and the Cities* (Brookings Institution, 1971), pp. 19–20.

can federalism different in nature from those that worried Madison? Are they not less susceptible of remedy? Is not the economy more interdependent and therefore more sensitive? Are not social and welfare problems more national? If the answers are affirmative, does this mean that the states as governmental units are obsolete? The preceding pages support no such conclusion; rather do they present evidence of an opposite tenor.

Yet it would be rash to allow belief—not to say dogmas—rooted in past experience to retard search for the ways by which American federalism can be strengthened. Confident complacency would be misplaced because evidence of new flaws is in full view. What, for instance, should the states do concerning the serious economic and social problems of metropolitan areas? Even if federal help is necessary for adequate remedy, state governments should not default on their manifest responsibilities. Must not the states invent ways to cooperate effectively among themselves? Must they not yield sovereignty to the other states as an alternative to loss to the federal level? Should not the states somehow devise rules of tax behavior that will be uniform across the nation?

James Madison, surely a classic federalist, once observed:

If . . . the people should in future become more partial to the federal than to the State governments, the change can only result from such manifest and irresistible proofs of a better administration, as will overcome all their antecedent propensities. And in that case, the people ought not surely to be precluded from giving most of their confidence where they may discover it to be most due.[8]

8. *The Federalist,* ed. Henry Cabot Lodge (Putnam's, 1888), no. 46, pp. 293–94.

Statistical Tables

Table A-1. General Expenditure for Civil Functions, by Classification of Intergovernmental Payments and Level of Government, Selected Years, 1902–73[a]

Classification of payments and level of government	1902	1927	1938	1948	1958	1968	1973
Intergovernmental payments charged to the level of government making the final disbursement							
Millions of dollars							
Federal	230	1,421	5,045	8,713	15,165	33,716	57,838
State and local	1,013	7,210	8,757	17,684	44,851	102,411	181,086
Total	1,243	8,631	13,802	26,397	60,016	136,127	238,924
Percentage of total							
Federal	18.5	16.5	36.6	33.0	25.3	24.8	24.2
State and local	81.5	83.5	63.4	67.0	74.7	75.2	75.8
Total	100.0	100.0	100.0	100.0	100.0	100.0	100.0
Intergovernmental payments charged to the orginaing level of government							
Millions of dollars							
Federal	237	1,544	5,807	10,484	20,000	51,769	99,504
State and local	1,006	7,087	7,995	15,913	40,016	84,358	139,420
Total	1,243	8,631	13,802	26,397	60,016	136,127	238,924
Percentage of total							
Federal	19.1	17.9	42.1	39.7	33.3	38.0	41.6
State and local	80.9	82.1	57.9	60.3	66.7	62.0	58.4
Total	100.0	100.0	100.0	100.0	100.0	100.0	100.0

Sources: U.S. Census Bureau, *Historical Statistics of the United States: Colonial Times to 1957* (Government Printing Office, 1960), pp. 725 and 727; and Census Bureau, *Governmental Finances in 1972–73*, pp. 17–18, and relevant preceding issues. In all tables, years are fiscal unless otherwise noted, and figures are rounded.

a. General expenditure excludes expenditures of utilities, liquor stores, and insurance trusts, and includes intergovernmental transactions net of duplicative transactions between levels of government. Civil functions exclude national defense and international relations, veterans' services not elsewhere classified, and interest on the federal debt. See notes to table 1-1 for additional details.

Table A-2. Tax Collections, by Type of Tax and Level of Government, 1902, 1927, 1938, 1948, and 1973

Level of government	Income	Consumption	Property	Other	Total
		Tax collections			
		Millions of dollars			
Federal					
1902	...	487	0	26	513
1927	2,138	1,088	0	137	3,364
1938	2,610	2,021	0	713	5,344
1948	28,983	7,650	0	1,243	37,876
1973	139,399	19,722	0	6,372	165,493
State					
1902	0	28	82	46	156
1927	162	445	370	631	1,608
1938	383	1,674	244	831	3,132
1948	1,084	4,042	276	1,340	6,743
1973	21,012	37,123	1,312	8,622	68,069
Local					
1902	0	0	624	80	704
1927	0	25	4,360	94	4,479
1938	0	120	4,196	157	4,473
1948	51	400	5,850	298	6,599
1973	2,406	4,924	43,970	1,731	53,032
All					
1902	0	515	706	152	1,373
1927	2,300	1,558	4,730	862	9,451
1938	2,993	3,815	4,440	1,701	12,949
1948	30,118	12,092	6,126	2,881	51,218
1973	162,818	61,769	45,283	16,726	286,595
		Percentage of total			
Federal					
1902	...	95	...	5	100
1927	64	32	...	4	100
1938	49	38	...	13	100
1948	77	20	...	3	100
1973	84	12	...	4	100
State					
1902	...	18	53	29	100
1927	10	28	23	39	100
1938	12	53	8	27	100
1948	16	60	4	20	100
1973	31	55	2	13	100
Local					
1902	...	...	89	11	100
1927	...	1	97	2	100
1938	...	3	94	4	100
1948	1	6	89	5	100
1973	5	9	83	3	100

Table A-2 (*continued*)

Level of government	Tax collections				
	Income	*Consumption*	*Property*	*Other*	*Total*
All					
1902	...	38	51	11	100
1927	24	16	50	9	100
1938	23	29	34	13	100
1948	59	24	12	6	100
1973	57	22	16	6	100

Sources: *Historical Statistics*, pp. 722–24 and 727–29; and *Governmental Finances in 1972–73*, p. 20.

Table A-3. General Expenditure for Civil Functions as Percentage of Gross National Product, by Level of Government, Selected Years, 1902–73

Year	Gross national product, in billions of dollars	Expenditure as percentage of GNP		
		Federal	*State-local*	*Total*
1902	21.6	1.1	4.7	5.8
1927	96.3	1.5	7.5	9.0
1938	85.2	5.9	10.3	16.2
1948	257.6	3.4	6.9	10.2
1958	447.3	3.4	10.0	13.4
1968	864.2	3.9	11.9	15.8
1973	1,294.9	4.5	14.0	18.5

Sources: Table A-1, using data for intergovernmental payments charged to the level of government making final disbursement; *Historical Statistics*, p. 139; and *Economic Report of the President, February 1975*, p. 249. Figures are rounded.

Table A-4. Direct General Expenditure for Civil Functions by All Levels of Government, Selected Years, 1902–73

Millions of dollars

Function	1902	1927	1938	1948	1958	1968	1973
Education	258	2,243	2,653	7,721	16,836	43,614	75,690
Highways	175	1,819	2,150	3,071	8,702	14,654	19,173
Public welfare	41	161	1,233	2,144	3,777	11,245	26,967
Hospitals	45	347	496	1,398	3,849	7,801	13,662
Health	18	84	182	536	806	2,778	5,007
General control	175	526	725	1,325	2,536	2,400	4,582
Police	50	290	378	724	1,769	3,700	7,331
Other	481	3,161	5,985	9,478	21,739	49,935	86,512
Total	1,243	8,631	13,802	26,397	60,014	136,127	238,924

Sources: *Historical Statistics*, pp. 723 and 727; *Governmental Finances in 1972–73*, pp. 23 and 24, and relevant preceding issues.

Table A-5. General Expenditure for Civil Functions by State and Local Governments, Selected Years, 1902–73
Millions of dollars

Classification of payment and function	1902	1927	1938	1948	1958	1968	1973
Intergovernmental payments charged to the level of government making final disbursement							
Education	255	2,235	2,491	5,379	15,919	41,158	69,573
Highways	175	1,809	1,650	3,036	8,567	14,481	18,615
Public welfare	37	151	1,069	2,099	3,729	9,857	23,582
Health	17	76	151	292	546	1,264	2,732
Hospitals	43	279	400	937	3,005	6,282	11,112
Other	486	2,660	2,996	5,941	13,085	29,369	55,472
Total	1,013	7,210	8,757	17,684	44,851	102,411	181,086
Intergovernmental payments charged to the originating level of government							
Education	254	2,225	2,379	4,961	15,266	36,431	60,907
Highways	175	1,726	1,386	2,718	7,089	10,190	13,339
Public welfare	36	150	851	1,375	1,930	4,450	11,485
Health	17	76	151	292	484[a]	701[a]	1,168[a]
Hospitals	43	279	400	937	2,959[a]	6,128[a]	10,910[a]
Other	481	2,631	2,828	5,630	12,288	26,458	41,611
Total	1,006	7,087	7,995	15,913	40,016	84,358	139,420

Sources: *Historical Statistics*, pp. 725 and 727; and *Governmental Finances in 1958*, pp. 16–18, in 1967–68, pp. 18, 19, 22, and 24, and in 1972–73, pp. 22–24.
a. In 1958, 1968, and 1973, "hospitals" are allocated $1 million, $2 million, and $50 million, respectively, designated as "other" under "health and hospitals" in the Census classification.

Table A-6. State and Local Expenditures as a Percentage of Total Direct General Expenditure for Civil Functions, Selected Years, 1902–73

Classification of payment and function	1902	1927	1938	1948	1958	1968	1973
Intergovernmental payments charged to the level of government making final disbursement							
Education	98.8	99.6	93.9	69.7	94.6	94.4	91.9
Highways	100.0	99.5	76.7	98.9	98.4	98.8	97.1
Public welfare	90.2	93.8	86.7	97.9	98.7	87.7	87.4
Health	94.4	90.5	83.0	54.5	67.7	45.5	54.6
Hospitals	95.6	80.4	80.6	67.0	78.1	80.5	81.3
Intergovernmental payments charged to the originating level of government							
Education	98.4	99.2	89.7	64.3	90.7	83.5	80.5
Highways	100.0	94.9	64.5	88.5	81.5	69.5	69.6
Public welfare	87.8	93.2	69.0	64.1	51.1	39.6	42.6
Health	94.4	90.5	83.0	54.5	60.0	25.2	23.3
Hospitals	95.6	80.4	80.6	67.0	76.9	78.6	79.9

Source: Tables A-4 and A-5.

Table A-7. State-Local Per Capita General Expenditure Including and
Excluding Federal Grants, by State, 1973

State	Expenditure including federal grants, in dollars	Amount of federal grants, in dollars	Expenditure excluding federal grants		
			Net expenditure, in dollars	Rank	Expenditure relative
United States	862.93	204.81	658.12	...	100
Alaska	2,376.36	616.95	1,759.41	1	267
Hawaii	1,311.04	249.56	1,061.48	2	161
New York	1,319.42	261.04	1,058.38	3	161
Delaware	1,117.01	211.14	905.87	4	138
Nevada	1,098,48	227.74	870.74	5	132
Washington	1,053.37	237.39	815.98	6	124
Wyoming	1,084.91	269.27	815.64	7	124
California	1,023.31	224.26	799.05	8	121
Massachusetts	986.89	215.63	771.26	9	117
Minnesota	965.62	199.13	766.49	10	116
Michigan	948.85	191.61	757.24	11	115
Maryland	940.75	193.01	747.74	12	114
Connecticut	900.46	178.57	721.89	13	110
Oregon	950.98	231.49	719.49	14	109
Wisconsin	888.88	171.47	717.41	15	109
New Jersey	876.42	167.15	709.27	16	108
Illinois	873.33	191.38	681.95	17	104
Vermont	964.53	294.86	669.67	18	102
Colorado	847.18	211.48	635.70	19	97
Arizona	818.93	193.56	625.37	20	95
Pennsylvania	814.97	197.14	617.83	21	94
Montana	887.42	300.96	586.46	22	89
Iowa	735.36	151.27	584.09	23	89
Nebraska	731.02	155.14	575.88	24	88
Kansas	746.84	171.87	574.97	25	87
Utah	789.68	226.03	563.65	26	86
Georgia	746.73	190.00	556.73	27	85
Rhode Island	801.18	245.70	555.48	28	84
North Dakota	804.84	252.71	552.13	29	84
Ohio	698.60	147.41	551.19	30	84
Indiana	677.06	127.12	549.94	31	84
Virginia	713.33	173.06	540.27	32	82
Florida	689.31	153.06	536.25	33	81
New Hampshire	715.78	185.69	530.09	34	81
South Dakota	818.44	290.04	528.40	35	80
Maine	760.73	238.01	522.72	36	79
Idaho	739.53	222.04	517.49	37	79
Louisiana	765.63	251.52	514.11	38	78
Missouri	680.64	177.01	503.63	39	77
Oklahoma	724.34	222.93	501.41	40	76
Texas	669.40	175.87	493.53	41	75
New Mexico	793.42	306.12	487.30	42	74
West Virginia	743.72	299.96	443.76	43	67
Tennessee	638.21	197.58	440.63	44	67
North Carolina	618.28	179.24	439.04	45	67
Kentucky	670.11	232.67	437.44	46	66
South Carolina	632.80	207.92	424.88	47	65
Alabama	636.93	223.96	412.97	48	63
Mississippi	666.06	298.05	368.01	49	56
Arkansas	548.81	235.49	313.32	50	48

Sources: *Governmental Finances in 1972–73*, p. 45; and *Social Security Bulletin*, vol. 37 (October 1974), p. 32.

Table A-8. State Ranks in Per Capita Income, 1972, and Per Capita Governmental Expenditure, Excluding Federal Grants, 1973

State	Rank Per capita income	Rank Per capita governmental expenditure	Difference between income and expenditure ranks −	Difference between income and expenditure ranks +
Connecticut	1	13	12	...
New York	2	3	1	...
New Jersey	3	16	13	...
Delaware	4	4	0	0
Alaska	5	1	...	4
Illinois	6	17	11	...
Nevada	7	5	...	2
Hawaii	8	2	...	6
California	9	8	...	1
Maryland	10	12	2	...
Michigan	11	11	0	0
Massachusetts	12	9	...	3
Colorado	13	19	6	...
Ohio	14	30	16	...
Rhode Island	15	28	13	...
Washington	16	6	...	10
Pennsylvania	17	21	4	...
Kansas	18	25	7	...
Florida	19	33	14	...
Indiana	20	31	11	...
Nebraska	21	24	3	...
Wyoming	22	7	...	15
Iowa	23	23	0	0
Virginia	24	32	8	...
Minnesota	25	10	...	15
Missouri	26	39	13	...
Oregon	27	14	...	13
Arizona	28	20	...	8
Wisconsin	29	15	...	14
New Hampshire	30	34	4	...
Montana	31	22	...	9
Texas	32	41	9	...
Georgia	33	27	...	6
North Carolina	34	45	11	...
Oklahoma	35	40	5	...
Idaho	36	37	1	...
North Dakota	37	29	...	8
Utah	38	26	...	12
South Dakota	39	35	...	4
Vermont	40	18	...	22
Tennessee	41	44	3	...
Maine	42	36	...	6
Kentucky	43	46	3	...
West Virginia	44	43	...	1
New Mexico	45	42	...	3
Lousiana	46	38	...	8
South Carolina	47	47	0	0
Alabama	48	48	0	0
Arkansas	49	50	1	...
Mississippi	50	49	...	1

Sources: Table A-7; and *Governmental Finances in 1972–73*, p. 52. The per capita income data are figured on the basis of the calendar year, the grants on the basis of the fiscal year.

Table A-9. General Revenue of State and Local Governments Collected from Own Sources per $1,000 of Personal Income, by State, 1973

State	General revenue per $1,000 of income, in dollars	Effort relative
United States	161.36	100
Vermont	207.01	128
New York	203.66	126
Alaska	200.20	124
Minnesota	193.63	120
Wisconsin	193.04	120
Nevada	188.17	117
North Dakota	184.35	114
Wyoming	184.27	114
Hawaii	182.60	113
California	180.66	112
New Mexico	180.51	112
Louisiana	177.58	110
South Dakota	175.09	109
Washington	174.09	108
Arizona	172.87	107
Massachusetts	170.64	106
Utah	167.75	104
Oregon	167.72	104
Maine	167.62	104
Montana	167.40	104
Mississippi	166.46	103
Michigan	163.12	101
Colorado	161.86	100
Maryland	161.50	100
Connecticut	157.41	98
Iowa	156.34	97
Idaho	155.63	96
Nebraska	153.89	95
Florida	153.21	95
Georgia	152.82	95
Pennsylvania	152.71	95
Delaware	152.45	94
South Carolina	151.55	94
Kansas	149.47	93
Kentucky	147.57	91
Oklahoma	146.65	91
West Virginia	146.62	91
Alabama	146.40	91
Tennessee	145.62	90
Rhode Island	145.28	90
New Jersey	144.80	90
Texas	140.83	87
Virginia	140.70	87
Arkansas	140.40	87
North Carolina	140.17	87
Illinois	139.31	86
Indiana	138.13	86
New Hampshire	135.83	84
Missouri	134.43	83
Ohio	134.19	83

Source: *Governmental Finances in 1972–73*, p. 50.

Table A-10. Percentage of State Tax Revenue Collected from Selected Taxes, by State, 1973

State	Total sales and gross receipts[a]	General sales and gross receipts	Individual income
South Dakota	84.9	42.6	...
Washington	79.6	53.4	...
Nevada	77.3	32.6	...
Florida	75.4	41.9	...
Mississippi	75.2	48.0	10.6
West Virginia	73.3	43.2	15.5
Maine	73.2	38.7	10.3
Connecticut	71.7	40.9	4.4
Wyoming	71.7	42.0	...
Texas	71.1	32.9	...
Tennessee	69.2	40.2	1.5
Alabama	67.7	31.1	15.3
New Jersey	67.1	35.5	1.3
Indiana	66.5	38.5	22.7
Georgia	65.0	35.1	20.9
Arkansas	64.2	32.1	17.1
Hawaii	63.6	48.7	31.2
South Carolina	63.6	34.7	22.2
North Dakota	63.0	39.0	15.2
New Mexico	62.8	39.7	12.8
Arizona	61.5	39.2	15.9
Nebraska	61.5	29.0	22.7
Ohio	61.3	30.2	14.0
Kentucky	61.2	31.0	17.6
Rhode Island	59.6	30.7	21.7
Kansas	59.6	32.8	18.7
New Hampshire	58.1	...	4.9
Illinois	57.5	32.5	24.3
Missouri	57.0	32.9	25.8
Utah	56.4	37.8	24.6
Colorado	55.2	33.0	27.9
North Carolina	52.7	22.3	26.0
Oklahoma	52.2	18.1	15.2
Louisiana	51.8	26.0	9.2
Idaho	51.7	27.1	25.6
Vermont	51.4	14.5	28.4
Virginia	50.9	20.9	31.6
Iowa	50.6	28.5	28.4
California	49.3	29.9	25.8
Pennsylvania	49.2	25.4	23.1
Michigan	49.1	31.0	26.2
Maryland	48.1	22.4	35.4
Minnesota	43.3	18.3	35.8
Wisconsin	40.7	23.2	39.0
New York	39.7	21.2	39.3
Massachusetts	36.0	11.2	42.7
Montana	33.7	...	41.2
Delaware	23.5	...	33.8
Alaska	23.0	...	39.8
Oregon	22.8	...	50.4

Source: Census Bureau, *State Government Finances in 1973*, pp. 19 and 21.
a. Includes revenue from both general and selective sales and gross receipts taxes.

Table A-11. Personal Income Per Capita, 1972, and Federal Grants Per Capita, 1973, by State

State	Per capita income, in dollars	Federal grants per capita, in dollars	State rank Per capita income	State rank Per capita grants
United States	4,492	204.81		
Connecticut	5,328	178.57	1	39
New York	5,242	261.04	2	9
New Jersey	5,232	167.15	3	45
Delaware	5,188	211.14	4	27
Alaska	5,141	616.95	5	1
Illinois	5,140	191.38	6	35
Nevada	5,078	227.74	7	19
Hawaii	5,031	249.56	8	12
California	4,988	224.26	9	21
Maryland	4,882	193.01	10	33
Michigan	4,881	191.61	11	34
Massachusetts	4,855	215.63	12	25
Colorado	4,574	211.48	13	26
Ohio	4,534	147.41	14	49
Rhode Island	4,483	245.70	15	13
Washington	4,472	237.39	16	15
Pennsylvania	4,465	197.14	17	31
Kansas	4,455	171.87	18	43
Florida	4,378	153.06	19	47
Indiana	4,366	127.12	20	50
Nebraska	4,355	155.14	21	46
Wyoming	4,330	269.27	22	8
Iowa	4,300	151.27	23	48
Virginia	4,298	173.06	24	42
Minnesota	4,296	199.13	25	29
Missouri	4,293	177.01	26	40
Oregon	4,287	231.49	27	18
Arizona	4,263	193.56	28	32
Wisconsin	4,255	171.47	29	44
New Hampshire	4,241	185.69	30	37
Montana	3,999	300.96	31	3
Texas	3,991	175.87	32	41
Georgia	3,909	190.00	33	36
North Carolina	3,799	179.24	34	38
Oklahoma	3,795	222.93	35	23
Idaho	3,780	222.04	36	24
North Dakota	3,738	252.71	37	10
Utah	3,728	226.03	38	20
South Dakota	3,699	290.04	39	7
Vermont	3,686	294.86	40	6
Tennessee	3,671	197.58	41	30
Maine	3,610	238.01	42	14
Kentucky	3,609	232.67	43	17
West Virginia	3,594	299.96	44	4
New Mexico	3,564	306.12	45	2
Louisiana	3,543	251.52	46	11
South Carolina	3,477	207.92	47	28
Alabama	3,420	223.96	48	22
Arkansas	3,365	235.49	49	16
Mississippi	3,137	298.05	50	5

Sources: *Governmental Finances in 1972–73*, p. 52; and *Social Security Bulletin*, vol. 37 (October 1974), p. 32. The per capita income data are figured on the basis of the calendar year, the grants on the basis of the fiscal year.

Table A-12. Estimated Per Capita Incidence of Federal Taxes, by State, 1972

State	Tax incidence, in dollars	Ratio of state incidence to U.S. incidence
United States	934	1.00
Connecticut	1,338	1.43
Nevada	1,216	1.30
Delaware	1,175	1.26
New York	1,164	1.25
New Jersey	1,143	1.22
Illinois	1,132	1.21
Massachusetts	1,081	1.16
California	1,071	1.15
Maryland	1,069	1.14
Alaska	1,044	1.12
Hawaii	1,026	1.10
Michigan	989	1.06
Ohio	967	1.04
Washington	955	1.02
Pennsylvania	949	1.02
Rhode Island	943	1.01
Florida	876	0.94
Missouri	876	0.94
Indiana	873	0.93
Colorado	869	0.93
Minnesota	864	0.93
Wisconsin	861	0.92
New Hampshire	860	0.92
Oregon	857	0.92
Wyoming	851	0.91
Kansas	845	0.90
Nebraska	841	0.90
Virginia	838	0.90
Texas	827	0.89
Iowa	818	0.88
Arizona	813	0.87
Vermont	800	0.86
Montana	789	0.84
Oklahoma	753	0.81
Georgia	752	0.81
Maine	749	0.80
Idaho	711	0.76
Tennessee	705	0.75
West Virginia	704	0.75
North Carolina	700	0.75
Louisiana	685	0.73
Utah	683	0.73
Kentucky	675	0.72
New Mexico	673	0.72
South Dakota	662	0.71
North Dakota	648	0.69
Alabama	626	0.67
South Carolina	623	0.67
Arkansas	595	0.64
Mississippi	511	0.55

Source: Tax Foundation, *Facts and Figures on Government Finance, 1973* (New York: Tax Foundation, 1973), p. 123.

Table A-13. Per Capita Redistribution of Income Attributable to Federal Grant
Formulas and Federal Tax Incidence, by State, 1973

Dollars

| | | Cause of redistribution | |
State	Total redistribution	Grant formula	Tax incidence
Alaska	+387.56	+412.14	−24.58
Mississippi	+185.41	+93.24	+92.17
New Mexico	+158.66	+101.31	+57.35
West Virginia	+146.35	+95.15	+51.20
South Dakota	+144.63	+85.23	+59.40
Montana	+128.92	+96.15	+32.77
Vermont	+118.72	+90.05	+28.67
North Dakota	+111.39	+47.90	+63.49
Arkansas	+104.41	+30.68	+73.73
Louisiana	+102.01	+46.71	+55.30
Alabama	+86.74	+19.15	+67.59
Kentucky	+85.21	+27.86	+57.35
Wyoming	+82.89	+64.46	+18.43
Utah	+76.52	+21.22	+55.30
Maine	+74.16	+33.20	+40.96
South Carolina	+70.70	+3.11	+67.59
Idaho	+66.39	+17.23	+49.16
Oklahoma	+57.03	+18.12	+38.91
Tennessee	+43.97	−7.23	+51.20
Oregon	+43.07	+26.68	+16.39
Rhode Island	+38.84	+40.89	−2.05
Washington	+28.48	+32.58	−4.10
Georgia	+24.10	−14.81	+38.91
North Carolina	+25.63	−25.57	+51.20
Hawaii	+24.27	+44.75	−20.48
Colorado	+21.01	+6.67	+14.34
Arizona	+15.38	−11.25	+26.63
Minnesota	+8.66	−5.68	+14.34
New York	+5.03	+56.23	−51.20
New Hampshire	−2.73	−19.12	+16.38
Texas	−6.41	−28.94	+22.53
Virginia	−11.27	−31.75	+20.48
California	−11.27	+19.45	−30.72
Pennsylvania	−11.77	−7.67	−4.10
Kansas	−12.46	−32.94	+20.48
Missouri	−15.51	−27.80	+12.29
Wisconsin	−16.96	−33.34	+16.38
Massachusetts	−21.95	+10.82	−32.77
Michigan	−25.49	−13.20	−12.29
Iowa	−28.96	−53.54	+24.58
Nebraska	−29.19	−49.67	+20.48
Nevada	−38.51	+22.93	−61.44
Florida	−39.46	−51.75	+12.29
Maryland	−40.47	−11.80	−28.67
Delaware	−46.92	+6.33	−53.25
Illinois	−55.44	−13.43	−43.01
Indiana	−63.35	−77.69	+14.34
Ohio	−65.59	−57.40	−8.19
New Jersey	−82.72	−37.66	−45.06
Connecticut	−114.31	−26.24	−88.07

Source: Tables A-11 and A-12.

Table A-14. **State Intergovernmental Expenditure,**
by Function, 1902, 1927, 1938, 1948, and 1973

Function	1902	1927	1938	1948	1973
		Millions of dollars			
Education	45	292	656	1,554	23,316
Highways	2	197	317	507	2,953
Public welfare	...	6	346	648	7,532
Other	5	101	197	574	7,021
Total	52	596	1,516	3,283	40,822
		Percentage distribution			
Education	86	49	43	47	57
Highways	4	33	21	15	7
Public welfare	...	1	23	20	18
Other	10	17	13	18	17
Total	100	100	100	100	100

Sources: Census Bureau, *Census of Governments, 1957*, vol. 4, no. 2, *State Payments to Local Governments* (1959), p. 100; and *Governmental Finances in 1972–73*, p. 22.

Table A-15. **State Intergovernmental Expenditure as Percentage of Local**
Expenditure, by Function, 1902, 1927, 1938, 1948, and 1973

Function	1902	1927	1938	1948	1973
Public welfare	...	5.4	56.2	57.0	79.8
Education	18.9	14.5	30.6	37.2	45.5
Highways	1.2	15.2	38.0	33.2	45.1
Other	1.0	3.4	5.9	9.0	15.1
All functions	5.4	9.4	22.0	24.6	35.9

Sources: *Census of Governments, 1957*, vol. 4, no. 3, *Historical Summary of Governmental Finances in the United States* (1959), pp. 20–23, and no. 2, p. 100; and *Governmental Finances in 1972–73*, p. 22.

Table A-16. State Individual Income Tax and General Sales Tax Collections Per Capita, Ranked by State, 1973

State	Individual income tax Rank	Amount, in dollars	General sales tax Rank	Amount, in dollars
New York	1	175.85	21	94.94
Hawaii	2	162.18	1	253.23
Wisconsin	3	159.31	23	94.65
Delaware	4	155.65	...	...
Massachusetts	5	150.63	45	39.59
Minnesota	6	150.43	38	76.81
Oregon	7	135.08	...	...
Alaska	8	131.40	...	...
Maryland	9	126.76	35	80.02
Vermont	10	107.22	43	54.88
Montana	11	106.89	...	...
Michigan	12	102.30	11	120.77
Virginia	13	91.85	42	60.71
California	14	91.57	16	106.24
Pennsylvania	15	84.93	25	93.19
Iowa	16	83.63	31	83.97
North Carolina	17	81.78	41	70.08
Illinois	18	79.63	15	106.44
Utah	19	76.53	12	117.44
Colorado	20	76.24	28	90.16
Idaho	21	74.92	36	79.22
Rhode Island	22	69.62	19	98.67
South Carolina	23	67.21	17	104.99
Missouri	24	66.22	30	84.61
Georgia	25	59.53	18	99.75
Nebraska	26	55.21	40	70.58
Kentucky	27	53.63	22	94.75
Indiana	28	53.59	27	91.09
Arizona	29	52.78	8	129.86
Kansas	30	50.14	29	87.64
West Virginia	31	49.31	6	136.89
New Mexico	32	44.76	5	138.75
Arkansas	33	43.86	32	82.40
North Dakota	34	42.68	14	109.52
Alabama	35	40.19	34	81.76
Oklahoma	36	39.45	44	47.00
Ohio	37	34.81	39	75.30
Mississippi	38	30.69	4	139.12
Maine	39	30.46	13	114.38
Louisiana	40	29.07	33	82.05
Connecticut	41	16.46[a]	3	151.76
New Hampshire	42	9.64[a]	...	...
Tennessee	43	3.66[a]	20	97.59
New Jersey	44	3.47[a]	26	92.64
Washington	...	...	2	200.56
Florida	...	...	7	135.63
Nevada	...	...	9	126.56
Wyoming	...	...	10	125.11
South Dakota	...	...	24	94.20
Texas	...	...	37	78.53

Source: *State Government Finances in 1973*, p. 11.
a. The state has a limited individual income tax.

Table A-17. Operating Revenue and Expenditure of Local Utilities, 1953, 1963, 1968, and 1973[a]

Year	Water supply Revenue	Water supply Expenditure	Electric power Revenue	Electric power Expenditure	Transit Revenue	Transit Expenditure	Gas supply Revenue	Gas supply Expenditure
				Millions of dollars				
1953	939	631	713	453	500	530	85	56
1963	1,865	1,273	1,728	1,111	639	723	242	202
1968	2,313	1,644	2,119	1,453	919	1,115	332	263
1973	3,463	2,650	3,355	2,513	1,267	1,946	536	439
				Expenditure as a percentage of revenue				
1953	67.2		63.5		106.0		65.9	
1963	68.3		64.3		113.1		83.5	
1968	71.1		68.6		121.3		79.2	
1973	76.5		74.9		153.6		81.9	

Sources: *Census of Governments, 1962*, vol. 6, no. 4, *Historical Statistics on Governmental Finances and Employment* (1964), pp. 45 and 50; and *Governmental Finances in 1963*, p. 27, in *1967–68*, p. 26, and in *1972–73*, p. 26.

a. Expenditure includes interest on utility debt.

Table A-18. Local Government User Charges, by Major Categories
of Governmental Service, 1953, 1963, 1968, and 1973

Governmental service	1953	1963	1968	1973
	Millions of dollars			
Nonhighway transportation	128	335	490	956
Air	42	216	331	682
Water	87[a]	119	159	274
Hospitals	230	815	1,411	3,405
Housing	225	446	514	689
Sewerage and other sanitation	154	633	678	1,951
Natural resources, parks, and recreation	91	238	243	443
Education	357	1,240	1,829	2,714
Highways	96	[b]	[b]	[b]
Other	343	932	1,729	2,128
Total	1,625	4,639	6,894	12,285
User charges as percentage of general revenue from own revenue	12.8	16.3	16.9	17.4
	Percentage of expenditure			
Nonhighway transportation	55.7	59.7	73.4	59.5
Air	n.a.	65.5	73.9	58.0
Water	n.a.	51.5	72.3	63.4
Hospitals	27.1	41.5	46.3	59.3
Housing	35.8	36.1	31.9	23.8
Sewerage and other sanitation	17.0	28.9	25.0	36.7
Natural resources, parks, and recreation	16.6	16.2	12.6	13.8
Education	4.6	6.5	6.1	5.3
Highways	4.3	[b]	[b]	[b]

Sources: Census Bureau, *Summary of Governmental Finances in 1954* (GPO, 1955), pp. 20, 22, and 27–28; *Governmental Finances in 1963*, pp. 22 and 25, *in 1967–68*, pp. 20 and 23, and *in 1972–73*, pp. 20 and 23.
n.a. = not available.
a. Includes "other" of $5 million.
b. Not separately available (dollar amounts included in "other").

Table A-19. State Government User Charges, by Major Categories of Governmental Service, 1953, 1963, 1968, and 1973

Governmental service	1953	1963	1968	1973
	Millions of dollars			
Nonhighway transportation	22	56	95	178
Air	2	13	27	73
Water transport and terminals	20	43	68	105
Education	410	1,260	2,742	4,891
Housing	...	8	7	19
Hospitals	111	333	741	1,306
Natural resources	81	118	170	275
Highways	103	461	691	975
Other	77	226	445	965
Total	804	2,462	4,891	8,609
User charges as percentage of general revenue from own sources	6.8	9.6	11.3	10.7
	Percentage of expenditure			
Nonhighway transportation	47.8	49.6	37.4	43.2
Air	n.a.	41.9	40.3	29.9
Water transport and terminals	n.a.	52.4	36.4	62.5
Education[a]	27.6	26.6	25.8	27.5
Housing	...	66.7	35.0	7.2
Hospitals	10.9	16.6	22.9	24.3
Natural resources	15.3	10.8	8.7	10.5
Highways	3.7	6.2	7.0	8.1

Sources: *Summary of Governmental Finances in 1954; Governmental Finances in 1963, in 1967–68,* and *in 1972–73;* and *State Government Finances,* relevant issues.

n.a. = not available.

a. Excludes payments to local schools.

Table A-20. Per Capita Personal Income and Per Capita Long-Term State and Local Debt Outstanding, by State, 1973

State	Personal income Rank	Personal income Amount, in dollars	Long-term debt outstanding Rank	Long-term debt outstanding Amount, in dollars
Connecticut	1	5,328	7	1,189.93
New York	2	5,242	5	1,453.60
New Jersey	3	5,232	18	858.79
Delaware	4	5,188	2	1,535.22
Alaska	5	5,141	1	2,443.15
Illinois	6	5,140	25	670.94
Nevada	7	5,078	12	950.91
Hawaii	8	5,031	3	1,518.79
California	9	4,988	15	883.81
Maryland	10	4,882	11	1,014.31
Michigan	11	4,881	24	716.09
Massachusetts	12	4,855	14	915.88
Colorado	13	4,574	34	595.76
Ohio	14	4,534	33	596.21
Rhode Island	15	4,483	22	741.65
Washington	16	4,472	4	1,457.79
Pennsylvania	17	4,465	13	949.97
Kansas	18	4,455	37	563.28
Florida	19	4,378	30	642.42
Indiana	20	4,366	43	452.77
Nebraska	21	4,355	6	1,315.31
Wyoming	22	4,330	23	734.18
Iowa	23	4,300	47	372.56
Virginia	24	4,298	35	584.56
Minnesota	25	4,296	17	871.17
Missouri	26	4,293	38	547.57
Oregon	27	4,287	16	873.54
Arizona	28	4,263	27	657.59
Wisconsin	29	4,255	28	653.28
New Hampshire	30	4,241	39	534.98
Montana	31	3,999	42	461.68
Texas	32	3,991	20	795.98
Georgia	33	3,909	29	645.15
North Carolina	34	3,799	48	353.29
Oklahoma	35	3,795	26	663.94
Idaho	36	3,780	49	233.95
North Dakota	37	3,738	46	405.63
Utah	38	3,728	44	428.76
South Dakota	39	3,699	50	205.52
Vermont	40	3,686	8	1,090.11
Tennessee	41	3,671	21	745.14
Maine	42	3,610	36	577.40
Kentucky	43	3,609	10	1,014.64
West Virginia	44	3,594	31	632.67
New Mexico	45	3,564	45	426.19
Louisiana	46	3,543	9	1,068.13
South Carolina	47	3,477	41	484.91
Alabama	48	3,420	19	798.36
Arkansas	49	3,365	40	508.39
Mississippi	50	3,137	32	626.14

Source: *Governmental Finances in 1972–73*, pp. 48 and 52.

Table A-21. Long-Term Debt of State and Local Governments Outstanding at End of Fiscal Year, 1949, 1963, 1968, and 1973

Year	State and local debt			State debt			Local debt		
	Total	Full faith and credit	Non-guaranteed	Total	Full faith and credit	Non-guaranteed	Total	Full faith and credit	Non-guaranteed
Billions of dollars									
1949	20.2	17.7	2.5	4.0	3.4	0.6	16.2	14.3	1.9
1963	83.2	50.7	32.4	22.8	10.7	12.1	60.4	40.0	20.4
1968	112.7	65.1	47.7	33.6	14.7	18.9	79.1	50.4	28.7
1973	172.6	102.9	69.7	55.7	28.4	27.3	116.9	74.5	42.4
Percentage of total									
1949	100.0	87.6	12.4	100.0	85.0	15.0	100.0	88.3	11.7
1963	100.0	60.9	38.9	100.0	46.9	53.1	100.0	66.2	33.8
1968	100.0	57.8	42.3	100.0	43.8	56.3	100.0	63.7	36.3
1973	100.0	59.6	40.4	100.0	51.0	49.0	100.0	63.7	36.3
Relative change in debt (base year 1949 = 100)									
1949	100	100	100	100	100	100	100	100	100
1963	412	286	1,296	570	315	2,017	373	280	1,074
1968	558	368	1,908	840	432	3,150	488	352	1,511
1973	854	581	2,788	1,393	835	4,550	722	521	2,232

Sources: Data for 1949 were provided by the Census Bureau; for other years, see *Governmental Finances*, relevant issues.

Table A-22. Distribution of States by Percentage of State Government Net Long-Term Debt in Full Faith and Credit Form, 1941, 1949, 1966, and 1973

Percentage of debt in full faith and credit form	Number of states			
	1941	1949	1966	1973
90 and over	18	21	4	2
80–89	7	2	3	6
70–79	4	1	4	5
60–69	2	2	4	7
50–59	3	1	5	2
40–49	2	0	2	4
30–39	1	3	3	3
20–29	4	3	5	5
10–19	0	3	2	3
Up to 10	1	6	9	1
None	6[a]	6[b]	9[c]	12[d]

Sources: Census Bureau, *Financial Statistics of States, 1941*, vol. 3, *Statistical Compendium* (1943), pp. 63–65; and *State Government Finances in 1949*, pp. 32–33, *in 1966*, p. 40, and *in 1973*, p. 40.
a. Florida, Indiana, Kentucky, Nebraska, Ohio, and Wisconsin.
b. Florida, Georgia, Indiana, Iowa, Nebraska, and Wisconsin.
c. Arizona, Colorado, Florida, Georgia, Nebraska, North Dakota, South Dakota, Wisconsin, and Wyoming.
d. Arizona, Arkansas, Colorado, Florida, Georgia, Indiana, Iowa, Kansas, Montana, Nebraska, South Dakota, and Wyoming.

Table A-23. Net Long-Term Nonguaranteed State Government Debt, Per Capita, of States without Full Faith and Credit Debt, 1941, 1966, and 1973

State	Debt, in dollars		
	1941	1966	1973
Arizona	...	26.40	36.44
Arkansas	...	...	49.40
Colorado	...	47.63	43.50
Florida	a	105.50	142.01
Georgia	...	123.67	145.16
Indiana	2.40	...	93.26
Iowa	...	...	39.31
Kansas	...	...	80.75
Kentucky	3.72	...	...
Montana	...	...	103.59
Nebraska	1.03	37.22	34.82
North Dakota	...	32.45	...
Ohio	1.82	...	...
South Dakota	...	26.30	56.08
Wisconsin	1.74	63.55	...
Wyoming	...	75.55	101.81

Sources: *Financial Statistics of States, 1941*, vol. 3, pp. 63–65; and *State Government Finances in 1966*, p. 15, and *in 1973*, p. 15.
a. Florida had no net long-term debt in 1941.

Bibliography

EXCELLENT SOURCES of statistical data on state and local public finance are prepared by the Bureau of the Census in the U.S. Department of Commerce. The important yearly publications are: *Governmental Finances; State Government Finances;* and *City Government Finances.* For historical material the most convenient sources are U.S. Census Bureau's *Historical Statistics of the United States: Colonial Times to 1957* published by the Government Printing Office in 1960, and later editions extending the data. The bureau's *Census of Governments,* taken in 1942, 1952, 1957, 1962, 1967, and 1972, is published in numerous volumes.

Descriptions of state functional organization, as well as statistical material, are to be found in *The Book of the States,* issued biennially by the Council of State Governments. The *Municipal Year Book,* issued by the International City Management Association, Washington, offers similar materials concerning local governments. *The Bond Buyer's Municipal Finance Statistics,* published annually by The Bond Buyer, New York, is a useful reference, and so also is *Facts and Figures on Government Finance* issued annually by the Tax Foundation, New York. The Commerce Clearing House of Chicago issues a looseleaf *State Tax Guide* showing rates and major state tax laws.

In 1959 the Advisory Commission on Intergovernmental Relations was established with twenty-six members drawn from Congress, the executive branch of the federal government, governors, state legislatures, mayors, elected county officials, and private persons. Its aim is to advance cooperation among levels of government and to improve the effectiveness of the federal system. It has prepared and issued numerous and valuable reports dealing with specific intergovernmental problems.

278

Periodicals

Most useful for the general reader are:

Governmental Finance. Quarterly. Chicago: Municipal Finance Officers Association.

National Civic Review (formerly *National Municipal Review*). Monthly. New York: National Municipal League.

National Tax Journal. Quarterly. Columbus, Ohio: National Tax Association–Tax Institute of America.

Proceedings of the Annual Conference on Taxation. Columbus: National Tax Association–Tax Institute of America.

Tax Administrators News. Monthly. Chicago: Federation of Tax Administrators.

Special Studies

Aaron, Henry J. *Who Pays the Property Tax? A New View.* Washington: Brookings Institution, 1975.

Advisory Commission on Intergovernmental Relations. *City Financial Emergencies: The Intergovernmental Dimension.* Washington: Government Printing Office, 1973.

————. *Federal-State-Local Finances: Significant Features of Fiscal Federalism, 1973–74 Edition.* Washington: GPO, 1974.

————. *Financing Schools and Property Tax Relief—A State Responsibility.* Washington: ACIR, 1973.

————. *Fiscal Balance in the American Federal System.* 2 vols. Washington: GPO, 1967.

————. *Local Revenue Diversification: Income, Sales Taxes and User Charges.* Washington: GPO, 1974.

————. *Measuring the Fiscal Capacity and Effort of State and Local Areas.* Washington: GPO, 1971.

————. *The Role of Equalization in Federal Grants.* Washington: ACIR, 1964.

————. *The Role of the States in Strengthening the Property Tax.* 2 vols. Washington: GPO, 1963.

————. *State Constitutional and Statutory Restrictions on Local Government Debt.* Washington: ACIR, 1961.

Aronson, J. Richard, and Eli Schwartz, eds. *Management Policies in Local Government Finance.* Washington: International City Management Association, 1975.

Benson, George C. S., and others. *Essays in Federalism.* Claremont, Calif.: Claremont Men's College, 1961.

Bird, Frederick L. *The General Property Tax: Findings of the 1957 Census of Governments.* Chicago: Public Administration Service, 1960.

Break, George F. *Intergovernmental Fiscal Relations in the United States.* Washington: Brookings Institution, 1967.

Due, John F. *Sales Taxation.* Urbana: University of Illinois Press, 1957.

————. *State Sales Tax Administration.* Chicago: Public Administration Service, 1963.

Heins, A. James. *Constitutional Restrictions Against State Debt.* Madison: University of Wisconsin Press, 1963.

Hillhouse, A. M., and S. K. Howard. *State Capital Budgeting.* Chicago: Council of State Governments, 1963.

Jensen, Jens P. *Property Taxation in the United States.* Chicago: University of Chicago Press, 1931.

Maxwell, James A. *The Fiscal Impact of Federalism in the United States.* Cambridge: Harvard University Press, 1946.

Moak, Lennox L., and Albert M. Hillhouse. *Concepts and Practices in Local Government Finance.* Chicago: Municipal Finance Officers Association of the United States and Canada, 1975.

Mushkin, Selma J., ed. *Public Prices for Public Products.* Washington: Urban Institute, 1972.

Mushkin, Selma J., and John F. Cotton. *Functional Federalism: Grants-in-Aid and PPB Systems.* Washington: State-Local Finances Project of the George Washington University, 1968.

Nathan, Richard P., Allen D. Manvel, Susannah E. Calkins, and associates. *Monitoring Revenue Sharing.* Washington: Brookings Institution, 1975.

Netzer, Dick. *Economics of the Property Tax.* Washington: Brookings Institution, 1966.

Oates, Wallace E. *Fiscal Federalism.* New York: Harcourt Brace Jovanovich, 1972.

Ott, David J., and Allan H. Meltzer. *Federal Tax Treatment of State and Local Securities.* Washington: Brookings Institution, 1963.

Ott, David J., Attiat F. Ott, James A. Maxwell, and J. Richard Aronson. *State-Local Finances in the Last Half of the 1970s.* Washington: American Enterprise Institute for Public Policy Research, 1975.

Pechman, Joseph A., and Benjamin A. Okner. *Who Bears the Tax Burden?* Washington: Brookings Institution, 1974.

Penniman, Clara, and Walter W. Heller. *State Income Tax Administration.* Chicago: Public Administration Service, 1959.

Ratchford, B. U. *American State Debts.* Durham, N.C.: Duke University Press, 1941.

Robinson, Roland I. *Postwar Market for State and Local Government Securities*. Princeton: Princeton University Press for the National Bureau of Economic Research, 1960.

Sigafoos, Robert A. *The Municipal Income Tax: Its History and Problems*. Chicago: Public Administration Service, 1955.

Smith, R. Stafford. *Local Income Taxes: Economic Effects and Equity*. Berkeley: University of California, Institute of Governmental Studies, 1972.

Studenski, Paul, and Herman E. Krooss. *Financial History of the United States*. 2d ed. New York: McGraw-Hill, 1963.

Tax Foundation. *Earmarked State Taxes*. Research Publication No. 2, New Series. New York: Tax Foundation, 1965.

————. *Retail Sales and Individual Income Taxes in State Tax Structures*. New York: Tax Foundation, 1962.

Twentieth Century Fund, Task Force on Municipal Bond Credit Ratings. *The Rating Game*. New York: Twentieth Century Fund, 1974.

U.S. Commission on Intergovernmental Relations. *A Report to the President*. Washington: The Commission, 1955.

U.S. Congress. House. Committee on the Judiciary. Special Subcommittee on State Taxation of Interstate Commerce. *State Taxation of Interstate Commerce*. 4 vols. Washington: GPO, 1964 and 1965.

Index

Aaron, Henry J., 140, 159n
ACIR. *See* Advisory Commission on Intergovernmental Relations
Adams, T. S., 92, 152
Admissions tax, 105
Advisory Commission on Intergovernmental Relations (ACIR), 6, 61, 162–63, 209; reports cited, 29, 30, 39n, 73n, 74, 89n, 90n, 93n, 95n, 96n, 97n, 99n, 100n, 101n, 102n, 105n, 119n, 145n, 150n, 154–55, 158n, 159, 161, 174n, 195n, 207n, 208n, 211n, 251n; reports quoted, 39n, 62, 116, 131–32, 154n, 155, 157–58, 159, 161, 163, 195, 208, 213–14
AFL-CIO, 108
Aged, 1, 2, 245, 246; assistance to, 27, 48, 49–50, 65, 89, 158, 244; exemptions for, 95; insurance for, 18; medical assistance to, 52; retirement benefits for, 9, 226, 228–36
Agricultural experiment stations, 47, 53
Agricultural extension service, 53
Agriculture, U.S. Department of, 79
Aid, federal and state. *See* Intergovernmental transfers
Aid to families with dependent children (AFDC), 48, 49, 50, 54–55, 65
Alabama, 115n, 128, 129, 131
Alaska, 3; expenditures, 31, 33n; state taxes, 43, 93, 95n, 96, 131

Alcoholic beverage tax, 41, 81, 98, 101, 221n, 227
Allen, Everett T., 229n
American Enterprise Institute, 236
Arizona, 157n
Arkansas, 126; expenditures, 33n, 34; state debt, 192n; state taxes, 131; tax exemptions in, 95
Aronson, J. Richard, 29n, 141n, 144n, 187n, 228n, 230n, 231n, 236n, 238n, 249n, 251n
Assessment. *See* Property assessment

Baltimore, 29
Banks, 27, 204–05
Benefits: spillover, 22, 23, 65n, 141, 179, 183; tax-related, 141, 221–22, 223
Benefit tax, 98
Benson, George C. S., 27n
Bird, Frederick L., 150
Bish, Robert L., 80n
Blind: assistance to, 48, 49, 50, 52, 65, 89, 244; exemptions for, 95
Block grants, 57–58, 75–76, 248
Boiteux, Marcel, 179n
Bollens, John C., 79n
Bonds, state and local: default on, 194; full faith and credit, 196, 209, 210, 211, 212; for industrial aid, 212–13, 251; interest rate on, 199, 206; non-

Delano, F. A., 129
Delaware, 187n; intergovernmental transfers in, 73n; local taxes in, 168; state debt, 214n; state taxes, 43, 95, 115n; tax exemptions in, 94, 143
Denver, 104
Depreciation in capital budgets, 237, 241
Depression of the *1930*s, 18–20, 56
Detroit, 168n
Dillon, John F., 11
Disabled: assistance to, 49, 50, 52, 65, 89, 244; retirement programs for, 229
District of Columbia: property assessment in, 160n; taxes, 93n, 96, 100, 104, 105, 116, 158; tax exemptions in, 95
Document tax, 45
Double taxation, 144
Drainage districts, 77
Due, John F., 106n

Earmarking, 8, 51, 81, 217, 220–28; defects of, 223–24; provisions for, 224–25; rationale for, 221–23; with special funds, 220, 228
Ecker-Racz, L. L., 243n
Education, 30, 217, 241; borrowing for, 210n; expenditures for, 1, 4, 22, 23, 24–26, 29–30, 37, 38, 84–85, 86, 88–89, 227, 245; intergovernmental transfers for, 47, 48, 53–56, 76, 88–89, 148–49; and state user charges, 186; vocational, 47, 53
Electric power systems, 177–78
Elementary and Secondary Education Act of *1965* (ESEA), 54, 55–56
Employee retirement programs. *See* Retirement systems, state and local government
Employment Act of *1946*, 20n
Environment, 58–59, 61n, 251
Environmental Protection Agency (EPA), 59
Equity in taxation, 63, 105, 106–10, 141. *See also* Income
Estate tax, 130. *See also* Death tax
Excises: as benefit taxes, 98; and intergovernmental transfers, 51, 81; on sales, 18, 41, 51, 81, 98–101, 181, 225, 246; as sumptuary taxes, 98–101, 221n–22n
Exemptions: for bonds, 7, 177, 193, 200–05, 212, 240n, 250–51; business, 156; government property, 142; homestead, 149, 156–57; income tax, 94–95, 167, 177, 250; nonprofit

group, 142, 155; personal property, 143; for veterans, 149, 156–57
Expenditure: and budgeting, 216, 217, 218, 220, 222, 223, 230, 233–34; federal, 1, 13–14, 18, 20, 23, 46–76, 89, 90, 182, 244; intergovernmental, 24, 83–84, 85; local, 1–2, 7, 13–14, 18, 20–21, 32–38, 65, 81, 83–84, 90, 141, 161–63, 210, 220, 222, 223, 224, 230, 233–34, 236–38, 240–42, 244, 245–46; per capita measure of, 3, 32–36, 47; related to per capita income, 3, 34–36; state, 1–3, 7, 13–16, 18, 20–21, 23, 29, 31–38, 64, 65, 77, 80–91, 162–63, 182, 222, 223, 224, 230, 233–34, 236–38, 240–42, 244–46, 250

Family assistance plan (FAP), 50
Federal aid. *See* Intergovernmental transfers
Federal-Aid Highway Act of *1956,* 51, 52, 182
Federal Civil Works Administration, 19
Federal Emergency Relief Administration, 19
Federal government: death tax, 18, 128–33; earmarked revenues of, 220–21; expenditures for civil functions, 1, 13–14, 18, 20, 23, 46–76, 89, 90, 182, 244; income tax, 4, 5, 17, 18, 27, 92, 94, 112, 117, 250; and intergovernmental transfers, 3–4, 14–15, 16, 46–76, 83, 89, 90, 182, 248–49; and jurisdictional conflicts, 19, 99–100, 250; and national defense, 22; and property tax, 134n–135n; relationship of local government to, 13–20, 60–61, 79, 90, 110, 200–02; relationship of state government to, 2, 10–30, 45, 75, 89, 110, 124–26, 128, 131–32, 200–02, 250; sales tax, 4–5, 18, 99–100; tax credits, 6, 125, 130; tax collection, 19, 21, 68n, 134; and tax equity, 63, 109; and user charges, 22, 100
Federal Highway Trust Fund, 51–52, 100, 182, 225
Federalism, 11–30, 60, 62–63, 252–53
Federal Water Pollution Control Act of *1956*, 59
Fire protection, 29, 141
Fisher, Glenn W., 36
Florida, 6; state taxes, 45, 93n, 116n, 126–27, 128, 129–30, 131; tax exemptions in, 157n
Formula grants. *See* Intergovernmental transfers